P9-DUK-582

THE SOCIAL PHILOSOPHY

OF

CARLYLE AND RUSKIN

THE SOCIAL PHILOSOPHY

OF

CARLYLE AND RUSKIN

BY

FREDERICK WILLIAM ROE

KENNIKAT PRESS
Port Washington, N. Y./London

TO MY WIFE
LUCY LEWIS ROE

THE SOCIAL PHILOSOPHY OF CARLYLE AND RUSKIN

First Published in 1921
Reissued in 1969 by Kennikat Press
Library of Congress Catalog Card No: 74-93069
SBN 8046-0682-X

Manufactured by Taylor Publishing Company   Dallas, Texas

FOREWORD

The following chapters have been written not only as an interpretation on important sides of two great and related literary personalities of the Victorian Era, but also as a contribution, however slight, to the history of social thought in England during a critical period. The writer would fain hope that the challenging message of these prophets, delivered in a time of profound transformations in the structure of society, might not be without inspiration and guidance for our own day, a day even more disturbed than theirs, more fraught with unrest and uncertainty, when men everywhere are listening for authentic voices that shall speak counsels worthy to be followed. For the social philosophy of Carlyle and Ruskin is not a matter of academic interest for a few leisured scholars and book-lovers alone. It is rather a trumpet-call to workers, old and young, workers alike with hand and with brain,—to put forth their utmost efforts, in the midst of the present confusion, for the purpose of effecting an ordered revolution of our industrial system, so that civilization in reality may become what for generations at least it has not been,—"the humanization of man in society."

The text of Carlyle used throughout the volume is the text of the *Copyright Edition*, published in England by Chapman and Hall, and sold in America by Scribner's. The text of Ruskin is that of the *Library*

Edition, edited by Cook and Wedderburn, and published by Longmans, Green & Co.

For much helpful criticism, the author wishes to record here his thanks to his long-time friend and college classmate, Dr. John Gowdy, President of the Anglo-Chinese College, Foochow, China.

F. W. R.

MADISON, WISCONSIN,
December, 1920.

CONTENTS

SOCIAL PHILOSOPHY OF
CARLYLE AND RUSKIN

CHAPTER I

THE NEW AGE

"On every hand, the living artisan is driven from his
workshop, to make room for a speedier, inanimate one.
The shuttle drops from the fingers of the weaver, and falls
into iron fingers that ply it faster. . . . Coal and iron, so
long unregardful neighbors, are wedded together; Birmingham and Wolverhampton, and the hundred Stygian forges,
with their fire-throats and never-resting sledge-hammers,
rose into day."—*Carlyle*.

No discussion of the social philosophy of Carlyle
and Ruskin can be understood without some account, however brief and incomplete, of the trans-
formation in modern life known as the industrial
revolution. The message of these great Victorians to
their contemporaries, their denunciations of present
evils as well as their prophetic vision of a better order,
were set forth against a background of social change
that took shape before their eyes. And they were not
only witnesses of this mighty drama of contending
industrial forces; they could also well remember
times, in their youth or early manhood, when the
English landscape was yet unsullied by factory-
smoke, and when many an English cottager lived

amidst beauty and peace and contentment and had not yet been infected by the fever of a modern manufacturing town. An account of these movements, therefore, even though it is more than a twice-told tale, must be placed before the reader, as an indispensable setting to the social philosophy which he is invited to consider. But it is a story fascinating in itself, fairly epical in its sweep and consequence, and one which the student of latter-day problems cannot know too well. The stream of events upon which it is borne along, moreover, flows onward from the beginning more unbrokenly in England than in any other country; for here all the older conditions existed in their fulness, and here the newer life first came into being in its power.

The man of to-day cannot easily picture that older world in which his ancestors lived less than two centuries ago. Measured as history measures them, changes have been so recent and so revolutionary that the England of the first Georges seems less removed from the times of the Pharaohs than from the England of the present, at least in nearly everything that is concerned with the daily activities of man. Commerce, manufacture, agriculture, travel, domestic economy, one and all, were carried on very much as they had been carried on centuries before. The world was bigger, cities were larger and more numerous, and the fruits of civilization were vastly more distributed, it is true, in the eighteenth century than in any previous age; and with these changes there were corresponding changes also in the external fashions and habits of life. But the business of the home, the field, and the market-place was not essentially different from what it had been when the heedful Penelope sat in her hall at Ithaca weaving the great web, or when Jacob drove shrewd bargains with his uncle Laban on the plains of Padan-Aram. In 1760—to take a convenient date—the old communal system of agriculture in England was in full swing. Land around a manor, or lord's house, was broken up into innumerable small strips, cultivated, fallow, and waste. The yeoman farmers of those days, some of them tenants, some of them freeholders (of whom there were about 180,000) tilled their scattered allotments, pastured their cattle, sheep, and swine on a common pasture, and lived in small clustered cottages. Most of their implements were wooden and therefore inadequate, and their methods of farming were almost hopelessly antiquated; for they did not rotate their crops nor fertilize, and they systematically allowed one-third of their arable land to lie fallow each year. Intervening between one community and another, moreover, there were likely to be immense tracts of undrained fen, waste moorland, or forest, which the enterprise or necessity of man had not yet reclaimed from their primeval state. Thus in these rural centers, lapped in a surrounding stillness of which we to-day can scarcely dream, these sturdy peasant proprietors lived from generation to generation, remote and slow no doubt, but, from all accounts not like Goldsmith's villagers, for they were neither unfriended nor melancholy. England in their times was an agricultural nation. Her lawmakers were her landlords and much of her physical and moral strength was in her yeomen.

The fields were not alone the source of livelihood. Otherwise these agricultural communities could not have been self-sufficient. Every farmer's cottage was his factory, where the family, old and young, not only made their own candles and leather, but spun and wove their own cloth from the wool of their own sheep. At least this was the custom in the beginning and for most peasants, although in some parts of England from Tudor times onward it was expanded into what has since been known as the "domestic system" of manufacture. "Every family spun from its own flock the wool with which it was clothed," says Wordsworth, speaking of the dalesmen of Westmoreland; "a weaver was here and there found among them; and the rest of their wants was supplied by the produce of the yarn, which they carded and spun in their own houses and carried to market, either under their arms, or more frequently on packhorses, a small train taking their way weekly down the valley or over the mountains to the most commodious towns." [1] It was the existence of these "commodious" towns, which were not self-sufficient, as were the earlier rural communities, that had brought about a development in "domestic" manufacture, only suggested in the passage just quoted from Wordsworth. Since the townspeople did not make their own cloth, they purchased it from the farmers, who therefore found it more and more to their profit to devote a larger share of their time to

[1] *Guide to the Lakes,* 60.

spinning and weaving than to farming, at least so long as farming went on in the old way. Spinning and weaving, moreover, might go on at any season and would furnish employment for the entire family instead of for a part only. "A family of four adult persons, with two children as winders," said Dr. Gaskell, in a book published in 1833, "earned at the end of the last and at the commencement of the present century, 4*l.* per week, when working ten hours per day."[1]

Thus there grew up entire communities of rural cloth-makers, some of them, like those of Yorkshire, where woollens were made, dating back to the days of the Tudors; others, like those of Lancashire, the home of cotton manufacture, probably not extending much back of the eighteenth century. In the prosperous expansion of this industry, we can trace the beginnings of capitalistic enterprise and division of labor. A hand-loom weaver would become the owner of four or five looms, which he worked with the assistance of journeymen and apprentices. His yarn would be spun in the neighboring cottages, whose families would thus be dependent upon him for their employment. If the master weaver were a maker of cotton cloth he would take the product of his looms thrice a week to the market at Manchester, offering his goods for sale, soliciting orders, and returning with a quantity of raw material for his spinners. "There was not a village within thirty miles of Manchester, on the Cheshire and Derbyshire side," says Chapman, in his *History*

[1] *Manufacturing Population of England*, 34.

of the Cotton Manufacture, "in which cotton manufacturing was not being carried on." [1] Defoe, in his
Tour of Great Britain (1727), has left us a vivid
picture of these vanished communities of workers,
in his description of the woollen industry in the
parish of Halifax, Yorkshire, and of the great cloth-
market at Leeds, where the weavers marketed their
goods. "The nearer we came to Halifax," he says,
"we found the houses thicker, and the villages
greater, in every bottom; and not only so, but the
sides of the hill, which were very steep every way,
were spread with houses; for the land being divided
into small enclosures, from two acres to six or seven
each, seldom more, every three or four pieces of land
had an house belonging to them. In short, after we
had mounted the third hill, we found the country
one continued village, though every way mountain-
ous, hardly an house standing out of a speaking-
distance from another; and as the day cleared up,
we could see at every house a tenter, and on almost
every tenter a piece of cloth, Kersey, or shalloon;
which are the three articles of this country's labor.
. . . Then, as every clothier (*i. e.*, weaver) must
necessarily keep one horse, at least, to fetch home
his wool and his provisions from the market, to
carry his yarn to the spinners, his manufacture to
the fulling-mill, and, when finished, to the market
to be sold, and the like; so every one generally keeps
a cow or two for his family. . . . Though we met
few people without doors, yet within we saw the
houses full of lusty fellows, some at the dye-vat,

[1] *Manufacturing Population of England*, 37.

some at the loom, others dressing the cloths; the women and children carding, or spinning; all employed from the youngest to the oldest; scarce anything above four years old, but its hands were sufficient for its own support. Not a beggar to be seen, nor an idle person, except here and there in an alms-house, built for those that are antient, and past working. The people in general live long; they enjoy a good air; and under such circumstances hard labour is naturally attended with the blessing of health, if not riches."

"The cloth-market held in cloth-hall at Leeds," continues Defoe, "is chiefly to be admired, as a prodigy of its kind, and perhaps not to be equalled in the world. The market for serges at Exeter is indeed a wonderful thing, and the money returned very great; but it is there only once a week, whereas here it is every Tuesday and Saturday. The Cloth-iers (*i. e.*, weavers) come early in the morning with their cloth; and, as few bring more than one piece, the market-days being so frequent, they go into the inns and public-houses with it, and there set it down. At about six o'clock in the summer, and about seven in the winter, the clothiers being all come by that time, the market bell at the old chapel by the bridge rings; upon which it would surprise a stranger, to see in how few minutes, without hurry, noise, or the least disorder, the whole market is filled, all the benches covered with cloth, as close to one another as the pieces can lie longways, each proprietor standing behind his own piece, who form a mercantile regiment, as it were, drawn up in a double line; in as great order as a military one. As soon as the bell has ceased ringing, the factors and buyers of all sorts enter the hall, and walk up and down between the rows, as their occasions direct. Most of them have papers with patterns sealed on them, in their hands; the colours of which they watch, by holding them to the cloths they think they agree to. When they have pitched upon their cloth, they lean over to the clothier, and, by a whisper, in the fewest words imaginable, the price is stated; one asks, the other bids, and they agree or disagree in a moment. . . . The buyers generally walk up and down twice on each side of the rows, and in little more than half an hour all the business is done. In less than half an hour you will perceive the cloth begin to move off, the clothier taking it upon his shoulder to carry to the merchant's house. At about half an hour after eight the market bell rings again, upon which the buyers immediately disappear, and the cloth which remains unsold is carried back to the inn. Thus you see 10 or 20,000*l*. worth of cloth, and sometimes much more, bought and sold in little more than an hour, the laws of the market being the most strictly observed that I ever saw in any market in England." [1]

Other accounts of these "golden times of manufacture," as Dr. Gaskell called them, it would be possible to give from various extant sources. For example, one of Ruskin's correspondents in the days of *Fors Clavigera* pictures the idyllic past that he knew at Wakefield before the advent of machinery

[1] Defoe, *Tour of Great Britain*, III, 155–6 and 131–2.

and the factory-system; and his picture sharply contrasts the brightness of the old times with the blackness of the new. "There was no railway then," he says, "only the Doncaster coach careering over the Bridge with a brave sound of horn; fields and farmsteads stood where the Kirkgate station is; where the twenty black throats of the foundry belch out flame and soot, there were only strawberry grounds and blossoming pear-orchards, among which the throstles and blackbirds were shouting for gladness. . . . On the chapel side there was the soft green English landscape, with woods and spires and halls, and the brown sails of boats silently moving among the flowery banks; on the town side there were picturesque traffic and life; the thundering weir, the wide still water beyond, the big dark-red granaries, with balconies and archways to the water, and the lofty white mills grinding out their cheering music. But there were no worse shapes than honest, dusty millers' men, and browned boatmen, decent people. I can remember how clean the pavement used to look there, and at Doncaster. Both towns are incredibly dirty now. . . . Market day used to be a great event for us all. I wish that you could have seen the handsome farmers' wives ranged round the church walls, with their baskets of apricots and cream cheese, before reform came. . . . You might have seen, too, the pretty cottagers' daughters, with their bunches of lavender and baskets of fruit, or heaps of cowslips and primroses for the wine and vinegar Wakefield housewives prided themselves upon. On certain days they stood to be hired as maid-servants, and were prized in the country round as neat, clean, modest-spoken girls. I do not know where they are gone now,—I suppose to the factories. . . . Tradespeople were different, too, in old Wakefield. They expected to live with us all their lives; they had high notions of honor as tradesmen, and they and their customers respected each other. They prided themselves on the 'wear' of their goods. If they had passed upon the housewives a piece of sized calico or shoddy flannel, they would have heard of it for years after. Now the richer ladies go to Leeds or Manchester to make purchases; the town tradesmen are soured and jealous. They put up big plate-glass fronts, and send out flaming bills; but one does not know where to get a piece of sound calico or stout linen, well spun and well woven." [1]

The more characteristic aspects of this attractive picture were no doubt reproduced in hundreds of towns all over the country. England had a foreign trade then, as she had had in the days of Chaucer, but commerce and manufacturing in the modern sense were unknown. Her people lived and worked under the old, old theory that each community was to be self-sustaining. Relations therefore were far less international than national, and even more parochial than national. Villages and towns lived largely unto themselves, shut out from the rest of the world, most of their inhabitants never seeing beyond the horizon that circled their ancestral homes. For in those days there were few roads, and those few were almost hopelessly bad. According to Adam Smith, it took

[1] Ruskin, *Works*, XXVIII, 380–2.

a broad-wheeled wagon, attended by two men and drawn by eight horses, about six weeks to carry and bring back between London and Edinburgh four tons weight of goods.[1] It took a coach longer to go the same distance than it now takes a liner to go from Liverpool to New York. In the summer season a journey by coach from London to Manchester occupied two days. Travel, therefore, was infrequent and only for the well-to-do. Traders went from community to community on horseback, or afoot, and bartered their goods on market days or at periodical fairs, as did the voluble Bob Jakin in *Mill on the Floss*. The beginnings of capitalistic enterprise at this period there were, as we have seen, but the captain of industry who systematically exploited his labor, purchasing it in the cheapest market, and who developed his industry in the British spirit of individualism had not yet come. Nor had the wage-earner, nor the factory-system. It was not an ideal world, far from it; and there were communities, such as the weavers of coarse cloth at Oldham, Lancashire, among whom conditions were wretched. But take it all in all, the world of those days was a world of contented toilers, for the most part independent and prosperous, owning their own wheels and looms, and on Sundays regularly attending the village church, because like Job "they feared God, and eschewed evil;"—a world, be it said, which furnished the quiet background in so much of Wordsworth's poetry and to which Carlyle and Ruskin and Morris reverted so often a half century and more afterward.

[1] *Wealth of Nations*, I, 20.

Then as if by magic came the flying shuttle, the spinning-jenny, and the power-loom, followed rapidly by the application of steam to all the uses of industry through new and marvelous machinery. Then came also a revolution in travel and transportation by means of canals, Macadam's turnpikes, railroads, and steamships. By a kind of simultaneous collaboration of wonder-working forces, a new world sprang into being, and the old world vanished like ghost at cock-crow.[1] "The spinning-wheel and the hand-loom were silenced, and manufactures were transferred from scattered villages and quiet homesteads to factories and cities filled with noise. Villages became towns, towns became cities, and factories started up on barren heath and deserted waste." Within fifty years English industry changed from medieval or semi-medieval to modern conditions. A new order of population was created. Commerce and manufacture went forward by leaps and bounds. And by the middle of the nineteenth century England became the wealthiest nation in the world, and her people found themselves in the midst of a gigantic industrial

---

[1] It is interesting to note the close sequence of dates respecting the principal inventions and improvements: the fly-shuttle by John Kay, 1733; the spinning-jenny by Hargraves, 1764; the water-frame by Arkwright, 1769; the "mule" by Crompton, 1779; Watt's steam-engine, first used to run spinning machines, 1785; Cartwright's power-loom, 1785; smelting iron by coal, 1740-1750; application of steam to blast furnaces, 1788; Davy's safety lamp, 1815; Duke of Bridgewater's canal, 1759; improvement of roads and bridge-building under Telford and Macadam, 1815-1830; first railroad, Stockton to Darlington, 1825; Fulton's *Clermont*, from New York to Albany, 1807; the *Comet*, first passenger steamer in Europe, launched on Clyde, 1812; Great Western, built by Cunard Company, the first steamship to cross the Atlantic, 1838.

system, with its myriad interests and its multitudinous problems.

A few figures may assist the reader's imagination to grasp the magnitude of these changes. The population of England and Wales in 1750 is estimated to have been 6,517,035; by 1821 it had nearly doubled. The increase in the population of England and Wales from 1770 to 1801 was 27½%; from 1801 to 1831 it was 56-3/5%.[1] The manufacturing towns expanded enormously. From 1801 to 1831, the population of Glasgow increased 161%, Manchester, 151%, Liverpool, 138%, Birmingham, 90%.[2] "The population of Lancashire, which is the great center of the cotton trade," says Dr. Gaskell, "in 1700, was 166,200; in 1750, 297,400; in 1801, 672,731; in 1811, 828,309; in 1821, 1,052,859; in 1831, 1,335,800."[3] In 1700 the agricultural population was double that of the manufacturing population; by 1830 the situation was reversed. In 1813 there were 2,400 power looms in use in Great Britain; in 1835 there were 116,801.[4] In 1760 in the cotton trade 3,000,000 pounds of cotton were manufactured; in 1833, 303,656,837 pounds were produced.[5] "One spinner," says Dr. Gaskell, writing in 1836, "produces as much in one day now as would have required a year's time to produce a century ago."[6] In 1787 there were 41 cotton mills in Lancashire alone; a half century later, there were 157,

[1] Porter, *The Progress of the Nation*, 13.
[2] Gaskell, *Manufacturing Population of England*, 220.
[3] *Ibid.*, 220.
[4] Chapman, *Lancashire Cotton Industry*, 28.
[5] Gaskell, *Artisans and Machinery*, 329.
[6] Gaskell, *Artisans and Machinery*, 329.

with operatives estimated at 137,000.[1] Perhaps
nothing shows more impressively the effect of the
new order of things than the growth in the importation of raw cotton: in 1815 it amounted to 82 million
pounds; in 1835 it was 318 million pounds; in 1851, 659
million pounds.[2] "The Briarean arms of the steam-
engine" reached into every industry and "British
science and British skill" made England, in the popular phrase of the Victorian era, the workshop of the
world. The soldiers of Napoleon who marched to
Moscow wore clothing made of cloth from English
looms, and manufactured goods from English factories
were carried by British merchantmen to the ends of
the earth. It is little wonder that many a contemporary writer should hail the new inventions as a special
dispensation of providence to British genius, and
should describe the new times in language that sounds
ludicrously extravagant to-day, even to American
ears. The transformations wrought upon society
were indeed more revolutionary, both actually and
potentially, than any which the world had hitherto
seen. The new distributions of property, the rapid
accumulations of private fortunes, the widespread
application of machinery and the consequent enormous multiplication of the conveniences and luxuries
of life, the disappearance of some classes and the
emergence of others, together with the deeper changes
in the habits and thoughts of a whole people,—all
these were circumstances sufficient to awaken the
attention of thoughtful men to the fact that a new

[1] Podmore, *Life of Owen*, I, 40.
[2] Slater, *The Making of Modern England*, 128.

order of life had come into being, bringing with it new conditions and new problems such as were destined to make rough sailing for the ship of state in the years ahead.

For the source of England's wealth was likewise the source of her most troublesome problems and her darkest conditions, the factory system. In the early days of machinery, before the application of steam to manufacturing and when the power-loom was operated by the force of water, factories sprang up in the country districts wherever a stream afforded sufficient power to turn the wheels. A little later, as soon as it was demonstrated that the power-loom could be profitably run by steam, factories were transferred to towns, where more workers lived or could live and where goods could be marketed more readily and more cheaply. It was not long before these factory towns presented an appearance with which the world of to-day is only too familiar,—myriads of rickety tenement buildings, housing a vast and crowded population of operatives with their families,—acres of factories, most of them hastily constructed and badly ventilated, and thrusting into the sky a forest of chimneys from which there poured a never-ceasing cloud of smoke that blackened the country for miles around. The population in these industrial centers grew rapidly on its own account, but it was augmented from two classes outside, the rural cloth-workers of the old order who were being thrown out of employment because of the introduction of new machinery, and the small farmers who were forced to leave their farms in consequence of

the movement in agriculture known as enclosures.[1]
How different was this new army of workers from the
old! Instead of an independent people, living mostly
in the country, owning their own cottages and tools,
and tilling their own small farms or gardens, there
grew up a vast aggregation of dependent city toilers,
—men, women, and children,—tenanting rented
houses, working in factories not their own, and
operating machinery that required less and less skill
and more and more merely monotonous "tending."
The day of the wage-earner had come. The day of
the exploiting captain of industry had come also.
Sprung in most cases from the ranks of operatives,
knowing little or nothing of what went on beyond the
four walls of his factory, frequently illiterate, usually
brutal and debased, the typical factory-owner of the
first quarter or so of the nineteenth century was
industrious and shrewd enough to accumulate a

---

[1] The old system of farming, described in the previous pages, was
found to be wasteful and backward in the extreme. In the eighteenth
century a few progressive landlords, like the Marquis of Rockingham,
the Duke of Bedford, Lord Townshend, and even George III himself,
began experimenting in new crops, new methods of rotation, drainage,
etc. They soon demonstrated the great value of these improvements.
But it was found that the new farming could not proceed without the
overthrow of the old. Hence, by act of parliament or by coercive act
of landlord, there went on from 1760 to 1843 a readjustment known as
enclosures. The small parcels of disconnected open land and the "commons" were re-apportioned into larger groups of *enclosed* lands, held by
fewer farmers under longer leases, or independently. The movement
which, considered in its broad aspects, is accurately described by Arthur
Young as "not merely beneficial to the individual" but "of the most
extensive national advantage," (*A Six Months Tour through the North
of England*, I, 258) was accompanied with great distress to hundreds
of the small, unprogressive farmers, who were now compelled to become
either dependent farm-laborers or to join the rising army of the proletariat in the factory towns.

fortune rapidly, whereby he could live in newly-built mansions furnished with all the tawdry accessories that money could buy. His position and his wealth gave him vast power, often exercised under the grossest forms of tyranny over the hordes of workers dependent upon him; so that he amply deserved the contemptuous nickname with which Carlyle dubbed him,—Plugson of Undershot, the modern buccaneer.[1]

The condition of the wage-earners operating under Plugson and his fellow masters has been the theme of novelists, prophets, reformers, and utopia-builders the world over. It would be difficult indeed to find in the annals of history a more dismal or distressing page than the one upon which is written the story of the early factory workers. The factories themselves, equipped with unprotected machinery and enclosing a damp over-heated atmosphere, were in the majority of cases wholly unfit for their swarming populations. They were of course unsanitary and uninspected, and the air in them was filled with floating particles of cotton "fluff." Far the greater number of operatives were women and children, since adult male labor was not needed to tend the machines. Child-labor was not only better adapted to the needs of the work; it was cheaper. In the earlier period before the apprentice system was abandoned, pauper children were re-

[1] The attitude of the mill-owner towards his operatives is well suggested in the remarks of a manufacturer who sold cloth to Francis Place, the famous Charing Cross tailor and radical reformer. "Damn their eyes," said he to Place, "what need you care about them? How could I sell you goods so cheap if I cared anything about them?" "I showed him the door," says Place, "and never purchased any of his goods afterwards." (Wallas, *Life of Francis Place*, 141.)

cruited from the workhouses and foundling hospitals
of London and other large cities, and were literally
sold into slavery to the mill-owners, whose brutal
overseers were wont to treat them in ways too
shocking to describe.[1]   Matters were scarcely improved when apprentice-children were withheld, or
when conditions under which they were allowed by
the magistrates to work were restricted, and "free"
children were employed; for the reason that parents,
in their ignorance and poverty, seemed glad enough
to have the meager wages of the household eked out
by the pittance which their children might earn.
Probably the most vivid—one should perhaps say
lurid—account of these early factory "hands" ever
written is that by Frederick Engels, life-long friend
and co-worker of Karl Marx, in his book called *The
Condition of the Working-Class in England in 1844*.
Describing child-labor, he refers to the parliamentary Factories' Inquiry Commission of 1833 in these
words: "The report of the Central Commission re-
lates that the manufacturers began to employ children rarely of five years, often of six, very often of
seven, usually of eight to nine years; that the work-
ing-day often lasted fourteen to sixteen hours, exclusive of meals and intervals; that the manufacturers
permitted overlookers to flog and maltreat children,
and often took an active part in so doing them-

---

[1] There were exceptions, perhaps the most notable one being the case
of Mr. Dale of New Lanark Mills, on the river Clyde.   Mr. Dale (father-
in-law of Robert Owen, afterwards himself proprietor of New Lanark)
took over some 500 pauper children, whom he clothed, fed, and lodged,
and for whom he established a night-school. (Podmore, *Life of Owen*,
I, 73.)

selves." [1]   As proof of his assertion that the active
work of the mills was done by women and children,
Engels quotes figures from a speech of Lord Ashley
made in support of the Ten Hours' Bill which Lord
Ashley introduced into the House of Commons in
1844: "Of 419,560 factory operatives of the British
Empire in 1839, 192,887, or nearly half, were under
eighteen years of age, and 242,296 of the female sex,
of whom 112,192 were less than eighteen years old.
. . . In the cotton factories, 56¼ per cent.; in the
woollen mills, 69½ per cent.; in the flax-spining mills,
70½ per cent. of all operatives are of the female sex." [2]

If factory conditions were bad, the home conditions of these operatives were inexpressibly worse.
Where all accounts agree, one should no doubt dismiss his skepticism; and yet the often-told tale of
human wretchedness and human degradation in
the tenement districts of the manufacturing towns
almost passes belief, even for the sophisticated
student of slum conditions. "From some recent
inquiries on the subject," says Gaskell, "it would
appear that upward of 20,000 individuals live
in cellars in Manchester alone." [3]   "A full fifth of

[1] 151.

[2] *Ibid.*, 142. Probably the only place where "model" factory conditions were to be seen was at the New Lanark mills under the management of Robert Owen. The weekly wages there for boys under 18 were
4s. 5d.; for women, 6s.; for men, 9s. 11d. Piece-workers received from
25 to 50 per cent. more. Owen fixed the minimum age at 10, and allowed
children from 5 to 10 to attend his school free of charge. For some time
the hours of labor were 14 per day. "It was not until January, 1816,
that he was enabled to reduce the hours to 12 a day, with 1 and ¼ hours
for meals, leaving 10 and ¾ hours for actual work." (Podmore, *Life of
Owen*, I, 92.)

[3] *Manufacturing Population of England*, 138.

the population, more than 45,000 human beings,
of Liverpool," says Engels, "live in cellar dwellings." [1] He found the situation as bad or worse in
other cities. Even at this distance of time one can
scarcely read without a shudder the descriptions of
endless ranges of houses along the "unpaved and
unsewered" back streets of the industrial centers,
into which the tired throngs of toilers poured at
the end of one day, and from which they emerged
at the dawn of the next. These rickety hovels were
not only filthy and over-crowded; they were centers
where the common decencies of life were hardly
known, or if they were known were not practiced.
Here vice and drunkenness, crime and poverty,
flourished in their natural habitat and throve as
weeds thrive in a neglected barnyard. [2] Readers of
Dickens and Disraeli, Mrs. Gaskell and Kingsley,
Bulwer-Lytton and Charles Reade—to mention only
the most famous names—will recall how vividly
these writers have set forth the state of society that
followed in the wake of the industrial revolution.
One institution after another of that day, the church,

[1] *Condition of the Working-Class*, 36.

[2] For prostitution and crime the reader is referred to Engels. On
drunkenness he says: "Sheriff Alison asserts that in Glasgow some
thirty thousand workingmen get drunk every Saturday night, and the
estimate is certainly not exaggerated; and that in that city in 1830, one
house in twelve, and in 1840, one house in ten, was a public-house. . . .
Gaskell estimates secret distilleries in Manchester alone at more than
a hundred. . . . When one has seen the extent of intemperance among
the workers in England, one readily believes Lord Ashley's statement
that this class annually expends something like twenty-five million
pounds sterling upon intoxicating liquor." (*Condition of the Working-
Class*, 126–128.) As to poverty we have the testimony of the historian
of the period: in England in 1815 "nearly one person in every eleven
of the population was a pauper." (Walpole, *History of England*, I, 186.)

the schools, the prisons, the workhouses, the factories, they held up to scorn and just condemnation; one class of operatives after another, the miners, the iron-workers, the textile-workers, the tailors, they introduced into their pages, together with all the attendant evils in the industrial system,—sweating, poisoning, "rattening," strikes, and the whole gamut of labor troubles. The distress of the iron-workers in the cutlery trades,—the employment of children in mines—those subterranean midgets who hauled tubs of coal from twelve to sixteen hours a day,—the tyranny of the "truck" system (*i. e.*, payment for wages in goods from the company store, with short weight, higher prices, adulteration, and falsification of account),—the reduction of wages by petty underhand means such as fines and rebates,—the work of the factory girls begun so early in the morning that watchmen were engaged by districts to tap on the windows in order to awaken them,—the ever-increasing irritation and distrust between masters and men,—and around all, like the coils of a venomous reptile, the stretch of dilapidated tenements with their countless holes and corners where the Fagins and Quilps held sway:—it was the telling of these and other facts like them that made the mid-Victorian novel a powerful instrument for reform.[1]

[1] The treatment of the industrial revolution by the novelists is a chapter or a book by itself. The best accounts are in the following: Bulwer-Lytton's *Paul Clifford*, Disraeli's *Sybil*, Dickens's *Oliver Twist* and *Hard Times*, Kingsley's *Yeast* and *Alton Locke*, Mrs. Gaskell's *Mary Barton* and *North and South*, Charles Reade's *Never Too Late to Mend* and *Put Yourself in His Place*. These novels present conditions, roughly speaking, before 1850. Mrs. Gaskell comes nearer to the actual

But the workers did not wait for the novelists to make known their conditions to the world. It was inevitable that their own growing sense of distress should lead to protests and rebellion. Their attitude of mind is nowhere better described than in the words of Francis Place, whose life in the borough of Westminster, London, was passed in the center of radicalism and agitation. "A great mass of our unskilled and but little skilled labourers (among whom are the handloom weavers), and a very considerable number of our skilled labourers," he says, "are in poverty, if not in actual misery; a large portion of them have been in a state of poverty and great privation all their lives. They are neither ignorant of their condition nor reconciled to it. They live amongst others who are better off than themselves, with whom they compare themselves; and they cannot understand why there should be so great a difference, why others who work no more or fewer hours than themselves at employment not requiring more actual exertion, and in many cases occupying fewer hours in the day, should be better paid than they are, and they come to the conclusion that the difference is solely caused by oppression—oppression of bad laws and avaricious employers. To escape from this state is with them of paramount importance. Among a vast

lives and thoughts of the working people; Reade offers most definite solutions; Kingsley describes the humbug of the established religion and applies the remedy of Christian socialism; Dickens (without suggesting specific cures) is the most vivid of all in his pictures of the haunts of vice and villainy in the cities. A valuable study of the whole field is to be found in *Le Roman Social en Angleterre*, by Cazamian, 1904.

multitude of these people not a day, scarcely an hour, can be said to pass without some circumstance, some matter exciting reflection, occurring to remind them of their condition, which (notwithstanding they have been poor and distressed from their infancy, and however much they may *at times* be cheerful) they scarcely ever cease, and never for a long period cease, to feel and to acknowledge to themselves with deep sensations of anguish their deplorable condition."[1] However ignorant and debased they might be, the unorganized workers were thus conscious of oppression and sullenly antagonistic toward their oppressors, and they therefore resorted to methods of personal violence and wanton lawlessness such as make the earlier history of industrialism a shameful record of crime and cruelty. Dynamiting, incendiarism, shooting, throwing of vitriol, persecutions of inventors of new machinery, persecutions of "knobsticks,"— these and other acts of barbarity were then the invariable concomitant of industry. For the first twenty-five years of the century, or before the repeal of the Combination Laws, the revolt of labor was individualistic rather than collective. Gradually the scattered masses drew together into organizations, at first secretly and often rather for the purposes of mutual benefit than for united effort against their employers. Then the era of trade unions and strikes began. It dawned upon the benighted consciousness of the proletariat that there was a mighty power in combination. Up and down Great

[1] Wallas, *Life of Place,* 382.

Britain unions were formed, and rebellion now became organized, persistent, and militant. "The incredible frequency of these strikes," says Engels, "proves best of all to what extent the social war has broken out all over England. No week passes, scarcely a day, indeed, in which there is not a strike in some direction."[1] Despite the bitterness and the persistence of the struggle, however, labor's fight during the second quarter of the century was nearly always a losing one. "In council they are idealists," say Mr. and Mrs. Webb, "dreaming of a new heaven and a new earth, humanitarians, educationalists, socialists, moralists: in battle they are still the struggling, half-emancipated serfs of 1825,— armed only with the rude weapons of the strike and boycott; sometimes feared and hated by the propertied classes; sometimes merely despised; always oppressed, and miserably poor." [2]

How could the situation be different when the odds against the laboring classes were so overwhelming? All the effective weapons belonged to the other side,—political power, education, the law and the courts, the prestige of wealth and position, and the immense force of organized public opinion. The operative of that day was not only desperately poor and illiterate,—he had no vote. And if he had his day in court, he found that the magistrate regarded him more as a chattel than as a human being.

---

[1] Engels, *Condition of the Working-Class*, 224.

[2] *History of Trade Unionism*, 138. In a sketch like the present one it is obviously out of the question to deal with labor wars in any detail. There are many books on the subject by authorities, *e. g.*, the Webbs, Cooke-Taylor, Innes, Hobhouse, Cunningham.

Worse still, society thought that it was better for all concerned, including the worker himself, that he should remain in servitude. Compulsory school attendance was unknown. There were in England some infant schools, and later on some mechanics' institutes and a few ineffectual private day schools; but the only educational agency that the upper classes really desired to sustain was the Sunday school. It did not matter if the ragged juveniles of the factory districts could neither read nor write, provided they could make a tolerable showing in recitation of the incomprehensible tenets of the Church of England. A knowledge of the Thirty-nine Articles would make for peace and contentment, so a benevolent aristocracy reasoned; whereas a knowledge of the "three r's" might provoke trouble.[1] Illiteracy, therefore, was the rule, literacy the exception. "Rather more than 570,000 were not wholly destitute of educational advantages," says Walpole, speaking of conditions from 1815 to 1820. "But there must, at the very least, have been 2,000,000 children requiring education. So that for one child, who had the opportunity of education, three were left entirely ignorant." [2] "In Birmingham," says Engels, writing in 1844, "more than half the children between five and fifteen years attend no school whatsoever. . . . In the Potteries district, . . . three-fourths of the children examined by the Commissioner could neither read nor write, while the

[1] For the attitude of the aristocracy see Wallas, *Life of Place*, 112; Walpole, *History of England*, I, 186–9.
[2] *History of England*, I, 186.

whole district is plunged in the deepest ignorance. Children who have attended Sunday school for years could not tell one letter from another." [1]

The ignorant worker and his ignorant family, therefore, received scant consideration from the law and the legislature. Non-interference, *laissez-faire*, were the order of the day. After the repeal in 1813–14 of the old Elizabethan statute of Apprenticeship (a law enacted in 1563 giving justices power to fix wages and prescribing certain regulations as to apprenticeship), "the last remnant of that legislative protection of the Standard of Life which survived from the Middle Ages" was swept away.[2] Free, individual bargaining was the sole method of fixing wages. "A single master," said Lord Jeffrey in 1825, "was at liberty at any time to turn off the whole of his workmen at once—100 or 1000 in number—if they would not accept the wages he chose to offer. But it was made an offence for the whole of the workmen to leave that master at once if he refused to give the wages they chose to require." [3] The spirit of the typical British legislator, as well as of the typical British employer, for a full half century, is well shown in the words of a parliamentary committee of 1806, which declare that "the right of every man to employ the capital he inherits, or has acquired, according to his own discretion, without molestation or obstruction, so long as he does not infringe on the rights or property of others, is one of those privileges

---

[1] *Condition of the Working-Class*, 200, 207.
[2] Webb, *History of Trade Unionism*, 55.
[3] *Ibid.*, 63.

which the free and happy constitution of this country has long accustomed every Briton to consider as his birthright."[1] The statement reminds one of the classical remark in 1829 of the Duke of Newcastle concerning his practice of selling rotten boroughs to the highest bidder: "Have I not the right to do what I like with my own?" It was to be expected, therefore, that the attitude of authority should be almost exclusively in favor of the propertied classes, and that the "ignorant and avaricious" workmen should be left to the tender mercies of the magistrates, who appear to have treated offenders much as Mr. Bumble, the beadle, treated juvenile paupers. "Justice was entirely out of the question," says Francis Place; "the workingmen could seldom obtain a hearing before a magistrate—never without impatience and insult; and never could they calculate on even an approximation to a rational conclusion. . . . Could an accurate account be given of proceedings, of hearings before magistrates, trials of sessions and in the Court of King's Bench, the gross injustice, the foul invective and terrible punishments inflicted, would not, after a few years have passed away, be credited on any but the best of evidence."[2] The culmination of these grievances was a complete political disability of the working classes. Arnold Toynbee stated the literal truth when he said that "except as a member of the mob, the labourer had not a shred of political influence."[3]

[1] Webb, *History of Trade Unionism*, 56.
[2] Wallas, *Life of Place*, 198.
[3] *Industrial Revolution*, 186. The state of the franchise prior to 1832, when the first Reform Bill was passed, is too well known to need dis-

This deplorable state of affairs in the new industrialism was not due to an irresponsible sovereign
and a parliament of reactionary landlords alone. It
was immensely furthered by the political and economic doctrines of the time. The eighteenth century
had been a period of rigid economic control, a policy
inherited from the centuries before and modified to
suit contemporary needs. By a system of bounties
on exports and duties on imports, by acts of parliament to regulate wages (in the interests of landlord
and corporation), by rigidly monopolistic control of
the corporations over trades, by cheap labor and
high corn, governmental authority was well-nigh
absolute.[1] It was the economic and political creed of
the propertied classes then in power. Against these
old repressive measures the thought of the new century set up a determined revolt. The fundamental
postulate of the economic teaching of the new age
was individual freedom and non-interference from the
state. One after another the old medieval restrictions were thrown overboard; for according to the
pilots of the new school the ship of state could make
no headway while loaded down with cumbrous and
obsolete machinery. The founders of this school

cussion, even if there were any good reason for entering into it here.
Toynbee's statement covers the whole ground. One of the best extended accounts of the old corrupt rotten borough system and the growing agitation against it is Walpole's, in his *History of England from 1815*.
See especially Ch. II of Vol. I, and pp. 314-342 of Vol. II; also pp. 208-
244 of Vol. III. For the attitude of the radicals, Chapters 9, 10, and
11 of Wallas's *Life of Place* are of great value.

[1] "They endeavoured to regulate the clothes which the living should
wear, and the shrouds in which the dead should be buried." (Walpole,
History, I, 215.)

were Adam Smith and Jeremy Bentham, one the
father of political economy, the other the father of
philosophical radicalism.[1] According to Bentham's
"gospel of enlightened selfishness," the end of action
was happiness, and happiness resulted from a selfish
pursuit of pleasure,—pleasure, too, that sprang from
"material consequences." When a man by dexterous
additions and subtractions of the fourteen pleasures
and the twelve pains to which he was liable could
deduct for himself a net surplus of pleasure he might
be accounted happy,—such was the calculation of
Bentham's arithmetical hedonism. And the end of
society was reached, upon this theory, when the
greatest number of individuals in it could secure the
largest net result of happiness:—a consummation
which would come, be it remembered, only when each
person was allowed unrestricted freedom in the pursuit of his own interests. The function of government, on this doctrine, was negative and restraining
only. It would see that the selfish desires of men did
not clash (if collisions were possible!), and it would
keep the way clear for the unfettered competition of
men in the race for the goods of life. The world, in
the thought of Bentham and his early disciples, was
thus a collocation of human units,—the idea is J. S.

[1] Bentham said of himself: "I am the spiritual father of James Mill,
James Mill is the spiritual father of Ricardo, therefore, I am the spiritual
grandfather of Ricardo." (Quoted by Toynbee, *Industrial Revolution*,
3.) James Mill, J. S. Mill, Grote, the Austins, all the intellectual radicals of the time go back to Bentham; so, too, do the parliamentary
leaders, Sir Francis Burdett, Sir J. Cam Hobhouse, and Joseph Hume;
and also the radical agitator, Francis Place. It was by Bentham's money
and initiative that the *Westminster Review*, the radical organ, was
founded in 1824.

Mill's also,—each following his own interest, and each kept from "jostling one another" by "law, religion, and public opinion." So conceived, society becomes, in Sir Leslie Stephen's apt phrase, a creation of "universal cohesion out of universal repulsion."

The political economy of Adam Smith rests upon assumptions practically identical with those of Bentham and the philosophical radicals. In fact the economists built upon foundations laid by the radicals, just as the radicals adopted the new doctrines of the "classical school." [1] The economic order,—such was the teaching of Smith,—springs spontaneously from self-interest, that is to say, from the innate desire of every man to better himself. "The natural effort of every individual to better his own condition, when suffered to exert itself with freedom and security, is so powerful a principle, that it is alone, and without any assistance, not only capable of carrying on the society to wealth and prosperity, but of surmounting a hundred impertinent obstructions with which the folly of human laws too often incumbers its operations; though the effect of these obstructions is always more or less either to encroach upon its freedom, or to diminish its security. . . . It is not from the benevolence of the butcher, the brewer, or the baker, that we expect our dinner, but from their regard to their own interest." [2] Such are the classic presuppositions of the father of political economy.

[1] I refer of course chiefly to Smith, Malthus, and Ricardo. Smith's *Wealth of Nations* came out in 1776; Malthus' *Essays* on population, in 1798; Ricardo's *Principles of Political Economy and Taxation*, in 1817.
[2] *Wealth of Nations*, II, 43; I, 16.

Man is best off when least disturbed in the pursuit of his own interests; and his own real interests do not collide with those of his neighbors, since what is best for him is best for them. Like Bentham's, it is another plea for freedom, and in Smith's doctrine (in a day of corrupt and inefficient government) a plea even more for the poor man than for the capitalist and the landlord.[1]

The economists who followed Smith—Malthus and Ricardo—adopted his presuppositions as axiomatic. But they went further and developed two doctrines which deserve to be singled out, because they so clearly suggest the influence of the new economic teaching upon the welfare of the working class,—the theory of population and the wage-fund theory, both of which were law and gospel among the intellectual radicals for a half century and more. It was Malthus who formulated the famous law of increasing population and of diminishing returns. The population, he said, increases in a geometrical progression, while the means of subsistence increase only in an arithmetical progression; and therefore the food-supply of the world always tends to be in-

[1] "The patrimony of the poor man lies in the strength and dexterity of his hands; and to hinder him from employing the strength and dexterity in what manner he thinks proper without injury to his neighbor, is a plain violation of this most sacred property." On this theory government was left with little to do but to keep its hands off. "The sovereign is completely discharged from a duty,"—and by sovereign Smith of course means the state— "in the attempting to perform which he must always be exposed to innumerable delusions, and for the proper performance of which no human wisdom or knowledge could ever be sufficient; the duty of superintending the industry of private people, and of directing it towards the employments most suitable to the interest of the society." (*Wealth of Nations*, I, 123; II, 184.)

sufficient to feed the people, unless checks are found
to reduce their numbers. Nature's check is death.
And the first to feel the rigors of its law are the poor.
But the poor are in the clutches of another law also,—
the law of wages,—which collaborates with its fellow
as smoothly as Spenlow collaborated with Jorkins in
David Copperfield. The theory of wages was set
forth by Malthus, but it was elaborated and popular-
ized by Ricardo. There is at any time, they said, a
fixed sum of money that can go for wages; it is just
sufficient to keep the wage-earners plodding along on
the lowest level of existence: for if it is increased so
that wages go up, the workers will multiply beyond
the demand for labor and the means of subsistence,
and the wage-fund will shrink to its old dimensions.[1]
These laws,—so it was thought and taught,—were
the creation of destiny, not to be altered by decree of
parliament.[2] The fate of the worker was in his own
hands. If he would better his condition, let him
abjure the old Hebraic command to increase and
multiply, and follow the new gospel of Malthus
and Ricardo.[3]

[1] The law refers of course to real wages, not to money wages. If the
wages go up, but the prices of food go up, too, then the actual conditions
remain the same. "The natural price of labor," said Ricardo, "is that
price which is necessary to enable the laborers one with another to sub-
sist and to perpetuate their race without either increase or diminution."
(Quoted by Gide and Rist, *History of Economic Doctrine*, 157.)

[2] The suggestions of Malthus and others that the poor might exercise
moral restraint to keep down their numbers were received with anathemas by the people of the regency and of the reign of George IV. Their
piety seems to have been in inverse ratio to their religion.

[3] "The people must comprehend that they are themselves the cause
of their own poverty," said Malthus. (Gide and Rist, *ibid.*, 119.) "Every
suggestion which does not tend to the reduction in number of the working
people is useless," said Francis Place. (Wallas, *Life of Place*, 174.)

The popularity of this latest evangel for the poor was a measure of its acceptance. Its golden rules were regarded as truisms which a child might understand. Harriet Martineau diluted them down to what she thought was the capacity of juvenile intelligence in her nine volumes of *Illustrations* (1832–34). Maria Edgeworth in her letters declared that ladies of fashion wanted governesses who were "competent" in political economy. "Political Economy," said Bagehot, "was a favorite subject in England from about 1810 to about 1840, and this to an extent which the present generation can scarcely comprehend." [1] In 1830 John Stuart Mill spoke of Ricardo's book as "immortal." Cobbett thought that Malthus held in political economy a position like that of Newton in astronomy; he considered the Malthusian principle one "which never can be shaken." [2] Francis Place, an equally devout Malthusian, regarded the economists of his day as "the great enlighteners of the people." [3] Their instant and enormous vogue is not indeed difficult to make out from the vantage ground of history. The doctrines they stood for suited the temper of the times, were abundantly supported by common sense, and appeared to rest upon unchanging foundations. Emanating chiefly from middle-class thinking, they furthered and fostered middle-class enterprises. "The economy of Ricardo and Mill," as Mr. Hobson says, "was never

[1] Bagehot, *Economic Studies*, 154.
[2] Melville, *Life and Letters of Cobbett*, I, 292–3.
[3] Wallas, *Life of Place*, 161; see also 166.

political. . . . It was simply the economy of the
shrewd Lancashire mill manager 'writ large' and
called political." [1] Again and again in their combats
with parliamentary committees, the manufacturers
used weapons that the radicals and economists had
forged. "Have I not a right to do what I will with
my own?"—this was their shibboleth when they
came down to Westminster to defend themselves
against obnoxious investigators. The typical factory-
owner of the early Victorian era was not concerned
with the condition of his workers, nor with any
purely "human" equations. What he wanted was
what the "hard-headed" business man has always
wanted,—the unchartered freedom to buy his raw
material in the cheapest market, sell it in the dearest,
pay only the wages he must pay to get the work
done, pocket his profits to do with as he liked, and
let his laborers, when paid, look out for themselves
as best they could. Was it possible for common
sense to deny the validity of such a position? And
if practice needed the support of precept, one had
only to turn again to the high priests of the sacred
science. "Political economy," said Nassau Senior,
holder at Oxford of the first chair of political economy
in England and author of one of the first text-books
on the subject, "political economy is not greedy
of facts; it is independent of facts."

Obviously, then, the social philosophy of the day
did not much concern itself with the wage-earner.
His status in life was fixed. His condition within
that status was subject to his personal control, a

[1] Hobson, *John Ruskin: Social Reformer*, 93.

matter of private, not of public, interest. He might bargain individually with his employer, and might take his chances with his fellows in the general scramble, but if he attempted to bargain collectively he was a menace to society. It is plain to-day that all this was anything but "free and unlimited competition"; for the workers as individuals were helpless against the organized power and wealth of the captains of industry. The situation was accurately stated by Arnold Toynbee, when he said that while the political economy of that day sought to establish *"free competition of equal industrial units,"* what it really helped to establish was "free competition of unequal industrial units." [1] Without the support, therefore, of justice-loving men from the upperclasses, who builded even better than they knew, the proletariat might not have risen from servitude except through revolution.

But during the first thirty years or so of the century, up to the period when Carlyle entered the field as a critic of industrial society, some progress towards an improved Standard of Life had been made. The Factory Acts of 1802, 1819, and 1833 were passed, and in 1824-5 the Combination Laws were repealed.[2] The repeal of these laws was of

---

[1] Toynbee, *Industrial Revolution*, 17.

[2] The Factory Act of 1802, introduced by Sir Robert Peel, father of the famous Sir Robert, applied only to apprentices in cotton mills. Among its provisions were: whitewashing of rooms in factories; instruction of apprentices in reading, writing, arithmetic, and limitation of working hours to 12. The act did not apply to "free" labor, and it did not in any way limit the age of employment. The Act of 1819 forbade employment of children up to nine years of age, restricted the hours of work for those under 16 years to 12 hours per day less 1½ hours for

immense importance to the working world. "The right of collective bargaining, involving the power to withhold labor from the market by concerted action, was for the first time expressly established." [1] Foremost among the men who led in the various movements for betterment were Place, Cobbett, Robert Owen, and, later, Lord Ashley, seventh Earl of Shaftesbury. Place and Cobbett, themselves sprung from the working classes, were the most practical of the reformers. To them real reform began with political reform. They saw the futility of any progress in the industrial and agricultural communities while parliament, under the sway of the old rotten borough system, was in the control of Tory landlords who accomplished their ends through the most open, wholesale, and shameless methods of bribery known in the political history of England. Cobbett, through his twopenny *Political Register* (1802–1836), and Place, largely through an extraordinary direct personal influence,

meals, and limited the total hours of work per week to 72. Like the previous act it applied only to cotton mills. It contained no provision for education, and none for inspection, leaving violations to be reported by common informers. The Act of 1833 "prohibited night-work to all young persons under eighteen; it allowed no child under nine to work except in silk mills, and it prescribed a limitation of hours of labor to nine in one day, or forty-eight in a week, for every child under eleven, on the first passing of the Act; a year later this restriction was to apply to all children under twelve, and, again, in a year's time to all children under thirteen." (Slater, *Making of Modern England*, 124.) Young people between thirteen and eighteen years of age were restricted to a twelve-hour day. This act applied to all textile industries, and was to be made effective by the appointment of four government inspectors.

The Combination Laws, passed in 1799 and 1800, made all combinations among operatives illegal on the ground of restraint of trade. They were a powerful weapon for the manufacturers up to 1825.

[1] Webb, *History of Trade Unionism*, 97.

incessantly advocated an extensive and thoroughgoing reform of parliament, including universal
manhood suffrage and voting by ballot.[1] Though
the Reform Bill of 1832 did not secure the relief which
these stout agitators demanded, it effectually broke
up the old system and was a long stride in the right
direction. The work of Owen, first great socialist,
though not so directly practical as that of Cobbett
and Place, was perhaps even more influential, at
least if its total effect is taken into account. A
dreamer, dreaming of a golden age, "to come suddenly like a thief in the night," as he said, Owen pictured a new terrestrial paradise, where through a
rational system of universal education, favorable
environment and "villages of co-operation and
equality," competition and capitalism would be no
more and mortals would live happily upon a plane
of mutual ownership and social equality. His
dreams faded into nothingness or vanished into
Utopia, where like other visions of other visionaries
they may be awaiting the slow upward march of
humanity. But he left behind him achievements
of a more substantial kind. He reformed conditions
in his own mills at New Lanark, so that these mills
became a model, in a distressing period, of what

---

[1] "In January, 1817, Cobbett's *Register* was selling 50,000 a week of
its twopenny edition." (Wallas, *Life*, 124.) Samuel Bamford, the radical,
wrote of Cobbett's paper: "They were read on nearly every cottage
hearth in the manufacturing districts of South Lancashire, in those of
Leicester, Derby, and Nottingham; also in many of the Scotch manufacturing towns. Their influence was speedily visible. He directed his
readers to the true cause of their sufferings—misgovernment; and to its
proper correction—parliamentary reform." (Melville, *Life of Cobbett*,
II, 75.)

factories should be. He labored unremittingly to
secure a decent Standard of Life in factories everywhere (by minimum time and minimum wage),
and he was directly influential in securing early
factory legislation. With the fervor of an apostolic
Christian, he went straight to the operatives all
over Great Britain, denouncing competition among
the capitalists and preaching union and co-operation
among the workers. For twenty years (1815–1835)
Owen was probably the greatest single force in
bringing the laboring world to a realization of its
collective strength; and the far-spread seed of his
planting bore fruit manyfold in the years to come.

Progress, then, there was. Competition and
laissez-faire had been openly attacked, and at some
points they were decisively routed. But the field
stretched interminably ahead toward the ultimate
objective, and there were unnumbered obstacles
looming up with every new advance. Even the most
radical reformers were largely guided by middle-class
ideals and could see the battle only from their own
point of view. Owen, with the temper of an intoler-
ant idealist who distrusts compromises and half-
measures, held aloof from all political activity, and
took no part in the reform movement of 1832, nor in
the long struggle for the repeal of the Corn Laws, nor
in the momentous Chartist agitations, although his
teaching told strongly upon many of the leading
Chartists, and upon the beginnings of trade-unionism.
His appeal for help was mainly addressed to benevolent members of the upper-classes, for his idea of
reform savored of the aristocratic method of reaching

down to the masses below, to alleviate, not to recon-
struct. The radicals, philosophical and political
alike, true to their creed, were willing to remove old
restrictions, but resisted the imposition of new.
James Mill regarded the middle-class as a model for
the masses; "the great majority of the people," said
he, "never cease to be guided by that rank." Ricardo believed in the repeal of the Combination Laws,
but did not favor the restrictions imposed by the
Factory Acts. His disciple, Joseph Hume, a leader
among the parliamentary radicals, and a co-worker
with Place, led in the fight for the repeal of the Combination Laws in 1824, while in 1833 he contended
that the passing of the Factory Acts was "pernicious
and a libel" upon the humanity of the masters.
Even Place himself, the most consistently practical
of all the agitators, and a fearless and open fighter
against injustice and tyranny, thought that after the
repeal of the Laws, combinations among workmen
would "fall to pieces," because workmen had combined only to resist the oppression of the old regulations, not to promote the creation of new. Middle-
class opinion continued to predominate in the halls of
legislature, in the councils of party, and in the circles
of the intellectual element for a good many years to
come. The worker of 1832, like the worker of 1800,
was without political rights; the education of his
children except for a few well-intentioned, but pietis-
tic and ineffectual efforts of experimenters and par-
sons, was wholly unprovided for; and government
was only making faint and hesitating headway in the
betterment of conditions in which he was fated to

live. Under the stress of circumstances, however, there was in him a growing sense of injustice and of the power of union with his fellows. Meantime, as the years went on and as industry, commerce, and wealth expanded to gigantic proportions, a knowledge of the worker's condition spread abroad in society and new champions came forward to espouse his cause. Among these were two men of genius, with whom the present study is concerned, Thomas Carlyle and John Ruskin, prophets of revolt and heralds of a new day of justice.

CHAPTER II

SANSCULOTTISM AND ITS PROPHET

"One can predict, without gift of prophecy, that the era of routine is nearly ended. Cost what it may, by one means or another, the toiling multitudes of this perplexed, over-crowded Europe must and will find governors. '*Laissez-faire*, Leave them to do'? The thing they will *do*, if so left, is too frightful to think of! It has been *done* once, in sight of the whole earth, in these generations: can it need to be done a second time?"—*Carlyle*.

THE life of Carlyle was coincident with the momentous events of the new era. Born in 1795 and living until 1881, he was a spectator of the social transformations that went on in England and in Europe during the better part of the century, and that brought men face to face with new conditions and forced upon them new and newer conclusions. Graduated from the University of Edinburgh in 1814, the year before Napoleon was overthrown at Waterloo, he saw the unfolding of a great social and political drama, action and reaction, revolution and counter-revolution, such as made Europe a battle-ground between the old order and the new for more than half a century. The distress and revolts following upon the Napoleonic era, the "Carbonari rebellions and other political tumults" in Italy and Spain, the revolutions of 1830 and 1848 in Belgium and France,—"lava-torrents of fever frenzy, and immense explosions of democracy," Carlyle called them,—the unification of

41

Italy and of Germany, and the giant onward stride
of industrialism and democracy everywhere;—these
were events, or rather angry portents, that followed
one upon another in the countries across the channel.
At home affairs were no less charged with ominous
meaning, and Carlyle watched them at close range.
He wrote his earliest essays at Edinburgh and at
Craigenputtock amid "the din and frenzy of Catholic
Emancipations and Rotten Boroughs." He was in
London in the winter of 1831–32, during the prolonged fight on the Reform Bill, having temporarily
left the solitude of Craigenputtock in the vain hope
of finding a publisher for *Sartor Resartus*. And after
1834 as a permanent resident in London he witnessed
with growing amazement and apprehension everything that went on about him in the political and
industrial world, from the Chartist movements, the
Corn Law agitations, and the rise of trade-unions, to
the passing of the Reform Bill of 1867, which the then
venerable prophet of Chelsea regarded as England's
final plunge over the precipice and into the whirlpool
of democracy. No spectator could have been more
alive to the momentousness of these changes than
Carlyle. To him the entire period was one of transition and unrest; an age in a state of flux, ever on the
verge of revolution, and nowhere resting upon sure
and settled foundations. "There is a deep-lying
struggle in the whole fabric of society; a boundless
grinding collision of the New with the Old," he said
in 1829.[1] Almost forty years later he read the signs
of the times to the same effect: "There probably

[1] *Signs of the Times*, 252.

never was since the Heptarchy ended, or almost since it began, so hugely critical an epoch in the history of England as this we have now entered upon." [1] And when he asked himself and his readers what was the nature of this crisis, what it was that "bursts asunder the bonds of ancient Political Systems, and perplexes all Europe with the fear of Change," his answer was ready: it was, he said, "the increase of social resources, which the old social methods will no longer sufficiently administer." [2]

Carlyle's interest in revolutionary movements was passionate and profound from the first. He was hardly out of college when "the condition of England question" became, and to the end of his days remained, the central theme of his thought, his inquiries, and his talk. It was a constant subject of discussion between him and his friend Edward Irving, in the early days when both were teaching at Kirkcaldy. His first political and social essay, *Signs of the Times*, 1829, found its way to Paris, where it aroused the interest of the Society of St. Simonians. These ardent dreamers of a new order at once began to solicit the attention of the mystic radical of Craigenputtock, and were hopeful that they might make a disciple of him. They dispatched a parcel of books and pamphlets to Carlyle, and for a time undoubtedly much engaged his interest in their doctrines, even though Goethe warned him to keep clear of their influence. He directed his brother John, then in London, to send him their books; and he translated St. Simon's chief work, *Nouveau Christian-*

[1] *Shooting Niagara*, 200.   [2] *Essays*, IV, 34.

isme, with a short introduction, and sent it to his brother to be sold to a publisher.[1] His mind was very evidently running on the social teachings of these enthusiasts when he set foot in London in 1831, for he records that at an eating-house on his arrival in August, he began discussing social problems among some Frenchmen, "one of whom ceases eating to hear the talk of the St. Simonians."[2] In that epoch the disciples of St. Simon were "stirring and conspicuous objects," and Carlyle came into personal contact with a number of them, notably Gustave d'Eichthal and Detrosier, the latter of whom was then lecturing to the working classes of Manchester. Although they may have wandered into strange paths, to the transcendentalist of Craigenputtock they seemed to have laid hold of momentous but neglected truths concerning the spiritual and social nature of man, and to have been a notable sign of the times. And when he returned to the solitude of his home, he offered to write an essay on the society, but magazine editors were again deaf to his proposals. Readers of *Sartor Resartus* will recall that the society transmitted its propositions to Teufelsdröckh (who comments: "here also are men who have discovered, not without amazement, that Man is still Man"), and that the strange disappearance of the clothes-philosopher was perhaps to be accounted for on the ground that he had gone to join the St. Simonians! But these heralds of a new Christianity from Paris

---

[1] Apparently without success. There is no evidence that it was published at that time, or that it has appeared since.

[2] *Two Note Books*, 193.

were by no means the only sources from which Carlyle, during his six months in London in 1831–1832,
added to his already abundant store of knowledge
and enthusiasm concerning the problems of the day.
A radical, even though a spiritual and speculative
one, he was not without some hopes of becoming
himself the center of a mystical school, to which
might be drawn the younger spirits of the radical
group then dominant in London political circles. He
had many walks and talks with John Stuart Mill,
"a fine clear enthusiast, who will one day come to
something." [1] He saw again on frequent occasions
his old pupil, the brilliant Charles Buller, soon to be a
rising member of parliament and the hope of the
parliamentary radicals. These two men, Mill and
Buller, together with Irving (now a popular London
preacher), brought Carlyle into somewhat close
touch with utilitarian circles;—with John Austin, the
legalist, with Bowring, the friend and biographer of
Bentham, and editor of the *Westminster Review;* with
Molesworth, founder of the *London Review,* and many
others. We may be sure that the outpouring of utilitarianism from these sources was more than met by
copious floods of "Teufelsdröckhist" mysticism from

---

[1] Froude, *Life of Carlyle,* II (Edition of 1882-4, by Scribner's), 162. In a
letter to John Sterling (October, 1831) Mill describes Carlyle, whom he
has just met. Among other things he says: "He has by far the widest
liberality and tolerance that I have met with in any one; and he differs
from most men, who see as much as he does into the defects of the age,
by a circumstance greatly to his advantage in my estimation, that he
looks for a safe landing *before* and not *behind;* he sees that if we could only
replace things as they once were, we should only retard the final issue, as
we should in all probability go on just as we then did, and arrive at the
very place where we now stand." (*Letters of John Stuart Mill,* I, 16.)

the lips of Carlyle, who was each day stronger in his conviction that what the times needed most was not Benthamism, but "the doctrine of the Phœnix, of Natural Supernaturalism, and the whole Clothes Philosophy!" [1] Through the offices of Francis Jeffrey, now no longer editor of the *Edinburgh Review* but member of parliament, he visited the old unreformed House of Commons, where he heard Althrop, Wetherell, and Joseph Hume, all of them protagonists in the struggle for better political conditions. It would be easy to extend the list of these contacts which Carlyle was fortunate enough to secure in the winter of 1831–32. A little later after he established his residence in London (1834) his house was for years a kind of shrine to which many of the most passionate spirits of the age made pilgrimage for guidance and inspiration;—among the most famous being Godfroi Cavaignac, in exile from France for conspiracy against Louis Philippe; Louis Blanc, the celebrated French socialist leader of 1848 days; and the beloved Mazzini, organizer and soul of new Italy. The oracle in those times was rather more apt to express himself in hoarse thunder,

"winged with red lightning and impetuous rage,"

than in articulate speech. But the worshipers came none the less, for they saw here a man who had passed through a profound spiritual experience and whose discussion of the times was lighted up with a passionate sense of social justice and with an equally passionate sympathy for the poor and oppressed. Emerson

[1] Froude, *Life of Carlyle*, II, 145.

had found this out when he made his pilgrimage to
Craigenputtock in 1833. "He still returned to
English pauperism," said Emerson, speaking of their
earnest talks together, "the crowded country, the
selfish abdication by public men of all that public
persons should perform. Government should direct
poor men what to do." [1]

Carlyle's interest in social and industrial conditions was altogether too serious to permit him to
remain satisfied with discussion among thinkers
and theorists and agitators alone. He wished to
see the working world with his own eyes and when-
ever possible to speak with the operatives face to
face. He began to carry out his wishes early. In
1818 while he and his friend Irving were still at
Kirkcaldy, they took a vacation walking tour through
the Trossachs and visited the celebrated model
school of Robert Owen at New Lanark Mills on the
Clyde; being already familiar with Owenite teachings
and wishing to see this earliest realization of them.
Two years later, when Irving had become assistant
pastor to the famous Dr. Chalmers of Glasgow,
Carlyle paid him a visit there, and talked with the
"Radical Weavers" who were spreading consterna-
tion and terror far and wide with their rioting. [2] For

---

[1] *English Traits*, 17 (Centenary Edition).

[2] It was during the 1817 vacation tour that Carlyle first saw steamers
on the water. It was at Greenock, on the Firth of Clyde: "queer little
dumpy things, with a red sail to each, bobbing about there and making
continual passages to Glasgow." At Liverpool in August, 1831, on his
way to London with the manuscript of *Sartor*, he had his first sight of
'steam-coaches,' on the Liverpool and Manchester railway, which had
been opened the year before. It was not until 1839 that he made his
first journey by rail, going from London to Preston: "the whirl through

many years, at least up to 1852, when he retired to
the seclusion of his sound-proof room for the long
grapple with the history of Frederick the Great,
he seems rarely to have missed an opportunity to
see for himself the storm-centers of the new era. In
1824 he spent two months in Birmingham, with its
"thousand funnels." In that roaring center of flame
and smoke, there must have been little which his
devouring eyes did not discover; for he inspected
the blast-furnaces and the iron-works ("where
150,000 men are smelting the metal"), and he de-
scended into the mines, "poking about industriously
into Nature's and Art's sooty arcana." Twenty-
five years later he visited the iron and coal industries at Merthyr Tydvil, Wales, where some 50,000
"grimy mortals" were "screwing out a livelihood
for themselves amid their furnaces, pits, and rolling
mills." [1] A little before this, in 1847, he had been
at Manchester, having stopped there on his way to
the old home at Scotsbrig, "to see iron works and
cotton mills; to talk with some of the leaders of the
working men, who were studying his writings with
passionate interest." [2] While at Manchester he took
a day to visit Rochdale and the mills of John Bright
and his brother Jacob. A talk between the distinguished anti-cornlaw leader and the gaunt mystic
of Cheyne Row appears not to have gone off very
smoothly: "John and I discorded in our views not

the confused darkness, on these steam wings, was one of the strangest
things I have experienced—hissing and dashing on, one knew not
whither." (Froude, *Life of Carlyle*, III, 144.)

[1] Froude, *Life of Carlyle*, IV, 44.

[2] *Ibid.*, III, 351.

a little, . . . the result was that I got to talking
occasionally in the Annandale accent, . . . and
shook peaceable Brightdom as with a passing earth-
quake." [1] At another time when visiting at Matlock
Bath, Carlyle walked out to have a look at Arkwright's Mills: "one of them, the Cromford one if
I mistake not, the *first* erected mill in England, and
consequently the Mother of all Mills." [2] He went
through the workhouses at St. Ives and the 'model'
prisons of London; and from workingmen and
agitators on all sides he learned about a great many
more English industries and institutions than he
could inspect for himself. In 1846 he spent six days
observing conditions in Ireland under the guidance
of some ardent "Young Irelanders," when he heard
a speech at Dublin by the great O'Connell, "chief
quack of the then world." Three years later he
gave up five weeks to a more extended tour of observation in Ireland, at a time when the plight of
the poor seemed desperate. His letters and journals
are strewn with comments and lamentations upon
the social disturbances everywhere, which seemed
to loom up as lurid portents of disaster. The rick-
burning in 1830 "all over the south and middle of
England."; "the frightful riots at Bristol" in 1831,—
"all the public buildings burnt, and many private
houses,"—suggesting to Carlyle that "a second
edition of the French revolution" was within the
range of chances; "the paupers of Manchester
helping themselves out of shops, great bands of them
parading with signals of want of bread," in 1837;

[1] Froude, *Life of Carlyle*, III, 352.   [2] *New Letters*, II, 41.

the poor almost at his own door in Chelsea tearing up the garden palings in the winter of 1842, and stealing them for fuel; the marching of the army of discontented Chartists in the streets of London in 1848,—these and many other outbursts of insurrectionary radicalism he made record of as ominous signs of the times during the disturbed decades of 1830, 1840, and 1850.[1]

The transformations wrought upon the surface of society, as well as in its structure, by the coming of this new order, were seen and understood by Carlyle. His descriptions of them are in language characteristically vivid and powerful. The canal building of Brindley, who "chained seas together," the spinning wheel of Arkwright, who gave England "the power of cotton," the steam-engine of Watt, who with grim brow and blackened fingers searched out in his workshop "the Fire-secret,"—these thaumaturgic instrumentalities of industry seemed to Carlyle fit theme for a modern epic, the epic of Tools and the Man! If not yet sung, it is at least written, he says, "in huge characters on the face of this Planet,—sea-miles, cotton-trades, railways, fleets and cities, Indian Empires, Americas, New Hollands; legible throughout the Solar System! . . . The Prospero evoked the singing of Ariel, and took captive the world with those melodies: the same Prospero can send his Fire-demons panting across all oceans; shooting with the speed of meteors, on cunning highways, from end to end of kingdoms; and make Iron his missionary, preaching *its* evangel

[1] Froude, *Life of Carlyle*, II, 74, 179; *New Letters*, I, 69.

to the brute Primeval Powers, which listen and obey: neither is this small. Manchester, with its cotton-fuzz, the smoke and dust, its tumult and contentious squalor, is hideous to thee? Think not so: a precious substance, beautiful as magic dreams, and yet no dream but a reality, lies hidden in that noisome wrappage;—a wrappage struggling indeed (look at Chartisms and such like) to cast itself off and leave the beauty free and visible there! Hast thou heard, with sound ears, the awakening of a Manchester, on Monday morning, at half-past five by the clock; the rushing-off of its thousand mills, like the boom of an Atlantic tide, ten-thousand times ten-thousand spools and spindles all set humming there,—it is per-haps, if thou knew it well, sublime as a Niagara, or more so. Cotton-spinning is the clothing of the naked in its result; the triumph of man over matter in its means. Soot and despair are not the essence of it; they are divisible from it. . . . It was proved by fluxionary calculus, that steamers could never get across from the farthest point of Ireland to the nearest of Newfoundland; impelling force, resisting force, maximum here, minimum there; by law of Nature, and geometric demonstration:—what could be done? The Great Western could weigh anchor from Bristol Port; that could be done. The Great Western, bounding safe through the gullets of the Hudson, threw her cable out on the capstan of New York, and left our still moist paper-demonstration to dry itself at leisure." [1]

The Scottish brassmith's *idea*, traveling on fire-

----

[1] *Past and Present*, 138; *Chartism*, 165, 174.

wings, was in truth swiftly overturning "the whole
old system of Society," as Carlyle saw; "and, for
Feudalism and Preservation of the Game, preparing
us, by indirect but sure methods, Industrialism and
the Government of the Wisest. . . . On every hand,
the living artisan is driven from his workshop, to
make room for a speedier, inanimate one. The
shuttle drops from the fingers of the weaver, and falls
into iron fingers that ply it faster. . . . Even the
horse is stripped of his harness, and finds a fleet fire-
horse yoked in his stead. . . . The giant Steam engine in a giant English nation will here create violent demand for labor, and will there annihilate demand. . . . English Commerce stretches its fibres
over the whole earth; sensitive literally, nay quiver-
ing in convulsion, to the farthest influences of the
earth. The huge demon of Mechanism smokes and
thunders, panting at his great task, in all sections of
English land; changing his *shape* like a very Proteus;
and infallibly, at every change of shape, *oversetting*
whole multitudes of workmen, and as if with the wav-
ing of his shadow from afar, hurling them asunder,
this way and that, in their crowded march and course
of work or traffic; so that the wisest no longer knows
his whereabout." [1] Very evidently from such accounts Carlyle was alive to the movements of society
that were going on underneath the surface. The
omnipotence of the new machinery, scattering workshops everywhere, creating "new ganglions of population," new multitudes of cunning toilers, and making Britain queen of the industrial world and mistress

[1] *Sartor*, 82; *Signs of the Times*, 233; *Chartism*, 130.

of the seas,—in all this splendid triumph of the British worker Carlyle could and did exult with his contemporaries. But he could not share in the unclouded optimism of Macaulay and the middle-class Liberals. His sense of the glory of material expansion was disturbed by what he saw taking place in the very structure of society. More than all else the ever-increasing separation, economic and social, between the rich and the poor filled him with alarm. "Wealth has accumulated itself into masses," he said; "and Poverty, also in accumulation enough, lies impassibly separated from it; opposed, uncommunicating, like forces in positive and negative poles. The Gods of this lower world sit aloft on glittering thrones, less happy than Epicurus's gods, but as ignorant, as impotent; while the boundless living chaos of Ignorance and Hunger welters terrific, in its dark fury, under their feet." Man has conquered the material forces of the world, but he reaps no profit from the victory. "Sad to look upon: in the highest stage of civilization, nine tenths of mankind have to struggle in the lowest battle of savage or even animal man, the battle against Famine. Countries are rich, prosperous in all manner of increase, beyond example; but the Men of these countries are poor, needier than ever of all sustenance outward and inward. . . . The frightful condition of a Time, when public and private Principle, as the word was once understood, having gone out by sight, and Self-interest being left to plot, and struggle, and scramble, as it could and would, difficulties had accumulated till they were no longer to be borne, and the spirit that should have fronted and conquered them seemed to have forsaken the World;—when the Rich, as the utmost they could resolve on, had ceased to govern, and the Poor, in their fast accumulating numbers, and ever widening complexities, had ceased to be able to do without governing." [1]

The many graphic pictures that Carlyle drew of the miserable poor leave the reader in no doubt as to the character of the impressions which their condition made upon his mind. He was not a sentimentalist; for a lifetime he preached and practiced the gospel of labor as an antidote to sentimentalism. But his soul was stirred to its depths by what he saw and read. Dante's vision of Hell is not more intense and hardly more vivid. "When one reads," he said in a letter, "of the Lancashire Factories and little children labouring for sixteen hours a day, inhaling at every breath a quantity of *fuzz*, falling asleep over their wheels, and roused again by the lash of thongs over their backs, or the slap of 'billy-rollers' over their little crowns, . . . one pauses with a kind of amazed horror, to ask if this be Earth, the place of Hope, or Tophet, where hope never comes!" . . . "Do you remember," he asked in a letter to his wife, describing the Manchester Mills, "do you remember the poor 'grinders' sitting underground in a damp dark place, some dozen of them? . . . Those poor fellows, in their paper caps with their roaring grindstones, and their yellow *oriflammes* of fire, all grinding themselves so quietly to death, will never go out of my memory." No less indelible was his memory of the Welsh miners.

[1] *Characteristics*, 18–19; *Corn-Law Rhymes*, 195.

"Such a set of unguided, hard-worked, fierce, and miserable-looking sons of Adam I never saw before. Ah me! It is like a vision of Hell, and never will leave me, that of these poor creatures broiling, all in sweat and dirt, amid their furnaces, pits, and rolling mills." With incomparable literary skill, with the "lightning's power to strike out marvellous pictures and reach to the inmost of men with a phrase," as George Meredith pithily says, Carlyle thus described the continents of squalid dwellings in the cities,—the crowds of gaunt and tattered Irish, swarming into the manufacturing towns and lowering the standards of life of the British workmen,—"the thirty-thousand distressed needle-women,—" the "half-a-million handloom weavers, working fifteen hours a day in perpetual inability to procure thereby enough of the coarsest food,"—the two million paupers in crowded Bastilles, or workhouses,—and worst of all the moral degradation of these grimy and discontented masses.

One or two masterly sketches of these wrecks of humanity, set adrift by the industrial upheaval, are too characteristic of Carlyle's spiritual reaction to be omitted. "Passing by the Workhouse of St. Ives, in Huntingdonshire, on a bright day last autumn, I saw sitting on wooden benches, in front of their Bastille and within their ring-wall and its railings, some half-hundred or more of these men. Tall robust figures, young mostly or of middle age; of honest countenance, many of them thoughtful and even intelligent-looking men. They sat there, near by one another; but in a kind of torpor, especially in a silence, which was very striking. In silence: for, alas, what word was

to be said? An Earth all lying round, crying, Come
and till me, come and reap me,—yet we here sit enchanted! In the eyes and brows of these men hung
the gloomiest expression, not of anger, but of grief
and shame and manifold inarticulate distress and
weariness; they returned my glance with a glance that
seemed to say 'Do not look at us. We sit enchanted
here, we know not why. The Sun shines and the Earth
calls; and, by the governing Powers and Impotences
of this England, we are forbidden to obey. It is impossible, they tell us!' There was something that reminded me of Dante's Hell in the look of all this; and
I rode swiftly away." Likewise for the operatives in
Glasgow the time was out of joint, and the world was
become not a home but a dingy prison-house: "Is it
a green flowery world, with azure everlasting sky
stretched over it, the work and government of a God;
or a murky-simmering Tophet, of copperas-fumes,
cotton-fuzz, gin-riot, wrath and toil, created by a
demon? The sum of their wretchedness merited and
unmerited welters, huge, dark, and baleful, like a
Dantean Hell, visible there in the statistics of Gin:
Gin justly named the most authentic incarnation of
the Infernal Principle in our times, too indisputable
an incarnation; Gin the black throat into which
wretchedness of every sort, consummating itself by
calling on delirium to help it, whirls down; abdication
of the power to think or resolve, as too painful now,
on the part of men whose lot of all others would require thought and resolution; liquid Madness sold at
ten-pence the quartern, all the products of which are
and must be, like its origin, mad, miserable, ruinous,

and that only! If from this black unluminous un-
heeded *Inferno*, and Prisonhouse of souls in pain,
there do flash up from time to time, some dismal
wide-spread glare of Chartism or the like, notable to
all, claiming remedy from all,—are we to regard it as
more baleful than the quiet state, or rather as not so
baleful?" What was threatening among the lower
orders as a result of these conditions the last sentence
in the passage clearly indicates. It was revolt.
"Revolt," says Carlyle, "sullen revengeful humor of
revolt against the upper classes, decreasing respect
for what their temporal superiors command, decreasing faith for what their spiritual superiors teach, is
more and more the universal spirit of the lower
classes. . . . To whatever other griefs the lower
classes labor under, this bitterest and sorest grief
now superadds itself: the unendurable conviction
that they are unfairly dealt with, that their lot in this
world is not founded on right." [1]

Even more intense than his sympathetic understanding of the workers, if it were possible, was
Carlyle's scorn of the idle and irresponsible rich,
the new rich as well as the old landed artisocracy.
The smug contentment and careless detachment
of an upper class, piling up wealth with miraculous
rapidity and spending it ostentatiously upon luxuries and selfish pleasures, were so utterly opposed
to every article in his social and spiritual creed that
his descripion of it at times seems rather a splutter
of rage than rational speech. Readers who have

[1] *Letters of Thomas Carlyle*, 356; Froude, *Life*, III, 351; *ibid.*, IV, 44;
Chartism, 130; *Past and Present*, 2; *Chartism*, 132, 136.

followed him in this field will remember the explosions of Sauerteig and Smelfungus against Mammonism and Dilettantism, against the monsters of opulence and the bloated nabobs of the new era,—Plugson of Undershot, Bobus of Houndsditch, and others of their ilk. "Are these your Pattern Men?" he asks. "They are your lucky (or unlucky) Gamblers swollen *big*. . . . Paltry Adventurers for most part; worthy of no worship. . . . Unfortunate creatures! You are fed, clothed, lodged as men never were before; every day in new variety of magnificence are you equipped and attended to. . . . Mount into your railways; whirl from place to place, at the rate of fifty, or if you like of five hundred miles an hour: you cannot escape from that inexorable all-encircling ocean-moan of Ennui." [1] For the most part the older aristocracy, the landowners, held themselves loftily aloof from the new industrialism and its problems. "What do these highly beneficed individuals *do* to society for their wages?"—asked Carlyle during his long quiet days of meditation at Craigenputtock: "Kill partridges," he answered. "*Can* this last? No, by the soul that is in man it cannot, and will not, and shall not. . . . Eleven thousand souls in Paisley alone living on three half pence a day, and the governors of the land all busy shooting partridges!" [2] England thus seemed to Carlyle, in his savage-satirical mood, to be made up of two sects, the sect of the drudge and the sect of the dandy,—a division running through

[1] *Latter-Day Pamphlets*, 223, 286.
[2] Froude, *Life of Carlyle*, II, 67; III, 243.

the entire structure of society and threatening it
with dissolution.

In the presence of such conditions, when great
issues were at stake and when men must be brought
back to first principles, he could not stand aloof,
indifferent and silent. Various special interests had
their voices and their organs,—the aristocracy, the
radicals, the Corn-law agitators, the Poor-law
reformers. But each group spoke for itself, and
spoke one-sidedly or selfishly. "The dumb poor,"
said Carlyle, "have no voice; and must and will
find a voice—other than Rick-burnings, Gunpowder,
and Chartism!" It was not enough, moreover, to
pile up parliamentary reports upon the condition
of England, with facts and figures as to the prosperity of the rich and the wretchedness of the poor.
Statistics and special pleadings were well enough
in their way—and Carlyle read them extensively,—
"but it must be the utterance of *principles*, grounded
on facts which all may see." Men must be led back
once more to the eternal foundations of life, to the
laws of God and Nature, to the dictates of justice,
to the rights of the governed and the duties of the
governors. The great solid *heart* of England must
be awakened! Otherwise reports and statistics were
as so much chaff before the wind. Carlyle occupied
a fortunate position from which to speak to the
conscience of his contemporaries with the voice
of the prophet. He was free from the trammels of
party, class, or sect, free to condemn any evil and
to advocate any remedy; and he gloried in his
freedom. "No King or Pontiff has any power over

me. . . . There is nothing but my maker whom I call Master under this sky," he wrote to his sister in 1842, in words that accurately express his convictions for any period of his life. It is true that at certain times and under certain circumstances he did cherish hopes that he might become identified with social problems and issues, in a practical way; as when in 1834 (a time of almost desperate uncertainty in his private fortunes), he would gladly have accepted from John Stuart Mill and Molesworth the editorship of the *London Review;* and in 1867, the year of the second reform bill, when he had some desire of starting an independent journal with Froude and Ruskin. Froude is indeed authority for the statement that Carlyle, after the publication of *Latter-Day Pamphlets* in 1850, imagined that he might be invited by the government "to assist in carrying out some of the changes which he had there insisted on." [1] It was fortunate that these hopes came to nothing, and that he was left with his independence. Carlyle called himself a Bedouin, and a Bedouin he remained to the end, unattached, unchartered, free to follow no will but his own, free to strike when and where he pleased.

Even during the first period of his literary career, the period of the critical essays, he was drawn further and further into discussions of the state of society.

[1] Froude, *Life of Carlyle*, IV, 48. The suggestion, implied in the above statement, of Carlyle's holding public office reminds one of the offer to him of a clerkship by Basil Montagu, on his first London visit in 1824: "the faith of Montagu wishing *me* for his clerk; thinking the polar bear, reduced to a state of dyspeptic dejection, might safely be trusted tending rabbits."

He could not remain content to write reviews when he saw, as he said in *Sartor*, "a world becoming dismantled." Poetry, literary criticism, art, and philosophy must give way to more pressing issues. "How can we *sing* and *paint*," he asks, "when we do not yet *believe* and *see?*" [1] "He thinks it the only question for wise men," reported Emerson, "instead of art and fine fancies and poetry and such things, to address themselves to the problems of society." [2] From 1830 onward Carlyle, in his essays, referred more and more to "our age." It would be possible indeed to regard all of the later and greater essays as tracts for the times, though to do this would be to lay emphasis upon certain aspects at the expense of others. In the *Voltaire* (1828) he declared against skepticism and denial; in the *Diderot* (1833) he warned his readers of mechanism and a mechanical age. Even in the *Scott* (1837), last of the critical essays, Carlyle wrote with his eye upon worldliness and a worldly era. On the other hand the essay on *Boswell's Life of Johnson* (1832) was written partly for the purpose of setting before a drifting social order the figure of a man who held fast to integrity and duty; while in the second *Goethe* (1832) there was presented the true prophet and ideal character,— the builder who had wrought out for himself a *complete* life, in contrast to the *halfness* in the lives of men of Carlyle's own time. In the *Signs of the Times* (1829) and *Characteristics* (1832) the attack upon contemporary thought was more direct and open.

[1] Froude, *Life*, II, 299.
[2] Emerson, *Lectures and Biographical Sketches*, 497.

The monumental histories themselves, although built upon a solid foundation of documentary material, were inspired by a very definite social philosophy. The *French Revolution* (1837) set forth the frightful dangers that inevitably threatened a nation whose social order was founded upon class privilege and ancient injustice; while the *Cromwell* (1845) and the *Frederick the Great* (1858–1865) reflected Carlyle's stern conviction that the ship of state could not come through the storms that beat upon it, unless its course was directed by a great captain. The writing, however, in which his social philosophy is most fully set forth and which form the basis of the present study are the following: *Sartor Resartus* (1831); *Chartism* (1839); *Heroes and Hero-Worship* (1841); *Past and Present* (1843); *Latter-Day Pamphlets* (1850); with which should be included *Shooting Niagara* (1867), a parting volley at advancing democracy. In these books it is not the political propagandist nor the partisan who speaks. It is not even mainly the advocate of special remedies, although very special remedies were urged, as will be shown in the next chapter. The voice heard oftenest is the voice of the moralist and seer, speaking directly to the hearts of Englishmen upon the plain facts of greedy wealth and grim poverty, and proclaiming with an assurance born out of fiery trial the authentic principles of justice and truth as the basis of a better social order. It was a voice that grew harsher with the passing of events, but to the last it never wavered from its conviction that there could be no other foundation of constitutions and creeds alike

than the righteousness of the individual soul. It
was this voice, says Froude, that came to the young
generation of Englishmen like the sound of ten
thousand trumpets, "amidst the controversies, the
arguments, the doubts, the crowding uncertainties"
of mid-Victorian England.[1]

Carlyle's criticism of his age starts with a profound
dissent from its fundamental beliefs, and from the
tendencies which, as he thought, sprang from them.
That the times were sick and out of joint discerning
thinkers could see for themselves. According to the
great majority of these observers the *cause* of social
disorders lay in bad social arrangements, and the
cure in right arrangements. The panacea, in other
words, was proper *machinery*,—a word that Carlyle
caught up, in a time of enormous material expansion,
and made use of as the symbol of his entire attack.
The epoch, in its work, its ways, its thought and its
ideal, was mechanical,—that was its primal eldest
curse. There was a pervading belief in the outer, visible, practical, and physical, a belief that the possibility of reform and regeneration rested in statistics,
workhouses, model prisons, acts of parliament, phil-
anthropical and co-operative societies, organizations,
constitutions, and thirty-nine articles alone. "Do
you ask why misery abounds among us?" he inquired.
"I bid you look into the notion we have formed for
ourselves of this Universe, and of our duties and destinies there. . . . Faith, Fact, Performance in all
high and gradually in all low departments, go about
their business; Inanity well tailored and upholstered,

[1] Froude, *Life*, III, 249.

mild-spoken Ambiguity, decorous Hypocrisy which is astonished you should think it hypocritical, taking their room and drawing their wages: from zenith to nadir, you have Cant, Cant,—a Universe of Incredibilities which are not even credited, which each man at best only tries to persuade himself that he credits. Do you expect a divine battle, with noble victories, out of this?" [1] The reiterated cry of the prophet is familiar. Religion is waning, or gone; men have closed their eyes to the eternal Substance of things and opened them only to the Shows and Shams. They believe only in "a great unintelligible Perhaps." Their only hell is the hell of not succeeding—"a somewhat singular Hell." Faith in the vital, invisible, infinite; faith in love, fear, wonder, enthusiasm; faith in the expression of these mystic forces through literature, art, and religion, has vanished from society, leaving it sick, introspective, and self-conscious. The vital has retreated before the mechanical. "A man's religion," Carlyle said, "consists not in the many things he is in doubt of and tries to believe, but of the few he is assured of, and has no need of effort for believing." [2] But what is the religion of the average Britisher? "He believes in the inalienable nature of purchased beef, in the duty of the British citizen to fight for himself when injured, and other similar faiths." [3] His faith is faith in stomach and purse, not in heart and head. He believes that happiness depends upon circumstances without, not upon spirit within; and he looks, if he looks at all, to political and economic adjustments for salvation. For his sacred

[1] *Latter-Day Pamphlets*, 252.   [2] *Ibid.*, 266.   [3] *Ibid.*, 267.

"interests" must be preserved whatever else is lost. His gospel, therefore, is a gospel of Mammonism and dilettantism,—a very ancient religion!

This materialistic faith found complete expression, according to Carlyle, in the current ethical and social philosophy of the time; in the utilitarianism of Bentham and his disciples, in the parliamentary radicalism of this group and their followers, and in the blind dogmatism of the "Dismal Science," as Carlyle nicknamed political economy. To the creeds of this school of thought he was opposed by every intuition of his nature. Its very shibboleths proved that its foundations were mechanistic:—"cause and effect," "profit and loss," "cash-payment," "competition," "*laissez-faire*," "pleasure and pain," "self-interest," and all the rest of the labels attached by a generation of quacks to their nostrums,—as though the ills of a stricken society could be instantly cured by some "Morrison's Pill!" The corner-stone of this machine-made philosophy was the "steam engine Utilitarianism" of Bentham, which Carlyle regarded as the inevitable creed of an epoch of gigantic material growth; but which he none the less condemned as the negation of every principle by which the world must be reformed. For it identified virtue with self-interest; it made ethics into a system of checking and balancing by which the self-regarding accountant might extract a net surplus of pleasure as against pain; it insisted upon rights before duties, wages before obligations; it promoted the physical and finite ends of man at the expense of his spiritual nature, considering him a compound of clashing de-

sires and fears instead of a creature dependent upon a
God whom he should reverence and obey. Carlyle
was never weary of venting his scorn and anger upon
men who hoped to regenerate society with such a
creed. For a man to fancy himself, he said, "a dead
Iron-Balance for weighing Pains and Pleasures on,
was reserved for this latter era. There stands he, his
Universe one huge Manger, filled with hay and this-
tles to be weighed against each other; and looks long-
eared enough."[1] Vitally linked with this individualistic hedonism were the teachings of Malthus and the
doctrine of *laissez-faire*, which drew down Carlyle's
anathemas no less scornfully; for they, too, left the
toiling masses without guidance, with ominous results. "How often," he said, "have we read in Malthusian benefactors of the species: 'The working
people have their condition in their own hands; let
them diminish the supply of laborers, and of course
the demand and the remuneration will increase!'
Yes, let *them* diminish the supply: but who are they?
They are twenty-four millions of human individuals,
scattered over a hundred and eighteen square miles
of space and more; weaving, delving, hammering,
joinering; each unknown to his neighbour; each distinct within his own skin. *They* are not a kind of
character that can take a resolution, and act on it,
very readily. . . . O, Wonderful Malthusian prophets! Millenniums are undoubtedly coming, must
come one way or another: but will it be, think you, by
twenty millions of working people . . . passing, in
universal trade-union, a resolution not to beget any

[1] *Sartor Resartus*, 152.

more till the labor-market become satisfactory?"
A shade more rational would it be, continued Carlyle
in acrid Swiftian vein, to supply a "Parish Extermi-
nator, or Reservoir of Arsenic, kept up at the public
expense, free to all parishioners." [1] To the same
effect was his condemnation of *laissez-faire*, which left
the workers to scramble along as best they could:
"Whoever in the press is trodden down, has only to
lie there and be trampled,"—a monstrous doctrine
and an abrogation of every duty on the part of the
governors of society. Carlyle's hostility to these and
the allied tenets of the schools grew more vehement
as he saw conditions on all sides becoming worse. He
fulminated against a soft-hearted philanthropy that
coddled criminals in model-prisons and left uncared
for the needy and deserving. Your scoundrel, he
declared, could not be reformed by applications of
rose-water! He fulminated against parliamentary
radicalism that debated eight years in a reformed
parliament and left the English workingmen wringing
their hands and breaking out into "five-point Chartism," amidst riots and hootings. He broke forth in
anger, too, against a ceremonious officialism that
heaped up mountains of red-tape and made a great
fuss about smaller matters; while the "Condition of
England Question" was left to take care of itself under
the guidance of "enlightened selfishness." Wherever Carlyle looked he saw a world in the grip of
machinery. Mechanism had become the vampire of
national life.

The evil effects of this materialistic philosophy and

[1] *Chartism*, 183.

political economy were to be seen everywhere. They
were to be seen in bad leaders and in bad work. Most
of all they were evident in the distressed and discon-
tended workers. Much of Carlyle's severest condemnation of the age was directed, as has already been
pointed out, against the old aristocracy and the new.
Both classes wantonly neglected the duties of leadership. By every sign of the times, therefore, they
were doomed to extinction, unless they should speedily awaken to a sense of their responsibilities. "What
shall we say of the Idle Aristocracy, the Owners of the
Soil of England; whose recognized function is that of
handsomely consuming the rents of England, shooting the partridges of England, and as an agreeable
amusement, diletantte-ing in Parliament and Quar-
ter-Sessions for England? We will say mournfully,
in the presence of Heaven and Earth,—that we stand
speechless, stupent, and know not what to say!
That a class of men entitled to live sumptuously on
the marrow of the earth; permitted simply, nay
entreated, and as yet entreated in vain, to do nothing
at all in return, was never heretofore seen on the face
of this Planet. That such a class is transitory, exceptional, and, unless Nature's Laws fall dead, cannot
continue. . . . A High Class without duties to do is
like a tree planted on precipices; from the roots of
which all the earth has been crumbling." [1] The fat
luxury and the grasping brutality of the British
manufacturer on the other hand,—like Hudson, the
railway King, who swindled poor people out of their
savings and fared sumptuously upon plundered

[1] *Past and Present*, 153, 154.

wealth,—these too must be transitory, if there were any justice in creation. Relations between an upper class such as this and the laboring classes were of necessity impersonal and mechanical. The old feudal relations of master and servant on manor or in guild had given place to what Carlyle called the "nomadic principle" in servantship. Between employers and men, in modern industry, there was no permanence of tenure, no permanence of relation anywhere. Cash-payment was the sole nexus. The laborer worked during long hours under bad conditions for *wages* alone. He was a mechanical cog in a mechanical wheel, in a world of machinery! "We have profoundly forgotten everywhere that Cash-payment is not the sole relation of human beings; we think, nothing doubting, that *it* absolves and liquidates all engagements of man. 'My starving workers?' answers the rich mill-owner: 'Did not I hire them fairly in the market? Did I not pay them, to the last sixpence, the sum covenanted for? What have I to do with them more?' " [1] The disastrous results of these unnatural relations were more and more evident in the soot and dirt and "squalid horror now defacing England," and in what Carlyle condemned as "cheap and nasty" work,—universal *shoddy* in all departments of industry. "Do you know the shop, saleshop, workshop, industrial establishment temporal or spiritual, in broad England, where genuine work is to be had?"—he asked. [2] How could there be a genuine product when the workman had no interest in his work and when the manufacturer, under the

[1] *Past and Present*, 126.   [2] *Shooting Niagara*, 227.

stress of competition, was only concerned in turning out ever *cheaper* and more *showy* articles for the trade? Under such conditions collapse of standards was inevitable.[1]

Bad as these things were, the growing discontent of the workers was infinitely worse. Without guidance from the upper classes, or from middle-class utilitarianism, and driven to desperation by their own worsening condition, they were beginning to demand political rights as their only hope and they were threatening to revolt if these rights were not forthwith granted. "The expectant millions," said Carlyle, "have sat at a feast of the Barmecide; been bidden fill themselves with the imagination of meat. What thing has Radicalism obtained for them; what other than shadows of things has it so much as asked for them? Cheap Justice, Justice to Ireland, Irish Appropriation-Clause, Rate-Paying Clause, Poor-Rate, Church-Rate, Household Suffrage, Ballot-Question 'open' or shut: not things but shadows of things; Benthamee formulas; barren as the east-wind! An Ultra-Radical, not seemingly of the Benthamee species, is forced to exclaim: 'The people are at last wearied. They say, Why should we be ruined

---

[1] *Cf.* "A newly built house is more like a tent than a house; no Table that I fall in with here can stand on its legs; a pair of good Shoes is what I have not been able to procure for the last ten years." This was Carlyle's entry in his notebook for 22 October, 1831, London. To this Professor Norton appends the following comment: "Even in later life Carlyle used to complain humorously that no tolerable shoes could be found in London, and to declare that his only pair of well-made shoes came from an old shoemaker in Dumfries, that he had worn them for years, 'had them upper-leathered and under-leathered,' and they would last a long while yet." (*Two Note Books*, 206–7.) He wore clothing also made at home, because of his faith in Annandale cloth and Annandale tailors.

in our shops, thrown out of our farms, voting for these men? . . . It is not a light matter when the just man can recognize in the powers set over him no longer anything that is divine; when resistance against such becomes a deeper law of order than obedience to them; when the just man sees himself in the tragical position of a stirrer-up of strife! " [1] The passage is significant, for it shows Carlyle's conception of the crisis towards which the drama of events must inevitably tend. The culminating phenomenon of the times, no less terrible than inevitable, was rebellion, widespread rebellion of the masses against a crushing mechanism. And this phenomenon, this threatened outburst of sansculottism, Carlyle called democracy!

To him as to many of his contemporaries the rise of democracy was the most momentous fact of the century. From year to year he watched its progress, at first not without sympathy and hope (he was in favor of Catholic emancipation and the first Reform Bill, and he looked upon extremes of wealth as unjust); [2] but as time went on his reaction changed to surprise and alarm, until democracy came to mean social and political ruin, and the negation of government. If the reader of Carlyle will call to mind the views expressed in the *French Revolution* (1837), then in *Chartism* (1839), *Past and Present* (1843), *Latter-*

---

[1] *Chartism*, 171–3.
[2] There are a good many evidences of a strong radicalism in Carlyle's earlier life: *e. g.* (1830) " *Le classe la plus pauvre* is evidently in the way of rising from its present deepest abasement: in time, it is likely, the world will be better divided, and he that has the toil of ploughing will have the first cut at the reaping." (*Two Note Books*, 158.)

Day Pamphlets (1850), and still later in *Shooting Niagara* (1867), together with the various opinions scattered up and down the published correspondence, he will have no difficulty to convince himself of the truth of this statement. Carlyle dated modern democracy from the French Revolution. The day of the procession of notables at Versailles in 1789 was "the baptism-day of democracy," as it was the "extreme unction day of Feudalism." From then onward, in the European revolutions of 1830 and 1848, in the Chartist disturbances at home, and in the steady upward push of the lower classes everywhere, he saw that the popular movement was "making rapid progress in these later times, and ever more rapid, in a perilous accelerative ratio." [1] Its progress was not only rapid, it was irresistible. "For universal *Democracy*, whatever we may think of it, has declared itself as an inevitable fact of the days in which we live. . . . The gods have appointed it *so;* no Pitt, nor body of Pitts or mortal creatures can appoint it otherwise. Democracy sure enough, is here: one knows not how long it will keep hidden underground even in Russia;—and here in England, though we object to it absolutely in the form of street-barricades and insurrectionary pikes, and decidedly will not open doors to it on those terms, the tramp of its million feet is on all streets and thoroughfares, the sound of its bewildered thousandfold voice is in all thinkings and modes and activities of men." [2]

What was the meaning of this inevitable move-

---

[1] *Chartism*, 145.   [2] *Latter-Day Pamphlets*, 7–8.

ment? How was the mighty advancing tide of the proletariat to be understood? This was the supreme question. "The whole social wisdom of the Present Time is summoned, in the name of the Giver of Wisdom, to make clear to itself, and lay deeply to heart with an eye to strenuous valiant practice and effort, what the meaning of this universal revolt of the European Populations, which calls itself Democracy, and decides to continue permanent, may be." [1] The answers that Carlyle made to this question have often been misunderstood. And with reason, since his opinions not infrequently must seem contradictory even to the devoted Carlylean; while by more than one casual or unfriendly reader they have been looked upon as hardly more than a jumble of ejaculations or inarticulate shrieks of despair.

Certain of Carlyle's social interpretations are wholly in the spirit of democracy. He believed in the worth of the individual, without regard to rank, creed, or capacity. Peasant-born himself, working his way to distinction from the humblest circumstances, he had good reason to disregard outer conditions in his estimates of men. His father, a stone mason of Ecclefechan, was to Carlyle a revered example of the wisdom and worth that may go with the lowliest duties. Burns and Johnson, two of his best loved literary heroes, taught him (if he needed to be taught) that genius could create an orbit for itself, regardless of the opinions of the literati. *Sartor Resartus*, his first book of importance, rings with the message that man is man, a child of

[1] *Latter-Day Pamphlets*, 8.

God, whether he be king, priest, poet, or toilworn craftsman. To the discerning eyes of Teufelsdröckh "the star of a Lord is little less and little more than the broad button of Birmingham spelter in a clown's smock. . . . Wouldst thou rather be a peasant's son that knew, were it never so rudely, there was a God in Heaven and in Man; or a duke's son that only knew there were two-and-thirty quarters on the family-coach?" [1] Because of such democratic opinions Carlyle called himself in 1831 a speculative radical. He habitually cut through rank and circumstances to the human being underneath. Like a poet, like another Burns, his soul was profoundly stirred by the thought of man the worker, man the sufferer, bearing within his nature mystic potentialities for better things. In such a mood, people were to him anything but an indiscriminate herd. "Masses indeed:—" he says in *French Revolution*, "every unit of whom has his own heart and sorrows; stands covered there with his own skin, and if you prick him he will bleed. . . . Every unit of these masses is a miraculous Man, even as thou thyself art; struggling, with vision or with blindness, for *his* infinite Kingdom (this life which he has got, once only, in the middle of Eternities); with a spark of the Divinity, what thou callest an immortal soul, in him!" [2] To these unawakened units Carlyle would give education as the one thing needful: "The poor is hungry and athirst; but for him also there is food and drink: he is heavy-laden and weary; but for him also the Heavens send Sleep, and of the

---

[1] *Sartor Resartus*, 19, 68.　　　[2] *French Revolution*, I, 30.

deepest; in his smoky cribs, a clear dewy heaven of
Rest envelopes him, and fitful glitterings of cloud-
skirted Dreams. But what I do mourn over is, that
the lamp of his soul should go out; that no ray of
heavenly, or even of earthly knowledge, should visit
him; but only, in the haggard darkness, like two
spectres, Fear and Indigestion bear him company.
Alas, while the Body stands so broad and brawny,
must the Soul lie blinded, dwarfed, stupefied, almost
annihilated! Alas, was this too a Breath of God;
bestowed in Heaven, but on earth never to be unfolded!—That there should one Man die ignorant
who had capacity for Knowledge, this I call a tragedy,
were it to happen more than twenty times in the
minute, as by some computations it does. The miserable fraction of Science which our united Mankind, in a wide Universe of Nescience, has acquired, why is not this, with all diligence, imparted
to all?" [1] Such passages contain the very essence
of democratic doctrine,—faith in the worth of the
individual irrespective of rank and in the power of
education to awaken and develop that worth!

Carlyle's democracy goes even further. He was a
vigorous and life-long champion of three great
principles which underlie modern progress and
which were established only after prolonged popular
struggle;—the right of private judgment as won by
the Protestant Reformation, the right of a people
to revolt against prolonged oppression, and the
right of the tools to him who can use them,—the
last two rights being the fruit of the French Revolu-

[1] *Sartor Resartus*, 158.

tion. Protestantism, of which Martin Luther was
the evangel, "was a revolt against spiritual sover-
eignties, Popes and much else," by which liberty
of private judgment in spiritual affairs was enthroned
among mankind; and, as such, Protestantism was
"the grand root from which our whole subsequent
European History branches out, . . . and the beginning of new genuine sovereignty and order." [1]
If the Reformation was for Carlyle the first act in
the struggle for freedom, the French Revolution was
the last, without which, he often declared, he could
not have understood the modern world. The most
memorable event "for a thousand years," it revealed to him facts of profoundest significance concerning democracy. It taught him that the people,
the *canaille*, may be trusted to rise up against immemorial privilege, and that position and power
belong not to a worn-out feudal aristocracy but,
regardless of rank, to those who can use them for
the good of the state. No extremest or leveler in
any age could have been more contemptuous than
was Carlyle towards the futile pomp and circumstance of ineffectual kingship. "Strip your Louis
Quatorze of his King-gear," he said, "and there *is*
left nothing but a poor forked radish with a head
fantastically carved. . . . To assert that in whatever man you chose to lay hold of (by this or the

---

[1] *Heroes and Hero-Worship,*115. Carlyle's recognition of the effects of
the Reformation in establishing an era of private judgment is weakened
by his attempt to explain that "liberty of private judgment must at all
times have existed in the world." Strong men like Dante, he says, must
always have followed their faith! Followed it, yes, but with what
'liberty'? Was there 'liberty' of private judgment for Galileo, Huss, or
Tyndale?

other plan of clutching at him); and clapt a round
piece of metal on the head of, and called king,—
there straightway came to reside a divine virtue, so
that *he* became a kind of god, and a divinity inspired
him with faculty and right to rule over you to all
lengths: this,—what can we do with this but leave
it to rot silently in the Public Libraries?" [1] If the
gods of this lower world will sit on their glittering
thrones, indolent and indifferent, while ignorant
and hungry humanity welters uncared for at their
feet, then the time must come when sansculottism
shall burst up from beneath and sweep away gods
and thrones alike, leaving their places cleared for
the institution of real government and real leaders.
Such is one of the Carlylean interpretations of the
French Revolution. It was exactly this kind of
portentous phenomenon which Carlyle saw threatening to return again, in the revolutions of 1830 and
1848, in the Chartist outbreaks, and in the Paris
revolution of 1871. Concerning this latest outbreak
of the populace he wrote to his brother: "One thing
I can see in these murderous ragings by the poorest
classes in Paris, that they are a tremendous proclamation to the upper classes in all countries:
'Our condition, after eighty-two years of struggling,
O ye quack upper classes, is still unimproved; more
intolerable from year to year, and from revolution
to revolution; and by the Eternal Powers, if you
cannot mend it, we will blow up the world, along
with ourselves and you.'" [2] The other principle

---

[1] *Heroes and Hero-Worship*, 170, 183.
[2] Froude, *Life of Carlyle*, IV, 346.

of modern democracy—the principle that the able
man does not belong exclusively to one rank but
may be found in any—was first victoriously proclaimed by Napoleon, who, said Carlyle, "in the
first period, was a true democrat. . . . The man
was a Divine Missionary though unconscious of it;
and preached, through the cannon's throat, that great
doctrine, *La carrière ouverte aux talens* (The Tools
to him that can handle them), which is our ultimate
Political Evangel, wherein alone can Liberty lie." [1] It
cannot be doubted, therefore, that Carlyle found
in sansculottism an indestructible right meaning, a
soul of truth which must live and work itself out
through the vicissitudes of time;—"till, in some
perfected shape, it embrace the whole circuit of the
world! For the wise may now everywhere discern
that he must found on his manhood, not on the
garnitures of his manhood." [2] It was this truth which
Burns had made immortal in the lines:

> "The rank is but the guinea's stamp,
>   The man's the gowd for a' that,"

and which was to be taken up as the battle-cry of
the new democracy.

Why, then, was Carlyle a foe of the popular movement? Why did he look upon sansculottism, or the
revolt of outraged masses, as an ebullition of bedlam?
How came he to believe that all the evils of his age,
social, industrial, political, were summed up in the
word democracy? For he, no less than Wordsworth
(the Wordsworth of 1820 and after), looked upon

---

[1] *Heroes and Hero-Worship*, 220; *Sartor Resartus*, 123.
[2] *French Revolution*, III, 264.

advancing democracy as upon a rising flood that threatened to sweep away the ancient landmarks and leave society in helpless confusion. The career must be open to the talents, yes, and every man should be free to become all that he was created capable of becoming,—to so much of the democratic creed he attached his undying faith. But this gifted son of an Annandale peasant had no faith in the capacity of the average man for independent collective action, whether industrial or political,—at least as he saw the average man in his own time. Hence his life-long opposition to the new movement. The individuals that made up the populations of the rising industrial centers were so many ignorant and servile units, without self-control and without vision, born to follow the guidance of wise leaders. Carlyle's creed with respect to the masses is graphically set forth in a characteristic passage from his essay on *Boswell's Life of Johnson:* "Mankind sail their life-voyage in huge fleets, following some single whale-fishing or herring-fishing Commodore: the log-book of each differs not, in essential purport, from that of any other: nay the most have no legible log-book (reflection, observation not being among their talents); keep no reckoning, only *keep in sight* of the flagship,—and fish. . . . Or, the servile *imitancy*, and yet also a nobler relationship and mysterious union to one another which lies in such imitancy, of Mankind might be illustrated under the different figure, itself nowise *original*, of a Flock of Sheep. Sheep go in flocks for three reasons: First, because they are of a gregarious temper, and *love* to be together: Secondly, because of their cowardice; they

are afraid to be left alone: Thirdly, because the common run of them are dull of sight, to a proverb, and
can have no choice in roads; sheep can in fact *see*
nothing; in a celestial Luminary, and a scoured pew-
ter Tankard, would discern only that both dazzled
them, and were of unspeakable glory. How like their
fellow-creatures of the human species! Men too,
as was from the first maintained here, are gregarious;
then surely faint-hearted enough, trembling to be left
by themselves; above all, dull-sighted, down to the
verge of utter blindness. Thus are we seen ever
running in torrents, and mobs, if we run at all; and
after what foolish scoured Tankards, mistaking them
for Suns! Foolish Turnip-lanterns likewise, to all
appearance supernatural, keep whole nations quak-
ing, their hair on end. Neither know we, except by
blind habit, where the good pastures lie: solely when
the sweet grass is between our teeth, we know it,
and chew it; also when grass is bitter and scant, we
know it,—and bleat and butt: these last two facts we
know of a truth and in very deed. Thus do Men and
Sheep play their parts on this Nether Earth; wander-
ing restlessly in large masses, they know not whither;
for most part, each following his neighbour, and his
own nose." [1] Over and over again, with increasing
fierceness as he grew older and often in Brobding-
nagian breadth of phrase, he returned to the charge
that the people were greedy blockheads, gullible and
bribeable, wholly incapable of anything but "beer
and balderdash," unless wisely directed by their
superiors, the Bell-weathers! "The poison of them,"

[1] *Essays*, IV, 88.

he said, "is not intellectual dimness chiefly, but torpid unveracity of heart: not mistake of road, but want of pious earnestness in seeking your road. Insincerity, unfaithfulness, impiety:—careless tumbling and buzzing about, in blind, noisy, pleasantly companionable 'swarms,' instead of solitary questioning of yourself and of the Silent Oracles, which is a sad, sore and painful duty, though a much incumbent one upon a man. . . . Certain it is, there is nothing but vulgarity in our People's expectations, resolutions, or desires, in this Epoch. It is all a peaceable mouldering or tumbling down from mere rottenness and decay; whether slowly mouldering or rapidly tumbling, there will be nothing found of real or true in the rubbish-heap, but a most true desire of making money easily, and of eating it pleasantly." [1]   Although some of Carlyle's explosions were repented of in the silences of old age, they suggest even better than less splenetic outbursts the depth of his distrust of the people: as for example his well-known description of Americans as "eighteen millions of the greatest *bores* ever seen in this world before"; and the hardly less familiar characterization of his own countrymen as "twenty-seven millions mostly fools." [2] Such were the creatures, so thought the prophet in his ultra-atrabiliar moods, whom all our yesterdays have lighted the way to dusty death.

Amidst these stupid millions, called the populace or the mob, there smouldered the dreadful fire of rebellion, useful enough on occasions when it should flare up and consume histrionic kings, immemorial

[1] *Essays*, VII, 223, 216.   [2] *Latter-Day Pamphlets*, 18, 177.

privilege, and centenarian abuses, as it did in the
French Revolution. But how if the power which
dethroned Kings should end by enthroning itself?
How if the "multitudinous canaille" were to follow
the beheading of Louis XVI with the Terror? The
Reign of Terror, in fact, was to Carlyle a perfect
symbol of democracy triumphant,—"Dominant Sansculottism," he called it. Referring to the September
Massacres and the work of the National Convention
which declared France a republic, he said: "France
has looked upon Democracy; seen it face to face. . . .
Liberty, Equality, Fraternity: not vestures, but the
wish for vestures! The Nation is for the present,
figuratively speaking, *naked;* it has no rule or vesture;
but is naked,—a Sancullotic Nation." [1] Democracy,
then, was revolt trying to govern. The result was
anarchy. This was the lesson which Carlyle learned
from the French Revolution and by which he interpreted the popular uprisings throughout his century.
Repeatedly he likened the mob outbursts of Chartism,
as well as later disturbances, to the Parisian mobs in
revolutionary days. "Democracy," he wrote in 1867,
"the gradual uprise, and rule in all things, of roaring,
million-headed, unreflecting, darkly suffering, darkly
sinning 'Demos,' come to call its old superiors to
account, at *its* maddest of tribunals." [2] "We are,"
he said in his Edinburgh University rectorial address,
which may be taken as his farewell utterance to the
British public, "we are in an epoch of anarchy." [3]
This address was delivered during the agitation pre-

---

[1] *French Revolution*, III, 57, 58.   [2] *Reminiscences*, II, 271.
[3] *Essays*, VII, 194.

ceding the reform bill of 1867, which proposed a further extension of the suffrage and which therefore meant to Carlyle fresh floods of sanscullotism. And democracy meant to him not only a method of rebellion, a consummation of no government and *laissez-faire;* it meant also the despair of finding any leaders to guide men. In casting out false leaders it cast out also belief in leadership and fostered the horrible delusion that men could do without guidance. The freedom which democracy substituted was freedom to the appetites of base men, who would henceforth run their course "in the career of the cheap and nasty." Worse still, democracy was the throwing off of all right relations between man and man, keeping society down to the basis of cash-nexus and *laissez-faire.* "Certainly the notion everywhere prevails among us too," said Carlyle, "and preaches itself abroad in every dialect, uncontradicted anywhere so far as I can hear, that the grand panacea for social woes is what we call 'enfranchisement,' 'Emancipation'; or, translated into practical language, the cutting asunder of human relations, wherever they are found grievous, as is like to be pretty universally the case at the rate we have been going for some generations past. Let us all be 'free' of one another; we shall then be happy. Free, without bond or connection except that of cash-payment; fair day's wage for the fair day's work; bargained for by voluntary contract, and law of supply-and-demand: this is thought to be the true solution of all difficulties and injustices that have occurred between man and man." [1]

[1] *Latter-Day Pamphlets,* 21.

Carlyle's disbelief in democracy thus carried with it a disbelief in the machinery of democracy,—the franchise and the ballot,—together with a growing distrust in the capacity of even limited representative assemblies to transact business. His deliberate opinion is well summarized by Froude, who says: "Under any conceivable franchise the persons chosen would represent the level of character and intelligence in those who chose them, neither more nor less, and therefore the lower the general average the worse the government would be."[1] Universal suffrage would place political power into the hands of the majority; and if the majority were stupid and debased, your result would not be government but anarchy. The ballot for all, therefore, was to Carlyle a perfect consummation of political evil. It gave liberty to bad men to inflict their badness upon society; it subjected wisdom to folly; it reduced all men to "equality," making "the vote of a Demerara Nigger equal and no more to that of a chancellor Bacon," and "Judas Iscariot to Jesus Christ."[2] The majority were foolish small men and they would never choose above their own heads. "There are such things as multitudes all full of beer and nonsense, even of insincere factitious nonsense, who by hypothesis cannot but be wrong. . . . Your Lordship, there are fools, cowards, knaves, and gluttonous traitors true only to their own appetite, in immense majority, in every rank of life; and there is nothing frightfuler than to see these voting and deciding. . . . No people or populace, with never such ballot-boxes, can select

---

[1] Froude, *Life of Carlyle*, IV, 296.   [2] *Essays*, VII, 91, 203.

such man for you (*i. e.*, a true leader); only the man of
worth can recognize worth in man;—to the commonplace man of no or of little worth, you, unless you
wish to be *mis*led, need not apply on such an occasion.
Those poor Tenpound Franchisers of yours, they are
not even in earnest; the poor sniffing, sniggering
Honourable Gentlemen they send to Parliament are
as little so. . . . I can tell you a million blockheads
looking authoritatively into one man of what you call
Genius, or noble sense, will make nothing but nonsense out of him and his qualities, and his virtues and
defects, if they look till the end of time." [1] Carlyle
regarded the parliaments of his day as representing
not the collective wisdom of the nation, but its con-
densed folly. He had no antagonism to the ballot if
exercised by loyal, genuine men; but "if of ten men
nine are recognizable as fools, which is a common
calculation, how, in the name of wonder, will you ever
get a ballot-box to grind you out a wisdom from the
votes of these ten men?" [2]

Democracy, therefore, or the rule of undisciplined
masses, must inevitably lead to the rule of the auto-
crat, whether benevolent or despotic; since anarchy
is a self-canceling business. Cromwell had to order
the Rump Parliament to quit, and Napoleon had to
quell the Parisian mobs with a whiff of grapeshot.
"More tolerable is the drilled Bayonet-rank," said
Carlyle, "than the undrilled Guillotine. . . . While
man is man, some Cromwell or Napoleon is the
necessary finish for a Sansculottism." [3]

---

[1] *Latter-Day Pamphlets*, 206, 120.   [2] *Ibid.*, 202.
[3] *French Revolution*, III, 244; *Heroes*, 188.

CHAPTER III

THE NEW CHIVALRY OF LABOR

"A man perfects himself by working. Foul jungles are cleared away, fair seedfields rise instead, and stately cities; and withal the man himself first ceases to be a jungle and foul unwholesome desert thereby. . . . No Working World, any more than a Fighting World, can be led on without a noble Chivalry of Work, and laws and fixed rules which follow out of that,—far nobler than any Chivalry of Fighting was."—*Carlyle.*

In spite of his sweeping denunciations of sansculottic radicalism, Carlyle knew that there was more, far more, in the popular uprisings of his time than mere rebellion against false gods. He had vision keen enough to see in the democratic movement not only a determined revolt against leaders that were false, but an effort, albeit blind and groping, to discover leaders that were true. So understood, democracy had in it a ray of hope, even though centuries of confusion might pass before the promise should be realized. "But oppression by your Mock-Superiors well shaken off, the grand problem yet remains to solve: That of finding government by your Real-Superiors! Alas, how shall we ever learn the solution of that, benighted, bewildered, sniffing, sneering, God-forgetting unfortunates as we are? It is a work for centuries; to be taught us by tribulation, confusions; insurrections, obstructions; who knows if not by conflagration and despair! It is a lesson inclusive of all

other lessons; the hardest of all lessons to learn. . . .
Cannot one discern, too, across all democratic tur-
bulence, clattering of ballot-boxes and infinite sorrow-
ful jangle, needful or not, that this at bottom is the
wish and prayer of all human hearts, everywhere and
at all times: 'Give me a leader; a true leader, not a
false sham-leader; a true leader, that he may guide me
on the true way, that I may be loyal to him, that I
may swear fealty to him and follow him, and feel
that it is well with me.' . . . All that Democracy
ever meant lies there: the attainment of a truer and
truer *Aristocracy*, or government again by the *Best*." [1]
The tragic mistake of democracy was that it taught
people to believe that the end of government could be
secured by the ballot alone and by other mere political and economic arrangements such as parliamentary speeches, causes, debatings, universal hip-hip-
hurrahing, oceans of beer and balderdash, copiously
supplemented with laws, statistics, reports, and co-
operative societies. Could the ballot ever raise the
best to places of control, so long as it was exercised by
a dim-eyed greedy multitude who always voted for
their kind? Your dull clod-pole and your haughty
featherhead alike must be made to discern and respect talent before they will raise it to positions of
leadership. It takes a man of worth' to recognize
worth in men. "It is the noble People that makes
the noble Government." Accordingly, to Carlyle,
political reform as a panacea, or a Morrison's Pill,
for the social evils of the times was futile unless

[1] *Past and Present*, 189 (*cf. ibid.*, 215); *Chartism*, 146 (*cf. Latter-Day
Pamphlets*, 92); *Latter-Day Pamphlets*, 102.

founded upon moral reform. The ancient mischief
was not that men could not *vote*, but that they were
weak, foolish, and sinful. Social evils arose from a
debased social order, and a debased social order was
only another way of saying that men as individuals
were self-centered and evil. "We may depend upon
it," said Carlyle characteristically, "where there is a
Pauper, there is sin; to make one Pauper there go
many sins. Pauperism is our Social Sin grown manifest." [1] Moral reform, therefore, should precede political reform, and moral reform must begin with the
individual. Here was the rock upon which the new
order must be built.

It is not too much to say that the central aim of
Carlyle's life-work, into the accomplishments of
which he threw the weight of all his great powers, was
to save man (of whatever class or station) from the
crushing effects of industrialism by restoring to him
faith in his humanity; and thus to create through him
and his fellows a new society resting upon humane
relations. To mechanics he opposed dynamics. To
the logical, calculating, scientific, severely rationalistic temper, he opposed the mystical, spontaneous,
poetic, and imaginative temper. He pleaded for personal inner freedom, for a spirit of reverence, for a
reawakening of faith in the inarticulate, unfathom-
able forces of the soul. He pleaded for a renewal in
man of his ancestral sense of wonder in the common
things of life, since the truly supernatural is forever
the natural. He wished to see men rediscover the
wisdom and heroic worth of their forefathers, the

[1] *Latter-Day Pamphlets*, 134.

generations of workers who builded better than they knew. Most of all, like a prophet of Israel, he called upon his contemporaries to re-enthrone righteousness and justice in their hearts as the source of every energy which could permanently recreate the world in which they lived. No less passionately than Wordsworth, Carlyle believed that the "high instincts" in human nature must be kept alive, if man is to survive the extraordinary risks of an industrial age. He recognized the value of machinery as frankly as did Arnold, but he saw just as clearly its dangers to the moral interests of man. "It seems clear enough," he said, "that only in the right co-ordination of the two, and the vigorous forwarding of *both*, does our true line of action lie. Undue cultivation of the inward or Dynamical province leads to idle, visionary, impracticable courses, and, especially in rude eras, to Superstition and Fanaticism, with their long train of baleful and well-known evils. Undue cultivation of the outward, again, though less immediately prejudiced, and even for the time productive of many palpable benefits, must, in the long-run, by destroying Moral Force, which is the parent of all other Force, prove not less certainly, and perhaps still more hopelessly, pernicious. This, we take it, is the grand characteristic of our age. By our skill in Mechanism, it has come to pass, that in the management of external things we excel all other ages; while in whatever respects the pure moral nature, in true dignity of soul and character, we are perhaps inferior to most civilised ages." [1]

[1] *Signs of the Times*, 245.

Carlyle's starting-point, then, for the solution of
the complex problems of society is characteristically
direct and simple. "All Reform except a moral one
will prove unavailing. . . . To reform a world, to
reform a nation, no wise man will undertake; and all
but foolish men know that the only solid, though a
far slower, reformation, is what each begins and perfects on *himself*. . . . We demand arrestment of the
knaves and dastards, and begin by arresting our own
poor selves out of that fraternity. There is no other
reform conceivable. Thou and I, my friend, can, in
the most flunky world, make, each of us, one non-
flunky, one hero, if we like: that will be two heroes to
begin with." [1] An ancient and familiar remedy for
the diseases of a modern age! But Carlyle found no
other and needed no other. Statistics, laws, organizations, mountains of red tape, were as nothing if
the individual were not transformed from the heart
outward. "It is the heart always that sees," he said,
"before the head *can* see." [2] He had measureless con-
fidence in the moral instincts which he believed to be
potential if not active in every healthy nature, and
he sought to arouse these instincts in man and to
inspire him to act upon them. The world, he thought,
needed nothing so much as good men, mystic creative
centers of virtue; each of whom should play his part
in the social drama, and so help to bring it nearer to
perfection.

It is important to note, however, that there was
nothing parochial in Carlyle's conception of moral-

---

[1] *Corn-Law Rhymes*, 205; *Signs of the Times*, 252; *Past and Present*, 31.
[2] *Chartism*, 135.

ity. To him man's moral life was the source alike of
man's proper relations with the world and with God.
When he said that "all talent, all intellect (was) in
the first place moral," and that "a thoroughly im-
moral *man* could not know anything at all," he
meant that the condition of getting knowledge, as of
all genuinely fruitful activity, was a right desire to
know. [1] The mind must reach out towards truth
positively, co-operatively, so to speak,—and this
mental attitude is moral. "To know a thing," he
said, "what we can call knowing, a man must first
love the thing, sympathize with it; that is, be *virtu-
ously* related to it. If he have not the justice to put
down his own selfishness at every turn, how shall he
know? His virtues, all of them, will lie recorded in
his knowledge. Nature, with her truth, remains to
the bad, to the selfish and the pusillanimous forever
a sealed book." [2] In thus making man's insight,
intellectual as well as moral, depend upon a right
state of the heart, Carlyle was at one with Ruskin,
who compressed the whole doctrine into a single
golden sentence: "The entire object of true education
is to make people not merely *do* the right things, but
enjoy the right things: not merely industrious, but
to love industry—not merely learned, but to love
knowledge—not merely pure, but to love purity—
not merely just, but to hunger and thirst after
justice." [3]

Morality is thus the basis of man's social relations.

---

[1] *Chartism*, 135; *Heroes and Hero-Worship*, 99.
[2] *Heroes and Hero-Worship*, 99. Cf. *ibid.*, 41
[3] *The Crown of Wild Olive, Works*, XVIII, 435.

It is likewise the basis of his religion. Immediate
contact with God through the conscience,—this was
the deepest fact that Carlyle professed to know concerning the nature of man. As a transcendentalist
he habitually interpreted the outer world, the *Not-
Me*, as phenomenal only, a daily manifestation of the
spiritual in the material and common. But revelation of the Over-Soul through nature, however miraculous, was secondary and mediate; revelation
through the conscience was primary and immediate.
"He who traces nothing of God in his own soul, will
never find God in the world of matter—mere circlings
of *force* there, of iron regulation, of universal death
and merciless indifference." [1] The true Shekinah is
man. He is the oracle of the unseen. Upon his heart
are written the laws of the Eternal more legibly than
upon stones, or even upon creeds and sacred books.
"Except thy own eye have got to see it, except thy
own soul have victoriously struggled to clear vision
and belief of it, what is the thing seen and the thing
believed by another or by never so many others?"
Carlyle was thus strictly Hebraic. He believed that
the secret of the Lord was with them that feared Him
and that only the upright should behold His face.
God did not manifest himself in images and rituals,
but in the "I ought" of each soul, a mystic impulse,
voiceless, formless, but "certain as Life, certain as
Death. . . . Such knowledge, the crown of his
whole spiritual being, the life of his life, let him keep
and sacredly walk by. He has a religion." [2]

The reformation of the individual was thus to be

---

[1] Froude, *Life*, IV, 329.   [2] *Past and Present*, 197.

achieved through his obedience to the first intimations of duty; for only so could man get his initial push in the right direction. " '*Do the Duty which lies nearest thee*,' which thou knowest to be a *Duty!* Thy second Duty will already have become clearer. . . . This day thou knowest ten commanded duties, seest in thy mind ten things which should be done, for one that thou doest! *Do* one of them; this of itself will show thee ten others which can and shall be done." [1] Self-realization, which is the aim of life, depends therefore upon action, upon work, and the call to duty becomes a gospel of labor, the corner-stone of Carlyle's social philosophy.

It is the worker who possesses the secret of life. Work is the one sure means of escape from unhappiness, from unbelief in self, from endless labyrinths of speculation. It is the pathway to a true knowledge of self, of the world, and of the eternal verities. From work done in obedience to duty springs faith, the faith that naturally grows up in a spirit that has lived both much and wisely. Through his work man advances step by step upon the kingdoms of darkness within and without, and creates good from evil, order from disorder. Each worker in his degree is a poet, discovering the ideal in the actual, and like the poet bodying forth the forms of things unseen and out of the flux fashioning the one thing that matters, a life, a bit of art, or a task faithfully done. [2] And so the worker

---

[1] *Sartor Resartus*, 135; *Past and Present*, 199.

[2] Many of Carlyle's best and most characteristic sayings are on work, as for examples: "He that has done nothing has known nothing. . . . The authentic insight and experience of any human being, were it but insight and experience in hewing of wood and drawing of water, is real

becomes a hero; for does not his toil, whether it be the toil of artist or of humblest craftsman, task all the capacity, all the loyalty, all the courage of his nature? He is therefore the indispensable beginning in the grand work of social reform, since through reform of self he has become qualified to discern worth and leadership in his fellow men. He has acquired an eye for talent; and he who sees talent must of necessity reverence it. He who is himself heroic may be trusted to choose heroes to govern him. Carlyle had no fear of a world made up of workers. In their hands ballots, elections, parliaments, "bills and methods," all the machinery of government, against which (when he thought of twenty millions, mostly fools and idlers) he raged so vehemently, were safe. "Given the men a People choose, the People itself, in Its exact worth and worthlessness, is given. A heroic people chooses heroes, and is happy; a valet or flunky people chooses sham-heroes, what are called quacks, thinking them heroes, and is not happy. The grand

knowledge, a real possession and acquirement, how small soever. . . . It is more honorable to have built a dog-hutch than to have dreamed of building a palace. . . . Doubt as we will, man is actually Here; not to ask questions, but to work. . . . Between vague wavering Capability and fixed indubitable Performance, what a difference! . . . . Our Works are the mirror wherein the spirit first sees its natural lineaments. . . . Work, never so Mammonish, mean, *is* in communication with Nature; the real desire to get Work done will itself lead one more and more to truth, to Nature's appointments and regulations, which are truth. . . . A small Poet every worker is. . . . Whatso we have done, is done, and for us annihilated, and ever must we go and do anew. . . . Not what I Have, but what I Do is my Kingdom. . . . No faithful workman finds his task a pastime. . . . All work of man is as the swimmers: a waste ocean threatens to devour him; if he front it not bravely, it will keep its word. . . . Ye know at least this, That the mandate of God to His creature man is: Work!"

summary of a man's spiritual condition, what brings out all his herohood and insight, or all his flunkyhood and horn-eyed dimness, is this question put to him, What man dost thou honour? Which is thy ideal of a man; or nearest that? So too of a People: for a People too, every People, *speaks* its choice,—were it only by silently obeying, and not revolting,—in the course of a century or so. Nor are electoral methods, Reform Bills and such like, unimportant." [1] Once we are a nation of workers, he declared, "By Reform Bills, Anti Corn-Law Bills, and thousand other bills and methods, we will demand of our Governors, with emphasis, and for the first time not without effect, that they cease to be quacks, or else depart; that they set no quackeries and blockheadisms anywhere to rule over us, that they utter or act no cant to us,—it will be better if they do not. For we shall now know quacks when we see them; cant, when we hear it, shall be horrible to us!" [2]

The workers, then, shall choose the leaders, who are to govern. An aristocracy of talent selected by hero-worshipers, a government of the wisest and best set up by a people with reverence for the wisest and best, this was Carlyle's second step in social reconstruction. "Find in any country the Ablest Man that exists there; raise *him* to the supreme place, and loyally reverence him: you have a perfect government for that country." [3] Here, therefore, we have the Carlylean gospel of the hero, a gospel no less famous than the gospel of work and integrating with

[1] *Past and Present*, 66.   [2] *Ibid.*, 30.
[3] *Heroes and Hero-Worship*, 182.

it to make a complete program for the regeneration of the social order. The one meaning for Carlyle, it will be remembered, in the popular disturbances of the time, which was of real significance for the future, was the effort to throw off sham leaders and to find real ones. Given now a society of workers as the basis of the new order, what manner of man should they choose for their governor? Who were the *aristoi* and where might they be found? A government of the best, could it be established, were beyond doubt "the one healing remedy" for an epoch grown sick and distracted.

Carlyle wrote so much and with so much repetition concerning his ideal leader that there ought to have been no confusion of mind as to what he meant. By calling his heroes *aristoi*, or best, he meant that they were to realize in the highest degree possible all the virtues that made a man in the truest sense human. The ideal hero is a *good* man. He is a worker, like those whom he represents or leads. He is the bravest, justest, noblest of his kind. Most of all he is a man of intellect, who by reason of his rectitude and his loyalty to the laws of life has been "initiated into discernment of the same." [1] Carlyle's hero is therefore one "who lives in the inward sphere of things, in the True, Divine and Eternal, which exists always, unseen to most, under the Temporary and Trivial."[2] He is one of those who in the words of Arnold, "have conquered fate" and

> "Through clouds of individual strife
> Draw homeward to the general life."

[1] *Latter-Day Pamphlets*, 91.   [2] *Heroes and Hero-Worship*, 144.

The lineaments of this heroic man are brought out with clearer precision in *Heroes and Hero-Worship* than elsewhere: he is, first, a man of sincerity, "the first characteristic of all men in any way heroic," and the basis of whatever originality may lie in him; he is, second, a man with the "seeing eye," or the poetic gift of vision which "looks through the *shows* of things into things,"—he cannot be duped nor misled by the false or the superficial; finally, he is a creative force, a source of order;—"his mission is order. . . . He is here to make what was disorderly, chaotic, into a thing ruled, regular;"—he is a maker, not a destroyer, and he comes like Goethe with a hammer to build, not like Voltaire with a torch to burn. He is, in truth, a servant of the people no less than their leader.[1]

But the Carlylean hero is also a man of power! Here we run upon the great rock of offense. For our leader turns out to be, say the critics, a Nietzschean superman, a Hohenzollern drill-sergeant, a vulgar strong Hercules or brawny Titan, anything but a wise and humane leader! It is true that as Carlyle grew older and saw no ebb in the rising tide of democracy, he likewise grew increasingly gloomy and impatient over the course of events. And he sometimes expressed himself in a manner that unfortunately gave justification to the protests of his critics, who seemed to have forgotten the wise teaching of the prophet (and the exaggerated humor of the talker!) and to remember more than all else the splenetic ejaculations of a wearied and saddened old

Past and Present, 222.

man. In these later years, especially, Carlyle displayed a readiness to praise the man who in a distracted time could get things *done*, like Frederick the Great, or like Bismarck, whether the methods he used were always the most proper or not. But it is to be remembered in the first place that he never claimed perfection for any of his historical heroes, whose strength suffered, he thought, by just in so much as it was an ignoble strength. "Napoleon," he said, "does by no means seem to me so great a man as Cromwell. . . . An element of blamable ambition shows itself, from the first, in this man; gets the victory over him at last, and involves him and his work in ruin." [1] It is well known that Frederick the Great was not one of his genuine heroes, much as he admired many aspects of his genius. "That terrible practical Doer with the cutting brilliances of mind and character, and the irrefragable common-sense," as Carlyle called the King, was "to the last a questionable hero" with "nothing of a Luther, of a Cromwell" in him.

In the second place Carlyle from first to last maintained that the only might that could endure must be founded upon justice. Any power resting upon brute force, upon mere will to power, could not last, however victorious it might be for the time. He was never an apostle of the horrible doctrine that dominion belonged to the man or the people who could conquer and rule by force of arms alone. The Carlyean hero must indeed be brave, for how else could he grow wise or his wisdom become effectual? "Your

[1] *Heroes and Hero-Worship*, 218-219.

Luther, your Knox, your Anselm, Becket, Abbot Samson, Samuel Johnson, if they had not been brave enough, by what possibility could they ever have been wise?"[1]   And just as the strength increases and makes operative the wisdom, so the wisdom directs the strength; the two virtues are complementary and inseparable in the heroic character. "The strong man, what is he if we will consider? The wise man; the man with the gift of method, of faithfulness and valour, all of which are the basis of wisdom; who has insight into what is what, into what will follow out of what, the eye to see and the hand to do; who is *fit* to administer, to direct, and guidingly command: he is the strong man. His muscles and bones are no stronger than ours; but his soul is stronger, his soul is wiser, clearer,—is better and nobler, for that is, has been and ever will be the root of all clearness worthy of such a name."[2] The victories of such a hero are not the victories of mere force: "Of conquest we may say that it never yet went by brute force and compulsion; conquest of that kind does not endure. Conquest, along with power of compulsion, an essential universally in human society, must bring benefit along with it, or men, of the ordinary strength of men, will fling it out."[3] To the end of his days Carlyle adhered to this belief in the divine strength of right. He never gave assent to the doctrine (as the historian Lecky described it) of the divine right of strength. "With respect to that poor heresy of might being the symbol of right," said he to Froude in 1873, "I shall have to tell Lecky one day that quite the converse or

---

[1] *Past and Present*, 208.   [2] *Chartism*, 135.   [3] *Ibid.*, 135.

re-verse is (my) real opinion—namely, that right is the eternal symbol of might; . . . and that, in fact, he probably never met with a son of Adam more contemptuous of might except where it rests on the above origin." [1]

It was of course easier for Carlyle to describe his able man, or hero, than to tell the British public how to find him,—a problem, he shrewdly declared, which belonged to the British public. The philistine mind has been much amused by the solemn declaration that the real superior is chosen by "divine right: he who is to be my Ruler, whose will is to be higher than my will, was chosen for me in Heaven." [2] Carlyle, it hardly needs to be said, was never an advocate of the historical doctrine of divine right of kings. The doctrine of hereditary privilege did not weigh heavily in the social philosophy of Diogenes Teufelsdröckh! What he meant in the passage just quoted and what he meant in numerous similar statements was that the truly able man, or leader, is the *gifted* man, who, living in the inward sphere of things, takes counsel of the Unseen and Silent and thus inevitably becomes

---

[1] Froude, *Life of Carlyle*, IV, 360. Numerous other passages to the same effect are to be found in Carlyle's books: *e. g.*— "Await the issue. In all battles, if you await the issue, each fighter has prospered according to his right. His right and his might, at the close of the account, were one and the same. He has fought with all his might, and in exact proportion to all his right he has prevailed. His very death is no victory over him. He died indeed; but his work lives." (*Past and Present*, 10.) "What Napoleon *did* will in the long-run amount to what he did *justly*. . . . The Ablest Man; he means also the truest-hearted, justest, the Noblest Man: what he *tells us to do* must be precisely the wisest, fittest, that we could anywhere or anyhow learn." (*Heroes and Hero-Worship*, 182, 222.) *Cf.* also *Chartism*, 134-5, 158; *Past and Present*, 164.

[2] *Sartor Resartus*, 225.

a spokesman of the Eternal Order. Now it was simply a vital element in Carlyle's faith in God and man that given a world in which men of superior capacity are born, and given a society in which the workers are a majority, the workers will perforce reverence and follow the leaders. It is in the nature of things that this should be so; "for the great soul of the world is just," and the workers must attach themselves to those who represent divine justice, namely, the men of superior brains and superior virtues, the heroes.[1] "Like people, like King" was thus an integral part of Carlyle's political creed, as we have seen. He feared democracy, he feared the ballot, he feared the widespread hue and cry for reform, only because he feared (had not the French Revolution taught him to fear?), far more, political power in the hands of a foolish, idle, intemperate, maddened, multitude;—a consummation quite the most catastrophic that he could conceive of, carrying with it the overthrow of every social principle and every accomplished fact of civilization. He condemned many philanthropic schemes for reform only because he was afraid that they would end by providing food and clothing and shelter for rascals and loafers. But political power in the hands of the *workers* he did not fear. Let these be left, he said, to choose their leaders by such machinery as would prove effectual,—the sole justification of political ways and means in any case. "To sift and riddle the Nation, so that you might extricate and sift-out the true ten gold grains, or ablest men, and of these make your Governors or

[1] *Past and Present*, 7, 164.

Public Officers; leaving the dross and common sandy
or silty material safely aside, as the thing to be governed, not to govern; certainly all ballot-boxes, cau-
cuses, Kensington-Common meetings, Parliamentary debatings, Red Republics, Russian Despotisms,
and constitutional and unconstitutional methods
of society among mankind, are intended to achieve
this one end. . . . The finding of your Ableman and
getting him invested with the *symbols of ability*, with
dignity, worship (*worthship*), royalty, Knighthood,
or whatever we call it, so that *he* may actually have
room to guide according to his faculty of doing it,—is
the business, well or ill accomplished, of all social
procedure whatsoever in this world! Hustings-
speeches, Parliamentary Motions, Reform Bills,
French Revolutions, all mean at heart this; or else
nothing." [1]

Out of a state composed of leaders and workers

---

[1] *Latter-Day Pamphlets*, 92; *Heroes and Hero-Worship*, 181. Carlyle
nowhere advocates the abolition of constitutional government. In fact
he everywhere implies the existence of such a government as the foundation for all the reforms he proposes: *cf. Chartism*, 164, also, *The English*
in *Past and Present*, Book III, ch. 5. He believed, however, that in
the field of *political*, as opposed to *industrial*, reform, what was needed
was reform in administration rather than in parliament; efficient exec-
utives were needed rather than extension of the franchise. He proposed
that the Crown should have power to elect "a few" members to Parliament, who, as Secretaries under the Prime Minister, should increase the
efficiency of administration. Chosen solely because of their ability for
special duties, these officers (minister of works, minister of justice, minister of education, etc.) ought immensely to improve and extend the services of the state. In this plan Carlyle saw no "risk or possibility" of
a bureaucracy. And why? Because of English democracy! "Democracy is hot enough here, fierce enough; it is perennial, universal, clearly
invincible among us henceforth. No danger it should let itself be flung
in chains by sham-secretaries of the Pedant species, and accept their
vile Age of Pinchbeck for its Golden Age!" (*Latter-Day Pamphlets*, 121.)

must come the new chivalry of labor. Carlyle called it a "chivalry" of labor, because he found in the old medieval social order a spirit which he wished to see revived in the new. The feudal past could teach the industrial present! The eleventh and twelfth centuries, the centuries of William the Conqueror, of Henry II, of Abbot Samson, were rough and rugged, and the methods of getting things done were not the smoothest. But Carlyle could never enough praise the bold vigor of the knights and the austere piety of the saints, whose leadership founded the order, the art, and the religion of the wonderful thirteenth century. The feudal workers did not live apart from their masters in isolation, dependent upon them for nothing but payment of wages. Gurth was thrall to Cedric, but for that very reason he was not left to starve in a workhouse or die of typhus-fever, under a system of *laissez-faire*. Rude and harsh as things were, there was yet fealty of man to man, up and down the feudal scale; baron protected dependent and dependent fought for baron. It was the age of the soldier, the fighting man,—immemorial type of training, obedience, order, and loyalty to superiors, without which a new chivalry of labor would be impossible. The true worker for Carlyle must ever be a fighter like one of the Conqueror's warriors. "Man is created to fight," said he; "he is perhaps best of all definable as a born soldier; his life 'a battle and a march' under the right general." [1] Looking at the statuesque lifeguardsmen who rode sentry at the Horse-guards, he was mournfully reminded of what

[1] *Past and Present*, 163.

at the moment seemed a sole surviving link between
the past and the present. Out of gray antiquity the
establishment of soldiery had come down to the
society of to-day as the obvious symbol of the power
of organization and the equally obvious proof of the
changes that could be wrought in human nature.
What promise was there in this venerable institution
for a new industrial order, a new chivalry of labor!
"These thousand straight-standing, firmest individuals, who shoulder arms, who march, wheel, advance,
retreat; and are, for your behoof, a magazine charged
with fiery death, in the most perfect condition of
potential activity: few months ago, till the persuasive
sergeant came, what were they? Multiform ragged
losels, runaway apprentices, starved weavers, thiev-
ish valets; an entirely broken population, fast tending
towards the treadmill. But the persuasive sergeant
came; by tap of drum enlisted, or found lists of them,
took heartily to drilling them;—and he and you have
made them this! Most potent, effectual for all work
whatsoever, is wise planning, firm combining and
commanding among men." [1]

But the drill sergeant as a professional man-killer
was not Carlyle's hero, despite the sneers of critics,
old and new. He abhorred war. "Under the sky,"
he declared, "is no uglier spectacle than two men
with clenched teeth, and hell-fire eyes, hacking one
another's flesh; converting precious living bodies,
and priceless living souls, into nameless mass of
putrescence, useful only for turnip-manure. How
did a Chivalry ever come out of that; how anything

[1] *Past and Present*, 225.

that was not hideous, scandalous, infernal?" [1] What Carlyle of course wished to see was the *spirit* of the fighting soldier, his courage, obedience, and loyalty, re-created in the worker of the new era, engaged in the warfare of modern industry. "It is forever indispensable for a man to fight: now with Necessity, with Barrenness, Scarcity, with Puddles, Bogs, tangled Forests, unkempt Cotton;—now with the hallucinations of his poor fellow Men. . . . O Heavens, if we saw an army ninety-thousand strong, maintained and fully equipt, in continual real action and battle against Human Starvation, against Chaos, Necessity, Stupidity, and our real 'natural enemies,' what a business it were! Fighting and molesting not 'the French,' who, poor men, have a hard enough battle of their own in the like kind, and need no additional molesting from us; but fighting and in- cessantly spearing down and destroying Falsehood, Nescience, Delusion, Disorder, and the Devil and his Angels!" [2] Nor was it the spirit of the feudal fighter alone that Carlyle would revive in the new age. It was the respect for superiorities, for old loyalties and pieties, and (not the least!) for the graces and courte- sies, the easy dignities and "kingly simplicities," that characterized lord and lady in the best times of the ancestral chivalry.

How to awaken and preserve these values in human nature "in conjunction with inevitable democracy" in an industrial era was, he knew, "a work for long

[1] *Past and Present,* 163. The reader will in this connection recall the famous satire on war in *Sartor.*

[2] *Ibid,* 164, 225.

years and centuries." For the old order must yield
to the new! The modern epic must be the epic of
Tools and The Man instead of *Arms and The Man*.
An age of fighting must give place to an age of working,—with "Captains of Industry" for leaders, instead of "Captains of Chivalry." The blind Plugson
of Undershot, modern capitalist cotton manufacturer,
who, like the medieval king, had hitherto been a
leader, but also, like the medieval pirate, a plunderer,
must be transformed into a fighting Chevalier, with
the nobleness of the feudal baron and the bravery of
the old-time bucanneer. So transformed, captains of
industry were to become in the future "the true
Fighters, henceforth recognisable as the only true
ones: Fighters against Chaos, Necessity and the
Devils and Yötuns; and (would) lead on Mankind
in that great, and alone true, and universal warfare.
. . . Let the Captains of Industry retire into their
own hearts, and ask solemnly, If there is nothing but
vulturous hunger for fine wines, valet reputation and
gilt carriages, discoverable there?" [1] The old slavery,
too, must give place to a new freedom or rather to a
new feudalism of the voluntary kind. No man is to
be *thrall* to another: "Gurth could only tend pigs;
this one will build cities, conquer waste worlds." [2]
Freely will he subject himself to the guidance, nay,
even to the authority, of his master, to whom he will
be attached by bonds quite other than the bonds of
servitude. He will be bound by the strong force of
good-will and justice, the only powers that can keep
men long together. Social progress in other words,

[1] *Past and Present*, 233.   [2] *Ibid.*, 215.

could not be effected, Carlyle held, unless men, leaders and workers alike, could be gradually transformed into a fuller and richer humanity.

The organization of the modern industrial world into the new chivalry of labor was the supreme task of the future.[1] In this task the *state* must lead. It must break up the régime of *laissez-faire* and must interfere between masters and men. It must *organize* industry and compel obedience to the principle of equal justice and equal opportunity for all. And in order to accomplish these ends, the state must guide and control human activity in ways yet scarcely dreamed of.[2] This was a work, as Carlyle well knew, that would require years, and perhaps even centuries. He harbored no dream of instantaneous social transformations, for he understood too clearly the nature of man and the magnitude of man's problems.[3] The ideals of social justice in their broad aspects might be easy to state and to defend, but the realization of these ideals throughout the complex structure of modern society was an enterprise of stupendous dimensions, infinitely too difficult to be undertaken or even imagined all at once. What Carlyle did urge

[1] Carlyle was alive to the difficulty of his position in making suggestions, and was not without hesitation in offering them. "Editors are not here, foremost of all, to say How. . . . An Editor's stipulated work is to apprise *thee* that it must be done. . . . All speech of positive enactments were hazardous in those who know this business only by the eye. . . . Of Time-Bill, Factory-Bill and other such Bills the present Editor has no authority to speak. He knows not, it is for others than he to know, in what specific ways it may be feasible to interfere, with Legislation, between the Workers and the Master-Workers." (*Past and Present*, 226, 231, 237.)

[2] *Past and Present*, 221, 226; *Latter-Day Pamphlets*, 31.

[3] *Past and Present*, 215.

from the beginning of his literary career was that the task should be started, and started upon the right lines. As a working basis for everything else he demanded investigation. "Our political Economists," he said in 1830, at a time of acute and widespread disturbance, "should collect statistical *facts* such as, 'What is the lowest sum a man can live on in various countries? What is the highest he gets to live on? How many people work with their hands? How many with their heads? How many not at all?' and innumerable such. What we all want to know is the condition of our fellow-men; and strange to say it is the thing least of all understood, or to be understood as matters go." [1] He vigorously assailed and ridiculed a government that debated endlessly on minor issues and left the major ones to take care of themselves: "The old grand question, whether A is to be in office or B, with the innumerable subsidiary questions growing out of that, courting paragraphs and suffrages for a blessed solution of that: Canada question, Irish Appropriation question, West-India question, Queen's Bedchamber question; Game Laws, Usury Laws; African Blacks, Hill Coolies, Smithfield cattle, and Dog-carts,—all manner of questions and subjects, except simply this the alpha and omega of all! Surely Honourable Members ought to speak of the Condition-of-England question too." [2] That Carlyle himself knew what this question involved we find in a passage closely following the preceding, a passage that reveals a grasp of the practical problems worthy of the best present-day investigators:—

[1] Froude, *Life of Carlyle*, II, 67.   [2] *Chartism*, 112.

"What constitutes the well-being of a man? Many
things; of which the wages he gets, and the bread
he buys with them, are but one preliminary item.
Grant, however, that the wages were the whole;
that once knowing the wages and the price of bread,
we know all; then what are the wages? Statistic
Inquiry, in its present unguided condition, cannot
tell. The average rate of day's wages is not correctly ascertained for any portion of this country;
not only not for half-centuries, it is not even ascertained anywhere for decades or years: far from insti-
tuting comparisons with the past, the present itself
is unknown to us. And then, given the average of
wages, what is the constancy of employment: what is
the difficulty of finding employment; the fluctuation
from season to season, from year to year? Is it
constant, calculable wages; or fluctuating, incalcu-
lable, more or less of the nature of gambling? This
secondary circumstance, of quality in wages, is perhaps even more important than the primary one of
quantity. Farther we ask, Can the laborer, by
thrift and industry, hope to rise to mastership; or is
such hope cut off from him? How is he related to
his employer; by bonds of friendliness and mutual
help; or by hostility, opposition, and chains of mutual
necessity alone? In a word, what degree of contentment can a human creature be supposed to enjoy in
that position? With hunger preying on him, his
contentment is likely to be small! But even with
abundance, his discontent, his real misery may be
great. The laborer's feelings, his notion of being
justly dealt with or unjustly; his wholesome compo-

sure, frugality, prosperity in the one case, his acrid
unrest, recklessness, gin-drinking, and gradual ruin
in the other,—how shall figures of arithmetic represent all this? So much is still to be ascertained; much
of it by no means easy to ascertain! Till, among the
'Hill Cooly' and 'Dog-Cart' questions, there arise in
Parliament and extensively out of it 'a Condition-of-
England question,' and quite a new set of inquirers
and methods, little of it is likely to be ascertained. . .
A Legislature making laws for the Working Classes,
in total uncertainty as to these things, is legislating
in the dark; not wisely, nor to good issues. The
simple fundamental question, Can the laboring man
in this England of ours, who is willing to labor, find
work, and subsistence by his work? is matter of mere
conjecture and assertion hitherto; not ascertainable
by authentic evidence: the Legislature, satisfied to
legislate in the dark, has not yet sought any evidence
on it." [1]

Here was work on a large scale for the state to
undertake. Until facts were available, Carlyle
insisted, it was folly to propose solutions to specific
problems. He did declare, however, not only that
there should be an organization of labor under the
new chivalry of workers and masters, and that the
work of organization should be mainly done by the
state; he confidently laid down also certain principles
by which he believed men should be guided in the
work of reconstruction and upon which all specific
measures should be based. To begin with, he repeated his old doctrines that government can only do

[1] *Chartism*, 117, 118.

what the people demand of it and that the first push, so to speak, in reorganization must come from the industrial workers themselves, masters and men, who see the problems as no others can. "The main substance of this immense Problem of Organizing Labor, and first of all of Managing the Working Class, will, it is very clear, have to be solved by those who stand practically in the middle of it; by those who themselves work and preside over work. Of all that can be enacted by any Parliament in regard to it, the germs must already lie potentially extant in those two Classes, who are to obey such enactment." [1] That is to say, there must grow up proper human relations between the captains of industry and their men. In the new order the captain will be a kind of servant, ready to do the greatest good to the greatest number, ambitious to be a just master rather than a rich master, one who knows his men and can win from them steadfast loyalty by reason of his fair and humane leadership. The cash-nexus as the sole connecting link must go. "Love of men cannot be bought by cash-payment; and without love men cannot endure to be together." [2] With love there must go justice. No worker in the new chivalry of labor must be dependent upon the charity of his superiors. "Not to be supported by roundsmen systems, by never so liberal parish doles, or lodged in free and easy workhouses when distress overtakes him; not for this, however in words he may clamor for it; not for this,

[1] *Past and Present*, 231.
[2] *Ibid.*, 233. *Cf.* "It is not by Mechanism, but by Religion; not by Self-interest, but by Loyalty, that men are governed or governable." (*Characteristics*, 37.)

but for something far different does the heart of him
struggle. It is 'for justice' that he struggles; for 'just
wages,'—not in money alone! An ever-toiling inferior, he would fain (though as yet he knows it not)
find for himself a superior that should lovingly and
wisely govern: is not that too the 'just wages' of his
service done? It is for manlike place and relation, in
this world where he sees himself a man, that he
struggles." [1]

But if, in the new order, masters and men are
united by relations of love and justice, other relations
and conditions will immediately spring up from these.
A fair cash payment for a fair day's work must be the
indispensable first step in all industrial and commercial operations whatsoever; and it will be the business
of the state to insure this. " 'A fair day's-wages for
a fair day's-work': it is as just a demand as Governed
men ever made of Governing. It is the everlasting
right of man. . . . The progress of Human Society
consists ever in this same, The better and better
apportioning of wages to work. Give me this, you
have given me all. Pay to every man accurately
what he has worked for, what he has earned and done
and deserved,—to this man broad lands and honors,
to that man high gibbets and treadmills: what more
have I to ask? Heaven's Kingdom, which we daily
pray for, *has* come; God's will is done on Earth even
as it is in Heaven! This *is* the radiance of celestial
Justice; in the light or in the fire of which all impedi-
ments, vested interests, and iron cannon, are more
and more melting like wax, and disappearing from the

[1] *Chartism*, 123.

pathways of men. A thing ever struggling forward; irrepressible, advancing inevitable; perfecting itself, all days, more and more,—never to be *perfect* till that general Doomsday, the ultimate Consummation, and Last of earthly Days." [1]

Compulsory universal Education is the second great task for the state. Intelligence must be diffused over the world like sunlight, if society is to be quickened into new life. The peasant-born Carlyle never forgot what knowledge might mean to the ignorant and poor. It was the prime necessity of man. To impart the gift of thinking to those who could not think was the first function of government. In a period when the British Empire had no system of national training, when parliament debated whether "a small fraction of the Revenue of one Day (30,000*l*. is but that)" should be expended upon education, when dissenters called for one scheme and the Church of England for another, and when illiteracy was universal, Carlyle came forward not only with a stern demand for general education, but with wise practical suggestions for realizing his demand. How, he asked, could twenty-four millions of striking, rick-burning, discontented, and illiterate toilers be brought into order and happy labor by the intellectual leadership of a mere handful of the *aristoi* alone? "The intellect of a Bacon, the energy of a Luther, if left to their own strength, might pause in dismay before such a task." It could not be done! The workers must themselves be educated to the extent of their capacity, so that their knowledge and energy might be

[1] *Past and Present*, 16, 17.

contributed collectively to the solution of great social problems. Some official, appointed by the state, working with a national committee, should send schoolmasters and "hornbooks" into every parish and hamlet of England to see that all were taught to read, under penalties and civil disabilities for those who should disobey the law!—"So that, in ten years hence, an Englishman who could not read might be acknowledged as a monster." [1]

A fair day's wage for a fair day's work and universal compulsory education were thus to be the foundations in the new chivalry of labor. But Carlyle's program of reform went very much further and included other aims and purposes of a comprehensive character, some of which have been carried out since his day, while others await fulfilment in times to come. Carlyle would hardly be called timid even by his most fanatical disciples; and yet (such was the force of public opinion in 1850 against state interference) he brought forward some of his most suggestive proposals in a tentative and hesitating spirit, lest they should be condemned out of hand as "visionary." On one principle, however, he was firm as adamant,— the principle of permanence of employment. The organization of industry upon the old basis of "nomadic" contract must be abandoned as hopeless. Employers and workers alike should be bound together in loyalty to a common cause, cherishing as their chief glory the glory of work well done, and as their chief disgrace the failure to perform their part in

---

[1] *Chartism*, 180; *cf.* also, *Past and Present*, 228; *Latter-Day Pamphlets*, 142; *Shooting Niagara*, 233.

the collective task. Only through permanent contract could this ideal be realized. A man must have *time*, if he is to come into possession of a house and home, if he is to strike his roots into congenial soil—not his "oak-roots" merely, but his "heart-roots" also! For it is only when such rootage has been established that nourishment can be drawn from the hidden sources of life, those memories and associations, both domestic and commercial, out of which are created the incorruptible stability essential to every worker. But the principle of permanent contract, Carlyle thought, depended upon another principle, which (writing in 1843) he seemed to regard as too advanced and too full of difficulties to be more than mentioned. He meant the principle of permanent economic *interest* in the management of the industry. "A question arises here," he says: "Whether, in some ulterior, perhaps some not far-distant stage of the 'Chivalry of Labor,' your Master-Worker may not find it possible, and needful, to grant his Workers permanent *interest* in his enterprise and theirs? So that it become, in practical result, what in essential fact and justice it ever is, a joint enterprise; all men, from the Chief Master down to the lowest Overseer and Operative, economically as well as loyally concerned for it?—Which question I do not answer. The answer, near or else far, is perhaps, Yes;—and yet one knows the difficulties. Despotism is essential in most enterprises; I am told they do not tolerate 'freedom of debate' on board a Seventy-four! Republican senate and *plebiscita* would not answer well in Cotton-Mills. And yet observe there too: Freedom, not nomad's or ape's Freedom, but man's Freedom, this is indispensable. We must have it, and will have it! To reconcile Despotism with Freedom:—well, is that such a mystery? Do you not already know the way? It is to make your Despotism *just*. Rigorous as Destiny; but just too, as Destiny and its Laws. The Laws of God: all men obey these, and have no 'Freedom' at all but in obeying them. The way is already known, part of the way,—and courage and some qualities are needed for walking on it!" [1] The note in this remarkable utterance, however hesitating, is the note of prophecy. The penetrating eye of the seer had a fleeting revelation of the far future, when control in industry should be democratic and the spirit in it, the spirit of fellowship.

But if English industries are to be set right, they must not only be created upon the principles of permanence of contract and co-operative control; they must recover from their paroxysm of competition and must undertake the tasks of distribution upon a wholly new basis. The England of Carlyle's day believed that national existence depended upon selling manufactured cotton at a farthing an ell cheaper than any other people,—with what disastrous effects upon English life both Carlyle and Ruskin have eloquently set forth. In the new era, under a chivalry of labor, inventive minds will quit their ceaseless efforts to sell cotton at cut-throat prices, and will turn their attention to the problems of fairer distribution at prices consistent with a just standard of life. "To be a noble Master, among noble

[1] *Past and Present*, 241.

Workers," said Carlyle, "will again be the first ambition with some few; to be a rich Master only the
second. How the Inventive Genius of England, with
the whirr of its bobbins and billy-rollers shoved somewhat into the backgrounds of the brain, will contrive
and devise, not cheaper produce exclusively, but
fairer distribution of the produce at its present
cheapness!" [1]

In truth, once you introduce the principle of governmental or social control, upon a basis of sounder
ethical values in human life, your field of reconstruction, both for private and for public enterprise,
becomes unlimited. It was in the wider and wider
establishment of this principle that Carlyle saw hope
for the society of the future. His vision of what
might be done was truly far-sighted, and perhaps
nothing so well evidences his prophetic sense of the
possibilities in store for some form of community
control as the following passage from *Past and Present*, written of course years before many of its proph-
ecies were even begun to be realized:—"Of Time-Bill,
Factory-Bill and other such Bills the present Editor
has no authority to speak. He knows not, it is for

[1] *Past and Present*, 232; *cf.* also, *ibid.*, 157-8. It is perhaps worth
while in this connection to note that Carlyle, in spite of his condemnation
of money-loving Captains of Industry of the unreformed Plugson type
and of his large emphasis upon the *moral* relations of business and industry, was not without sanity and practical sense respecting commerce
and its machinery: "I know Mammon too; Banks of England, Credit-
Systems, world-wide possibilities of work and traffic; and applaud and
admire them. Mammon is like Fire; the usefulest of all servants, if the
frightfulest of all Masters! . . . . Those Laws of the Shop-till are indisputable to me; and practically useful in certain departments of the
Universe, as the multiplication table itself." (*Past and Present*, 247;
Latter-Day Pamphlets, 38.)

others than he to know, in what specific ways it may
be feasible to interfere, with Legislation, between the
Workers and the Master-Workers;—knows only and
sees, what all men are beginning to see, that Legislative interference, and interferences not a few are
indispensable; that as a lawless anarchy of supply-
and-demand, on market-wages alone, this province
of things cannot longer be left. Nay interference has
begun: there are already Factory Inspectors,—who
seem to have no *lack* of work. Perhaps there might
be Mine-Inspectors too:—might there not be Furrow-
field Inspectors withal, and ascertain for us how on
seven and sixpence a week a human family does live!
Interference has begun; it must continue, must extensively enlarge itself, deepen and sharpen itself.
Such things cannot longer be idly lapped in darkness,
and suffered to go on unseen: the Heavens do see
them; the curse, not the blessing of the Heavens is on
an Earth that refuses to see them.

" Again, are not Sanitary Regulations possible for a
Legislature? The old Romans had their Ædiles; who
would, I think, in direct contravention to supply-and-
demand, have rigorously seen rammed up into total
abolition many a foul cellar in our Southwarks,
Saint-Gileses, and dark poison-lanes; saying sternly,
'Shall a Roman man dwell there?' The Legislature,
at whatever cost of consequences, would have had to
answer, 'God forbid!'—The Legislature, even as it
now is, could order all dingy Manufacturing Towns
to cease from their soot and darkness; to let in the
blessed sunlight, the blue of Heaven, and become
clear and clean; to burn their coal-smoke, namely,

and make flame of it.   Baths, free air, a wholesome
temperature, ceilings twenty feet high, might be
ordained, by Act of Parliament, in all establishments
licensed as Mills.   There are such Mills already
extant;—honor to the builders of them! The Legislature can say to others: Go ye and do likewise; better
if you can.

"Every toiling Manchester, its smoke and soot all
burnt, ought it not, among so many world-wide conquests, to have a hundred acres or so of free green-
field, with trees on it, conquered, for its little children
to disport in; for its all-conquering workers to take a
breath of twilight air in? You would say so! A
willing Legislature could say so with effect. A willing
Legislature could say very many things! And to
whatsoever 'vested interest,' or such like, stood up,
gainsaying merely, 'I shall lose profits,'—the willing
Legislature would answer, 'Yes, but my sons and
daughters will gain health, and life, and a soul.'—
'What is to become of our Cotton-trade?' cried
certain Spinners, when the Factory Bill was proposed; 'What is to become of our invaluable Cotton-
trade?' The Humanity of England answered stead-
fastly: 'Deliver me these rickety perishing souls of
infants, and let your Cotton-trade take its chance.
God Himself commands the one thing; not God
especially the other thing. We cannot have prosperous Cotton-trades at the expense of keeping the
Devil a partner in them!'" [1] In another passage,

[1] *Past and Present*, 226. Carlyle praised the new Poor Laws (of 1834)
for its substitution of government commissioners in place of the local
overseers of the old ineffectual corrupt system. (*Chartism*, 123). He
repeatedly advocated state aid to emigration as a sound means of reliev-

written in 1867, a passage that suggests the influence
of Ruskin even more than the passage just quoted,
Carlyle looked forward to very definite invasions of
British industrial and social "rights" through laws to
be enacted by a wise legislature. "Most certain it is,
an immense Body of Laws upon these new Industrial,
Commercial, Railway, etc. Phenomena of ours are
pressingly wanted; and none of mortals knows where
to get them. For example, the Rivers and running
Streams of England; primordial elements of this our
poor Birthland, face-features of it, created by Heaven
itself: Is Industry free to tumble out whatever horror of refuse it may have arrived at into the nearest
crystal brook? Regardless of gods and men and
little fishes. Is Free Industry free to convert all our
rivers into Acherontic sewers; England generally into
a roaring sooty smith's forge? Are we all doomed
to eat dust, as the old Serpent was, and to breathe
solutions of soot? Can a Railway Company with
'Promoters' manage, by *feeing* certain men in the
bombazeen, to burst through your bedroom in the
night-watches, and miraculously set all your crockery
jingling? Is an Englishman's house still his castle;
and in what sense?" [1]

But these and other great ends will not be realized
until the state shall have created the new chivalry
of labor. To this ideal Carlyle returned as his highest
conception of social reform. Again and again there

ing congested populations, and as an antidote to Malthusian doctrines.
(*Sartor*, 209; *Characteristics*, 35; *Chartism*, 182–186.) He urged, indeed,
the establishment of a government emigration service. (*Past and Present*, 225.)

[1] *Shooting Niagara*, 239.

rose up before him the vision of what a government *might* do that could drill thousands of discontented, idle, disunited individuals into an army of soldiers for the purposes of war,—obedient, united, loyal, brave! Why might not a vast and powerful collective effort such as this be applied to the infinitely tangled social problems of the modern world,—to the work of saving and beautifying life, instead of maiming or destroying it? Let Government, then, proceed to organize "industrial regiments of the New Era." Let there be soldiers of industry as well as soldiers of war. The paupers and idlers should be regimented first, and compelled to work, if they would not willingly do so. Gradually, year by year, decade by decade, generation after generation, the organization would spread outward and upward, until in all industries there would be captains and soldiers of the new chivalry. Thus directed by the state through wise masters and loyal, contented servants, government-controlled industries would furnish models for private enterprise,—which in turn would be compelled, through force of example and through force of associated workers, to regiment *its* workers and to substitute the spirit of co-operation for the spirit of competition in all its multitudinous ranks, until its reorganization were complete. "Wise obedience and wise command, I foresee that the regimenting of Pauper Banditti into Soldiers of Industry is but the beginning of this blessed process, which will extend to the topmost heights of our Society; and, in the course of generations, make us all once more a Governed Commonwealth, and *Civitas Dei*, if it please God! Waste-land

Industrials succeeding, other kinds of Industry, as cloth-making, shoe-making, plough-making, spade-making, house-building,—in the end, all kinds of Industry whatsoever, will be found capable of regimenting. Mill-operatives, all manner of free operatives, as yet unregimented, nomadic under private masters, they, seeing such example and its blessedness, will say: 'Masters, you must regiment us a little; make our interests with you permanent a little, instead of temporary and nomadic; we will enlist with the State otherwise!' This will go on, on the one hand, while the State-operation goes on, on the other: thus will all Masters of Workmen, private Captains of Industry, be forced to incessantly co-operate with the State and its public Captains; they regimenting in their way, the State in its way, with ever-widening field; till their fields *meet* (so to speak) and coalesce, and there be no unregimented worker, or such only as are fit to remain unregimented, any more." [1] The wonderful possibilities of appeal to the spiritual forces in human nature contained in such a reorganization of industry was suggested by Carlyle in his last political essay: "What is to hinder the acknowledged King in all corners of his territory, to introduce wisely a universal system of Drill, not military only, but human in all kinds; so that no child or man born in *his* territory might miss the benefit of it,—which would be immense to man, woman and child? I would begin with it, in mild, soft forms, so soon almost as my children were able to stand on their legs; and I would never wholly remit it till they had done

[1] *Latter-Day Pamphlets*, 141.

with the world and me. Poor Wilderspin knew
something of this; the great Goethe evidently knew a
great deal! This of outwardly combined and plainly
consociated Discipline, in simultaneous movement
and action, which may be practical, symbolical,
artistic, mechanical in all degrees and modes,—is one
of the noblest capabilities of man (most sadly under-
valued hitherto); and one he takes the greatest
pleasure in exercising and unfolding, not to mention
at all the invaluable benefit it would afford him if
unfolded. From correct marching in line, to rhythmic dancing to cotillion or minuet,—and to infinitely
higher degrees (that of symboling in concert your
'first reverence,' for instance, supposing reverence
and symbol of it to be both sincere!)—there is a
natural charm in it; the fulfilment of a deep-seated,
universal desire, to all rhythmic social creatures! In
man's heaven-born Docility, or power of being
Educated, it is estimable as perhaps the deepest and
richest element; or the next to that of music, of Sensibility to Song, to Harmony and Number, which some
have reckoned the deepest of all. A richer mine than
any in California for poor human creatures; richer by
what a multiple; and hitherto as good as never
opened,—worked only for the Fighting purpose."[1]

Thus "by degrees" there will come a renewed society, an ideal world towards which each generation,
playing its part, may hasten an approximation;—
a vast federated community of heroic workers, each
unit of which does its work in its appointed place.
"Give every man the meed of honor he has merited,

[1] *Shooting Niagara*, 235.

you have the ideal world of poets; a hierarchy of beneficences, your noblest man at the summit of affairs, and in every place the due gradation of the fittest for that place: a maximum of wisdom works and administers, followed, as is inevitable, by a maximum of success. It is a world such as the idle poets dream of,—such as the active poets, the heroic and the true of men, are incessantly toiling to achieve, and more and more realize. Achieved, realized, it never can be; striven after and approximated to, it must forever be,—woe to us if at any time it be not! Other aim in this Earth we have none. Renounce such aim as vain and hopeless, reject it altogether, what more have you to reject? You have renounced fealty to Nature and its almighty Maker. . . . To give our approval aright,—alas, to do every one of us what lies in him, that the honorable man every-where, and he only have honor, that the able man everywhere be put into the place which is fit for him, which is his by eternal right: is not this the sum of all social morality for every citizen of this world? This one duty perfectly done, what more *could* the world have done for it? The world in all departments and aspects of it were a perfect world; everywhere admin-istered by the best wisdom discernible in it, every-where enjoying the exact maximum of success and felicity possible for it." [1]

Carlyle's hope for the inauguration of this new order rested upon a "remnant" already in exist-ence,—the few noble masters and the small company of noble workers, to whom he made his final appeal.

[1] *Latter-Day Pamphlets,* 220, 221.

He called upon them, from the Prime Minister down to the least citizen, to lead in the huge task of resisting the rising tide of anarchy and unrest.[1] But his call was directed chiefly to the small company of *aristoi*, or noble few, who must at all costs keep in control the revolutionary spirit of the many. He looked for some response from the ranks of the titular aristocracy, but he believed that the burden of the work of wise social leadership in the future would fall upon the "natural" aristocracy. Of these, he said, there are two orders,—the men of genius (writers, poets, seers, sages), and the men of industry, since the true captain of industry is "already almost an Aristocrat by class." To these he called as to a select company of the *gifted*, men of vision, men of courage, men of natural nobility, each working in his proper field, according to his ability, each loyally co-operating to bring about the new chivalry of labor.[2] Under the leadership of these "industrial heroes," there shall be created an ever increasing company of workers who by their associated labors shall fashion the material for the new epic of the future. It shall not be another song of brutal victories over brother men, but a song of conquests over "Discord, Idleness, Injustice, Unreason, and Chaos." Carlyle's vision of a reconstructed social order culminates in a challenging chant to this militant fellowship of to-morrow:—
"But it is to you, ye Workers, who do already work, and are as grown men, noble and honorable in a sort,

[1] Carlyle regarded Sir Robert Peel as the man called by destiny to be foremost in the new movement. *Cf. Latter-Day Pamphlets*, 143–4; also *ibid.*, 108–142.

[2] *Shooting Niagara*, 212–219; *Past and Present*, 248–249, 253–255.

that the whole world calls for new work and nobleness. Subdue mutiny, discord, wide-spread despair,
by manfulness, justice, mercy, and wisdom. Chaos
is dark, deep as Hell; let the light be, and there is
instead a green flowery World. Oh, it is great, and
there is no other greatness. To make some nook of
God's Creation a little fruitfuller, better, more worthy
of God; to make some human hearts a little wiser,
manfuler, happier,—more blessed, less accursed! It
is work for a God. Sooty Hell of mutiny and
savagery and despair can, by man's energy, be made
a kind of Heaven; cleared of its soot, of its mutiny, of
its need to mutiny; the everlasting arch of Heaven's
azure overspanning *it* too, and its cunning mechanism
and tall chimney-steeples, as a birth of Heaven; God
and all men looking on it well pleased.

"Unstained by wasteful deformities, by wasted
tears or heart's-blood of men, or any defacement of
the Pit, noble fruitful Labor, growing ever nobler,
will come forth,—the grand sole miracle of Man;
whereby Man has risen from the low places of this
Earth, very literally, into divine Heavens. Ploughers,
Spinners, Builders; Prophets, Poets, Kings; Brind-
leys and Goethes, Odins and Arkwrights; all martyrs,
and noble men, and gods are of one grand Host;
immeasurable; marching ever forward since the beginnings of the World. The enormous, all-conquering,
flame-crowned Host, noble every soldier in it; sacred,
and alone noble. Let him who is not of it hide himself; let him tremble for himself. Stars at every
button cannot make him noble; sheaves of Bath-
garters, nor bushels of Georges; nor any other con-

trivance but manfully enlisting in it, valiantly taking place and step in it. O Heavens, will he not bethink himself; he too is so needed in the Host! It were so blessed, thrice-blessed, for himself and for us all. In hope of the Last Partridge, and some Duke of Weimar among our English Dukes, we will be patient yet a while."[1]

[1] *Past and Present,* 255.

CHAPTER IV

MASTER AND DISCIPLE

"The one soul now in the world who seems to feel as I do on the highest matters, and speaks *mir aus dem Herzen* exactly what I wanted to hear. . . . Many, many are the Phoebus Apollo celestial arrows you still have to shoot into the foul Pythons and poison our abominable Megatheriums and Plesiosaurians that go staggering about, large as cathedrals, in our sunk Epoch again."—*Carlyle* (letter to Ruskin, 1869).

"Only one man in England—Thomas Carlyle—to whom I can look for steady guidance. . . . Read your Carlyle with all your heart, and with the best of brain you can give; and you will learn from him first, the eternity of good law, and the need of obedience to it: then, concerning your own immediate business, you will learn farther this, that the beginning of all good law, and nearly the end of it, is in these two ordinances,—That every man shall do good work for his bread: and secondly, that every man shall have good bread for his work."—*Ruskin.*

IN 1850 Carlyle finished his *Latter-Day Pamphlets*. In 1852 he entered upon the long wrestle of thirteen years with his last great work, the *History of Frederick the Great*. He withdrew to the sound-proof room constructed upon the roof of his house at No. 5 Cheyne Row, as a refuge from the distracting noises of near-by fowls and pianos; and henceforth, "sucked by the mud-nymphs" into the depths of old folios and documents, he was little seen except by a small circle of admirers, who came regularly to hear his lamentations upon the swift down-

ward course of society,—lamentations lighted up by
the incomparably graphic sketches of men and events
for which the sage of Chelsea was by this time famous.
Always inclined to be a solitary student, Carlyle was
more than ever secluded during these later years of
haggard toil. True to his own gospel of labor to the
end, however, he completed the *Frederick* in 1865, in
five monumental volumes. But the task had nearly
broken him, and had left him an old man. He was
still further shattered in this year by the sudden
death of Mrs. Carlyle. Only once more, in 1867, the
year of the second Reform Bill, therefore, did he
really speak out in print on the condition of England,—in a kind of final latter-day pamphlet called
Shooting Niagara and After. His literary life was
practically over. An embattled veteran, he now
retired from the field and left the struggle to other
and younger leaders, of whom the most brilliant and
most effectual, in his opinion, was his disciple, John
Ruskin.

No other event in the literary history of the nineteenth century is at first thought more surprising
than that Ruskin, lover of beauty and evangelist of
art, should become in any sense a disciple of Carlyle,
who seldom spoke of art but with contempt and who
rarely regarded nature but as the somber and solemn
theater of man's struggles or as the mystical manifestation of a transcendental God. The contrasts are
indeed more conspicuous to us than the similarities,
particularly if we recall the first forty years in the life
of each. Carlyle, peasant born, reached success and
renown after years of effort along a pathway beset

with obstacles, and his struggles left him grim and defiant in temper and infinitely stern in his conception of the work that man was created to do. It was far otherwise with Ruskin. The road upon which he was destined to travel seems to have been marked out for him from the beginning and to have led him swiftly and brilliantly to fame. His parentage was Scotch, though he was born in London, the only child of a prosperous wine-merchant. The elder Ruskin was a gentleman-merchant of the olden time, a man of refined and cultivated tastes, who read the best literature, could put his son through two books of Livy, knew how to paint a little ("He never allowed me for an instant to look at a bad picture," said the son), delighted in architecture and landscape, and cherished a distant and romantic reverence for the nobility and for aristocratic environments. The intensely ethical spirit that was born in the boy and that forty years later attached him so strongly to Carlyle must have come mainly, although not entirely, from his mother. She was a severe and narrow-minded Puritan, proud, reserved and domestically devoted,—a woman, evidently, of great strength of mind, but very rigid, very formal, and very precise.

In his *Præterita* Ruskin has described with great fulness and charm the home and the education which these parents provided for him. The picture is not without its somber coloring, for the reader cannot overlook the "monastic severities and aristocratic dignities" of that sheltered household, where there were few playthings and no playmates, and where the puritanical gloom of recurring Sundays left a shadow upon the memory of the sensitive boy. But the youthful ecstasies would have lost something of their intensity, perhaps, without these tragic contrasts. At any rate no reader of Ruskin is likely to forget the autobiographical accounts of those fortunate influences and activities that had so much to do with the making of the man;—the early reading of Scott, Shakespeare, Pope's Homer, and the Bible, the drawing and sketching, the unsatiable curiosity over nature's ways, and the wonderful coaching tours all about England, Scotland, and Wales, and on the continent. His father, a "beautiful reader," was accustomed to read aloud, in the small home circle, from the best poetry and prose, always choosing what was most wholesome and noble. His mother with heroic resolution obliged him to read the Bible "every syllable through, aloud, hard names and all, about once a year," for at least sixteen times, and to commit long chapters to memory, thus teaching him, he says, to know that "accuracy of diction means accuracy of sensation." The influence of nature was ever more formative than that of books. Ruskin's passionate and life-long delight in natural beauty sprang from the deepest sources of his soul. "The habit of fixed attention with both eyes and mind," he says, was the "main faculty" of his life. He tells in *Præterita* of his "rapturous and riveted attention" to the ways of plants and running water; of his staring "all day long at the tumbling and creaming strength of the sea"; of his "indescribable rapture" when allowed to enter a cave in order to see its mineral deposits, for mineralogy always inspired him with its "romantic and visionary charm." He tells, too, of his watching the "rich color of the folds and creases" of the pulpit-cushion, when thumped by the tedious preacher, and of his looking with "closest attention" upon the "proceedings of any bricklayers, stone-sawyers, or paviers." These innate aptitudes of the boy were quickened and cultivated in the best of all possible ways. It was the annual custom of the elder Ruskin for many years to spend several weeks of the summer in traveling by coach about the country-side taking orders for sherry from aristocratic patrons. After the most delightful and leisurely fashion they visited castles, cathedrals, ruins, galleries, parks, lakes, and mountains, omitting nothing of historical or intrinsic interest the country over. These were days of "passionate happiness" for the youthful Ruskin, whose sensitive mind was all the while laying up an inexhaustible treasure of beautiful impressions. It was at this time that impulses were awakened in his heart, of which he spoke years after, when busy with art work in Verona: "There is a strong instinct in me which I cannot analyse to draw and describe the things I love—not for reputation, nor for the good of others, nor for my own advantage, but a sort of instinct like that for eating or drinking." And so he began to keep a diary and to write verses without number, and to draw (for drawing lessons had already commenced), recreating by word or line the scenes that never ceased to thrill him. Thus started in youth a career that continued without interruption for fifty-eight years (Ruskin's first printed book appeared in 1830, his last in 1889).

Meanwhile his formal education went on with the help of private tutors, until he was graduated in 1842 from Christ Church College, Oxford.

Ruskin's leap into fame the next year with the publication of the first volume of *Modern Painters* is inseparably connected with the name of Turner. By 1843, Turner's reputation as the first of landscape painters was established; he had long been a member of the Royal Academy, he had made a fortune from his pictures, and he was now living the life of an eccentric recluse. But he was passing into his later manner, and the critics were violently attacking his work. In the brutally frank language then current, they described his paintings as meaningless dreams, impossible and ridiculous. These attacks raised Ruskin to "the height of a black anger," and he at once rushed to the defense of his idol with the abandon of youth and genius. Young as he was, his enthusiasm for Turner was even then old. Perhaps the most precious gift he ever received was a copy of Roger's *Italy*, illustrated with vignettes by Turner, which came to him at his thirteenth birthday. He began copying the artist at fourteen, and at seventeen he flung off his first reply to Blackwood's criticism, a defense in which he spoke of Turner's art as "embodied enchantment, delineated magic," and as "seizing the soul and essence of nature." Before he was twenty-one, his father had given him two Turners, and when he was of age he began collecting for himself, until the Ruskin house contained one of the choicest collections in England, numbering even by 1860, says his biographer, "two oil pictures and more than a hundred drawings and sketches." "When I die," Ruskin said once to a visitor at Brantwood to whom he was showing the Turners in his bedroom, "I hope that they may be the last things my eyes will rest on in this world." They were to him a symbol of all the loveliness in nature and of all the mystery and tragedy in man,—"studied melodies of exquisite color" and "deeply-toned poems," an epitome of all that he best loved in nature and most revered in art.

The defense of a misunderstood and maligned painter, undertaken in an essay, grew into a book, and then into other books, leading Ruskin into ever-widening fields of interest and literary production. The interpretation and criticism of art was the main occupation of his life up to 1860. He was intermittently engaged upon *Modern Painters* for seventeen years, and he did not even then really complete the work. The first volume appeared in 1843; the second in 1846. Then came two works on architecture, *The Seven Lamps of Architecture* in 1849, and *The Stones of Venice*, in three volumes, 1851–1853. The third and fourth volumes of *Modern Painters* were published in 1856, and the fifth and last in 1860. In this year Ruskin's reputation, as Sir E. C. Cook, his biographer and editor, says, "stood probably at its highest point." In spite of severe criticisms upon his writings, many of them amply justified because of the paradoxes and dogmatisms which they contain, he was rightly regarded by the more judicious of his contemporaries as the man who had done more than any other to awaken the people of England to a feel-

ing for art and beauty, and was exalted by his fellow
writers as a master who, by his miraculous use of
words, had wrought new splendors into the fabric of
English prose. The younger artists, too, were capti-
vated by him. Holman Hunt sat up most of a night
reading a borrowed copy of *Modern Painters*, until
the "echo of its words" remained an enchantment to
his ears. William Morris and Burne-Jones hailed
him as a "Luther of the Arts," and to groups of Oxford friends Morris spouted passages of his prose in a
voice that fired his listeners with enthusiastic admiration. When the young Pre-Raphaelites were attacked in 1850 and 1851, Millais, in anger and despair,
went to Ruskin, who at once wrote a letter to the
Times in their defense, turning the tide in their favor;
and who made generous offers for their pictures to
Millais, Hunt, and Rossetti. Ruskin's achievement
had thus been in a high degree remarkable. At
twenty-three, in an ecstacy of indignation, he had
left his drawing and his mountain rambling to champion a maligned reputation, with little thought of the
way he was destined to go. At forty he stood upon
the summit of his power and his fame, the author of
more than a dozen books on painting and architecture,
and an acknowledged interpreter of the beautiful in
nature and art such as England had not hitherto
produced.

Then came a change. Ruskin now turned from a
study of art to a study of society, and his reputation
for a time collapsed. He has himself fixed 1860 as the
year of his apostasy. He had gone to Switzerland for
rest after finishing the fifth volume of *Modern Paint-*

ers. "I got this bound volume," he says, "in the Valley of St. Martin's in that summer, and in the Valley of Chamouni I gave up my art-work, and wrote this little book (*Unto this Last*), the beginning of the days of reprobation."[1] But the change which was announced to his astonished readers by the publication of some essays exclusively devoted to a discussion of social and economic problems had in reality been going on with increasing momentum for more than a decade. As far back as the earliest days of *Modern Painters*, when the Ruskin household received as guests the daughters (with their aristocratic husbands) of Mr. Domecq, Spanish partner in the wine trade, and the talk ran upon the management of the English market and the estates both in France and Spain, the surprised young author heard these foreign landlords speak "of their Spanish laborers and French tenantry, with no idea whatever respecting them but that, except as producers by their labor of money to be spent in Paris, they were cumberers of the ground." These discussions, he says, "gave me the first clue to the real sources of wrong in the social laws of modern Europe; and led me necessarily into the political work which has been the most earnest of my life. . . . It was already beginning to be, if not a question, at least a marvel to me, that these graceful and gay Andalusians, who played guitars, danced boleros, and fought bulls, should virtually get no good of their own beautiful country but the bunch of grapes or stalk of garlic they frugally dined on; that its precious wine was not

[1] *Works*, XXII, 512.

for them, still less the money it was sold for; but the one came to crown our Vandalic feasts, and the other furnished our Danish walls with pictures, our Danish gardens with milk and honey, and five noble houses in Paris with the means of beautiful dominance in its Elysian fields." [1]   Not many years later, in 1847, during a tour in Scotland, Ruskin describes in a letter his distressed mood when seeing some fishermen at Dunbar.   "I cannot understand how you merry people can smile through the world as you do.   It seems to me a sad one—more suffering than pleasure in it, and less of *hope* than of either—at least if the interpretations set by the most pious people on the Bible be true, and if not, then worse still.   But it is woeful to see these poor fishermen toiling all night and bringing in a few casks of herring each, twice a week or so, and lying watching their nets dry on the cliffs all day; their wives and children abused and dirty—scolding, fighting, and roaring through their unvarying lives.   How much more enviable the sea-gulls that, all this stormy day, have been tossing themselves off and on the crags and winds like flakes of snow, and screaming with very joy." [2]

Gradually this sheltered student, this lover of blue hills and Turnerian visions, began to observe men as well as mountains and to note that however much the glory of God might be revealed in nature it was but dimly reflected in the works and ways of His human creatures. He saw luxury and misery, unabashed, developing side by side at a prodigious rate in the decade 1848–1858, and at times he became prey to

[1] *Works*, XXXV, 409.   [2] Cook, *Life of Ruskin*, I, 214.

moods of acute depression, when his own pursuit of
art seemed to him not selfish merely, but utterly
useless. He was in France in 1848, the year of revolution, where he saw in the streets of Paris and Rouen
mobs of dissipated and desperate people moving
about as if ready to commit acts of violence, and he
was deeply agitated. His letters from this time on
contain reverberations of the inner disturbance and
clearly indicate that the "passionate happiness" of
earlier days was fast disappearing under pressure of
new moods. Nothing in the personality of Ruskin is
more significant than this late awakening to the
tragic contrasts between the beauty of nature on the
one hand, and the misery and folly of mankind on the
other. Signs of this awakening are to be found with
increasing frequency in every fresh book on art,
excepting only the first volume of *Modern Painters*.
His study of architecture in particular drew Ruskin
further and further into social problems, and, as we
shall see later, in his *Stones of Venice* he laid the
foundation of all his social philosophy. In 1854 he
began lecturing to drawing classes at the Working
Men's College in London, where for the inaugural
meeting a reprint of his chapter on Gothic in *Stones*
had been distributed as a manifesto of the aims of the
institution; and in 1857 he delivered two lectures at
Manchester on the political economy of art, in which
he attacked the *laissez-faire* economists within their
own stronghold. In the light of these multiplying
interests, which were more and more diverting him
from art, it is easy for the student of Ruskin's social
philosophy to accept as the literal truth a confession

which appears in the last volume of *Modern Painters*. His discussions of painters and pictures, he says, were "continually altered in shape, and even warped and broken, by digressions respecting social topics, which had for me an interest tenfold greater than the work I had been forced into undertaking" (*i. e.*, "forced" by his father to finish *Modern Painters*). "Nay," he says in a closing chapter, "I have many passages of history to examine, before I can determine the just limits of the hope in which I may permit myself to continue to labor in any cause of Art." [1]

Ruskin's books on political economy are *Unto This Last* (1860 in magazine, 1862 in book); *Munera Pulveris* (1862–1863 in magazine, 1872 in book); and *Time and Tide*, 1867. The first, which he called "that central book of my life" because it contains the substance of all that he had to say after 1860, is a collection of four papers written in the solitude of the Alps and published in the *Cornhill Magazine*, of which Thackeray was then editor. The series was abruptly stopped with the fourth number, owing to the storm of protests from the reading public.[2] A like fate awaited *Munera Pulveris*, composed of four articles which Froude, then editor of *Fraser's*, was bold enough to accept, but which the publishers refused to continue. *Time and Tide* is a series of twenty-five letters to Thomas Dixon, a cork-cutter of

[1] *Works*, VII, 257, 423.
[2] The position of the editor, as well as the state of public opinion, is suggested in the following sentence from a letter of Ruskin's father: "John was obliged to put 'J. R.,' as the Editor would not be answerable for opinions so opposed to Malthus and the *Times* and the City of Manchester." (Ruskin's *Works*, XVII, *intro.*, XXVI.)

Sunderland. They appeared in the *Manchester Examiner* and the *Leeds Guardian*, and contained the fullest statement that Ruskin had yet made concerning social reform. With these three central books should also be included *Sesame and Lilies* (1865), *Crown of Wild Olive* (1866), most of which were first given to the public in the form of lectures; and that amazing congeries of Ruskiniana, *Fors Clavigera*, a collection of ninety-six letters, appearing monthly, addressed "to the workmen and laborers of Great Britain." The first letter is dated January 1, 1871, and the last, Christmas, 1884,—the whole therefore covering a period of thirteen years and including, amid a mass of digressions and personalia, a succession of jeremiads on the shams and corruptions in modern life, besides many schemes and brilliant suggestions of social reconstruction.[1] Sir E. C. Cook, Ruskin's biographer, in some extracts from the contemporary press, has vividly suggested in what spirit the economic heresies of an art critic were accepted by the British public: "eruptions of windy hysterics," they were called, "intolerable twaddle," and "absolute nonsense,"—with many other verbal amenities of like import. The reviews railed at him as a quixotic rhapsodist who had suddenly lost his head, as an intruder into an alien field where sentimentalities were out of place. Friends withdrew from him in disgust. When *Unto This Last* appeared, Rossetti called it "bosh" and declared that Ruskin

[1] During these years, 1860-1880, Ruskin continued of course to write and lecture upon art;—he was Slade Professor of Fine Arts at Oxford from 1870 to 1878, and again in 1883. But he rarely spoke about art without launching into long digressions on social questions.

talked "awful nonsense." Ruskin himself wrote that
people were now accustomed to hear him spoken of
by artists as a " superannuated enthusiast," and by
philosophers and practical people as a "delirious
visionary." "As alone as a stone on a high glacier,"
is his description of himself to C. E. Norton in that
period. As Mr. Frederic Harrison aptly suggests,
Ruskin like Dante had found himself midway upon
his life's journey "in a dark wood where straight the
way was lost."

Out of the darkness of those years almost the only
voice of encouragement was the voice of Carlyle.
Carlyle was not blind to the weaknesses of Ruskin:
"sensitive," "flighty," "headlong," are some of the
terms which he used to describe the impetuous vivacity of his disciple, in whom he undoubtedly missed a
wholesome steadiness and robustness such as he
found in the earlier Tennyson or in Browning. Nor
did he unqualifiedly approve of all that Ruskin said
and did. Some of the fantastic schemes set forth in
the later numbers of *Fors* cooled his enthusiasm, and
the St. George's Company he regarded as "utterly
absurd," thinking it "a joke at first." But he recognized Ruskin's brilliant powers,—his "vivacity," his
"high and pure morality," his "celestial brightness";
and he dedicated to him his last book, *The Early
Kings of Norway*, in words that express the affectionate regard which had grown up between master and
disciple: "To my dear and ethereal Ruskin, whom
God preserve. Chelsea, 4 May, 1875. T. Carlyle."
Most of all Carlyle rejoiced in the bold frontal attacks
that Ruskin was making upon the "dismal" science of

political economy. "While all the world stands tremulous, shilly-shallying from the gutter," he wrote, "impetuous Ruskin plunges his rapier up to the very hilt in the abominable belly of the vast block-headism, and leaves it staring very considerably." [1] "There is nothing going on among us," he wrote to Emerson, "as notable to me as those fierce lightning-bolts Ruskin is copiously and desperately pouring into the black world of Anarchy all around him. No other man in England that I meet has in him the divine rage against iniquity, falsity, and baseness that Ruskin has." [2] He read the books on social and political economy as they appeared, and he applauded their style and truth in a way that immensely heartened Ruskin, who of all men living reverenced Carlyle most. That a man who had "entirely blown up" the hoary conventions in the world of art should now turn his guns upon "half a million dull British heads," "the Dismal-Science people" included, was something to fire the weary patriarch of Chelsea with new hope. [3]

[1] Froude, *Life of Carlyle*, IV, 280.
[2] *Carlyle-Emerson Correspondence*, II, 388.
[3] Carlyle's comments on Ruskin's books are characteristic. After reading one of the chapters of *Unto This Last*, he wrote: "I have read your paper with exhilaration, exultation, often with laughter, with bravissimo! . . . . I marvel in parts at the lynx-eyed sharpness of your logic, at the pincer-grip (red-hot pincers) you take of certain bloated cheeks and blown-up bellies. . . . If you dispose, stand to that kind of work for the next seven years, and work out then a result like what you have done in painting. . . . Meantime my joy is great to find myself henceforth in a minority of two, at any rate." (Ruskin, *Works*, XVII, intro. XXXIII.) Of *Munera Pulveris*, he said: "In every part I find a high and noble sort of truth, not one doctrine that I can intrinsically dissent from, or count other than salutary in the extreme, and pressingly needed in England above all. . . . There is a felicity of utterance in

The precise time when Ruskin first met Carlyle has not been fixed, although it must have been as early as 1850, for in his journal of that year Carlyle made note of an evening call from Ruskin. During the years immediately following, although Ruskin was already a devoted worshiper of Carlyle and often visited the Carlyles at Cheyne Row,[1] their intercourse could not have been intimate, for the parents of Ruskin were fearful of the 'perverting' influence of the older man who, they thought, was more than any one else responsible for leading their son "out of the way of fame—and into that of suffering." But after the death of John James Ruskin in 1864 and of Mrs. Carlyle in 1866, the two were drawn together into an almost uninterrupted relationship of mutual affection and admiration,—tempered on Ruskin's side with a profound veneration for the character and achievement of one whom he now habitually looked up to as his master.[2]

it, here and there, such as I remember in no other writer, living or dead, and it's all as true as gospel." (Ibid., LXX.) After finishing the fifth number of Fors, he wrote: "Every word of it as is spoken, not out of my poor heart only, but out of the eternal skies; words winged with Empyrean wisdom, piercing as lightning. . . . Continue, while you have such utterances in you, to give them voice." (Ibid., XXVII, intro. LXXXVI.) Carlyle was much struck with Ruskin's style, praising his "power of expression" again and again; e. g., "Passages of that last book, 'Queen of the Air,' went into my heart like arrows. . . . His description of the wings of birds the most beautiful things of the kind that can possibly be."

[1] Mrs. Carlyle once said: "No one managed Carlyle so well as Ruskin; it was quite beautiful to see him." Like many others Ruskin recognized the brilliancy of Mrs. Carlyle but did not like her sharp tongue. He once referred to her as a "shrew."

[2] There are characteristic touches of effusive sentiment on Ruskin's side: "I am your faithful and devoted son in the Florentine sense," he wrote in one of his almost daily letters from abroad to Carlyle in

Ruskin had felt the force of Carlyle's teaching in his early years, when the message of *Sartor* and *Heroes* had aroused him from a fit of uncertainty and made him resolve "to *do* something, to *be* something useful." Later on he read *Past and Present, Latter-Day Pamphlets,* and the histories, quoting repeatedly from them in his own books and referring to them and their creator in words that express the most enthusiastic appreciation. The "pure lightning" of Carlyle's style and the "white-hot fire" of energy and thought which it conveyed alike excited his wonder. The *French Revolution* and the *Frederick the Great* were to him "immortal" work done by "the greatest of historians since Tacitus." "All of your work is grandly done," he told Carlyle in 1871. The books that influenced him most, however, were *Past and Present* and *Latter-Day Pamphlets*. The first he evidently read and reread, for when he gave away his "much scored" copy to a friend he wrote: "I have sent you a book which I read no more because it has become a part of myself, and my old marks in it are now useless, because in my heart I mark it all." In the tenth *Fors* Ruskin recommended the reading of this much loved book to workingmen in these words: "Now, I tell you once for all, Carlyle is the only living writer who has spoken the absolute and perpetual truth about yourselves and your

1874. "Ever your most loving disciple," he wrote on another occasion. C. E. Norton entertained the two together at luncheon in 1872: "Each was delightful with the other, and each so perfectly at ease, so entirely free from self-consciousness of any disagreeable sort, so devoid of arrogance or disposition to produce false effect, each also was so full of humor and of thought, that the talk was of the best ever heard." (*Letters of Norton,* I, 441.)

business. . . . Read your Carlyle, then, with all
your heart." Upon the subject of social and political
reform, he came to the conclusion that in these two
books, together with *Sartor*, Carlyle had "said all
that needs to be said, and far better than I shall
ever say it again."[1]

[1] *Cf.* "I've been reading *Latter-Days* again, chiefly 'Jesuitism.' I
can't think what Mr. Carlyle wants me to write anything more for—if
people don't attend to that, what more is to be said? (*Letters*, I, 428.)
Ruskin's appreciations of Carlyle are almost too numerous to quote, and
yet the perusal of them greatly strengthens the reader's conviction of the
intimate relationship existing between the two men. "What can you say
of Carlyle," said Ruskin to Froude, "but that he was born in the clouds
and struck by lightning?" . . . "The greatest of our English thinkers
. . . our one quite clear-sighted thinker, Carlyle." Ruskin spoke of the
"mighty interests—its measureless pathos" of Carlyle's *Reminiscences*.
He was on the side of Froude, not of Norton, in the literary row that was
stirred up over the publications following Carlyle's death, and Froude
regarded him as the "only person to whom I can talk about Carlyle."
(Cook, *Life of Ruskin*, II, 505-6.) Ruskin in fact read Carlyle "so constantly, that, without wilfully setting myself to imitate him, I find myself
perpetually falling into his modes of expression, and saying many things
in a 'quite other,' and I hope, stronger, way, than I should have adopted
some years ago. . . . So that I find Carlyle's stronger thinking coloring
mine continually." (Ruskin, *Works*, V, 427-8.)
Of all the expressions of reverent appreciation that Ruskin avowed, the
following in which he urges Carlyle to a final work after the *Frederick* is
perhaps the best: "It seems to me," he wrote October 1, 1866, "that a
magnificent *closing* work for you to do would be to set your finger on the
turning points and barriers in European history, to gather them into
train of light,—to give without troubling yourself about detail or proof,
your own *final* impression of the courses and causes of things—and your
thoughts of the leading men, *who* they were, and *what* they were. If you
like to do this, I'll come and write for you a piece every day, if after
beginning it you still found the mere hand work troublesome. I have a
notion it would be very wholesome work for me, and it would be very
proud and dear for me." (*Works*, XXXVI, 518; *cf.* also 526.) In his own
closing days when his work was nearly over, Ruskin had plans of writing
about Carlyle. For one thing he proposed to collect and edit Carlyle's
descriptions of people (*ibid.*, XXXVII, 568); for another, he thought of
writing a small volume, as Cook says, "partly to vindicate, and partly to
supplement Froude." (*Ibid.*, XXXV, *intro.* XXIV.)

The influence of Carlyle upon Ruskin, therefore, particularly after 1860, was both continuous and powerful.[1] Accordingly when in 1872 Ruskin dedicated his *Munera Pulveris* "to the friend and guide who has urged me to all chief honor, Thomas Carlyle," he was stating the literal truth. For as the ethical and social interests gained ascendancy over the æsthetic in Ruskin, he was increasingly conscious of many links of sympathy between himself and his master. The similarities in the two men at this period are more striking than the differences. Both rested all their teaching on art, history, and life upon *fact*, as they liked to call it.[2] They sought to pierce through the shows and shams to the solid ground of eternal veracity beneath; and to show that it was in this soil alone, in the deep heart of our common humanity, that beauty and truth and goodness must have their roots if they were to live and flourish. Hence they could not tolerate a spirit of pretense or levity anywhere, and they were suspicious of anything in art or life that seemed to be created merely for amusement. Both believed in reverence, rever-

---

[1] As early as 1854 Ruskin in a lecture publicly acknowledged that he owed more to Carlyle than to any other writer. (*Works*, XII, 507.) In 1855 Ruskin wrote to Carlyle: "How much your general influence has told upon me, I know not, but I always confess it, or rather boast of it, in conversation about you." (*Ibid.*, XXXVI, 184.) Twenty-five years later he wrote to Miss Susan Beever: "We feel so much alike that you may often mistake one for the other now." (*Ibid.*, XXXVII, 320.)

[2] In a letter to Froude (1873) Ruskin said: "I am not the institutor, still less the guide—but I am the Exponent of the Reaction for Veracity in Art which corresponds partly to Carlyle's and your work in History, and partly to Linnæus's in natural science." (*Works*, XXXVII, 83.)

ence for the fundamental facts of life as well as for superior men; and Ruskin was as truly a hero-worshiper as Carlyle. Both stood staunchly for a gospel of work and held that the foundation of all religion is "in resolving to do our work well." Each had the same invincible and simple faith in the plain dictates of conscience, insisting that right is right and wrong is wrong in spite of the sophistications of dilettanti and wiseacres, and that "courage and chastity and honesty and patience bring out good; and cowardice and luxury and folly and impatience, evil." Ruskin, like Carlyle, reduced everything that he taught to the simple proposition that man has within him "that singular force anciently called a soul." Consequently they had much the same view and temper towards modern science, which, they thought, took the mystery out of things and was arrogant and assuming in its pretensions. Finally, they both looked backward to a medieval age for suggestions of a new social order; and, as we shall see in a subsequent chapter, they thought and preached alike upon many of the fundamental principles of social reconstruction. In the light of these many affinities, therefore, both in ideas and accomplishments, we can appreciate the accuracy of Ruskin's statement, when he spoke of Carlyle as having led in an attack upon the English Dagon, and of himself as merely fulfilling what Carlyle had already begun. The truth was exactly expressed by Froude, who knew well both master and disciple, when he said: "Ruskin seemed to be catching the fiery cross from (Carlyle's) hand, as his own strength was failing." The new chivalry of labor was thus to be championed by one who was more of a medievalist than Carlyle, and who, like a knight-errant of old time, went out alone into the wilderness of the modern world to slay the dragons and to restore the haunts of man to their ancient peace.

CHAPTER V

THE APOSTLE OF ART AND THE MODERN WORLD

"The first schools of beauty must be the streets of your cities, and the chief of our fair designs must be to keep the living creations round us clean and in human comfort. . . . Beautiful art can only be produced by people who have beautiful things about them, and leisure to look at them."
—*Ruskin*.

CASUAL readers of Ruskin have been puzzled to account for his apostasy from art to political economy. How was it, they ask, that one who could write eloquent rhapsodies about clouds and skies, about flowers and trees and mountains and all manner of living things, who could translate the golden visions of Turner into language that can only be compared with Shelley's in its ethereal splendor, whose extraordinarily sensitive nature was habitually thrilled by the glories of form and color alike in the world of nature and the world of art,—how was it that a writer with magic like this at his command should torment his spirit with thoughts of competition and co-operation, profit and loss, production, distribution, consumption, and all the dull lingo of the world of industry and commerce? Contemporaries of Ruskin were likewise puzzled over this question, and they turned upon him in derision and contempt, as we have seen. But a careful study of his work reveals a unity of purpose underneath a wide diversity of interests. In spite of the digressions—and they are legion—there is one principal aim in his voluminous writings, from *Modern Painters* to *Fors*, and it is this: that sound art, whether individual or national, is the expression of a sound life and depends for its nobleness and truth upon a noble spirit in the artist or in the age; and, further, that art, so understood, is not possible when it is thought of as a mere luxury created by a few highly gifted and highly paid virtuosos for the enjoyment of an aristocratic order alone, but only when it is conceived as the creative expression of a people, working, from humblest craftsman up to master artist, in response to impulses that spring from a happy and healthy community life. In his inaugural lecture at Oxford which he delivered in 1870 as the first professor of fine arts, Ruskin summarized his teaching in the following words: "the most perfect mental culture possible to men is founded on their useful energies, and their best arts and brightest happiness are consistent, and consistent only, with their virtue." It is necessary, he said, to find "in the laws which regulate the finest industries, the clue to the laws which regulate *all* industries. . . . The art of any country *is the exponent of its social and political virtues*." This, he explained to his audience, "is what I chiefly have to say to you,—one of the things, and the most important of all things, I can positively declare to you."[1] His doctrine of art is thus the root from which grew his social and economic ideals. Industry was inseparably connected with art

[1] *Works*, XX, 39-40.

in all his thinking. A brief analysis will make this clear.

Ruskin defined the art of man as "the expression of his rational and disciplined delight in the forms and laws of the creation of which he forms a part." Art is man's sense of beauty awakened and made creative. But what is beauty? Beauty, said Ruskin, is a special kind of pleasure communicated to man from the outer world, perceived first by the physical senses and then by the moral sense, or heart. "Any material object which can give us pleasure in the simple contemplation of its outward qualities without any direct or definite exertion of the intellect, I call in some way, or in some degree, beautiful." [1] This is sensuous beauty, or "that quality or group of qualities in objects by which they become pleasant to the eye considered merely as a sense. Pure and vivid colors, for instance, are to the eye precisely what musical sounds are to the ear, capable of intense expression, but also pleasant in themselves, and although wearisome if too long continued, possessing for a time a real charm, of which no account whatever can be rendered, but that the bodily sense is therein gratified. This is the first notion of beauty in the human mind." [2] But Ruskin did not stop here. He held that there is in material things a quality which conveys an idea of immaterial ones, that, for example, bright distance, curvature, or color gradation, is a type or reflection of infinity in the divine mind, just as material purity is a type of divine energy. This quality, which is essential to a complete notion of

[1] *Works*, III, 109.   [2] *Ibid.*, IV, 365.

beauty, can be fully apprehended only by the moral nature, or heart, "in its purity and perfection." [1] "As it is necessary to the existence of an idea of beauty," said Ruskin, "that the sensual pleasure which may be its basis should be accompanied first with joy, then with love of the object, then with the perception of kindness in a superior intelligence, finally, with thankfulness and veneration towards that intelligence itself; and as no idea can be at all considered in any way an idea of beauty, until it be made up of these emotions, any more than we can be said to have an idea of a letter of which we perceive the perfume and the fair writing, without understanding the contents of it; and as these emotions are in no way resultant from, or obtainable by, any operation of the Intellect;

[1] Ruskin regarded this "moral" aspect of beauty as the central feature of his theory of æsthetics, and to distinguish the faculty by which it is received from the merely sensuous nature of man, he took a hint from Aristotle and called it "theoretic." *Theoria* in Aristotle's *Ethics* means contemplation; and from this work Ruskin quotes a passage which, he says, "seems to have suggested the whole idea of my own essay" (*i. e.*, Volume II of *Modern Painters*), and which he translated as follows: "And perfect happiness is some sort of energy of Contemplation, for all the life of the gods is (therein) glad; and that of men, glad in the degree in which some likeness to the gods in this energy belongs to them. For none other of living creatures (but men only) can be happy, since in no way can they have any part in Contemplation." (*Works*, IV, 7.) Thirty years after the publication of the second volume of *Modern Painters*, in an unused letter written for *Fors* from Italy, he wrote: "Among the points of true value in the first and second volumes of *Modern Painters*, none were more vital than the distinction made between ordinary sight, and what—there being no English word for it—I was forced to call by the Greek one 'Theoria,' 'Contemplation'—seeing within the temple of the heart. . . . If you will look back to the chapters in Theoria in *Modern Painters*, you will see that the entire difference between the human sight of beauty and the animal scorn of it is shown to consist, in this concurrence, with physical sense, of Mental Religion. I use the word in its true meaning—the acknowledgment of Spiritual Power." (*Works*, XXIX, 575-7.)

it is evident that the sensation of beauty is not sensual on the one hand, nor is it intellectual on the other, but is dependent on a pure, right, and open state of the heart." [1] In the light of this account, beauty is not a mere pleasurable sensation of the eye or ear; it is rather a passionate and reverent joy excited in a pure mind by its contemplation of the external world of man and nature. It cannot be felt by mean and low spirits, nor by highly refined spirits in mean and low moments. "So much as there is in you of ox, or swine," said Ruskin, "perceives no beauty, and creates none: what is human in you, in exact proportion to the perfection of its humanity, can create it, and receive." [2] "Yes," we say, "but what of the licentious artists who are at once gifted and debased and who can yet create beautiful things? How absurd to contend that beauty depends upon morality!" Beauty, which is a good thing, Ruskin would reply, cannot come from vileness, which is an evil thing. "A bad woman may have a sweet voice; but that sweetness of voice comes of the past morality of her race. . . . A maiden may sing of her lost love, but a miser cannot sing of his lost money. And with absolute precision, from highest to lowest, *the fineness of the possible art is an index of the moral purity and majesty of the emotion it expresses*. . . . All æsthetics depend on the health of soul and body, and the proper exercise of both, not only through years, but genera-

[1] *Works*, IV, 48. By saying that the perception of beauty is not an *intellectual* activity, Ruskin means that such perception does not depend upon the combining powers of the imagination or the analytic powers of the reason.

[2] *Ibid.*, XX, 209.

tions. Only by harmony of both collateral and successive lives can the great doctrine of the Muses be received 'which enables men 'χείρειν ὀρθῶς', 'to have pleasure rightly.'" [1]

The full perception of beauty is thus conditioned upon a sound state of man's moral nature. And the primal source of greatness in art is accordingly the

---

[1] *Works* XIX, 393; XX, 74, 208. It would be possible to quote scores of passages from Ruskin in illustration of this fundamental dogma. His ethical interpretation of beauty no doubt owes much to his personal experience. The world of nature to Ruskin as to Wordsworth was apparelled in celestial light. His first sight of the Alps was like a direct revelation of heaven. In the midst of mountain solitudes, his soul was elevated to a solemn ecstasy and the very atmosphere seemed to thrill with the spirit of God. "I never climbed any mountain, alone," he said, "without kneeling down, by instinct, on its summit to pray." (*Works*, IV, 350.) "Whatever might be my common faults or weaknesses, they were rebuked among the hills; and the only days I can look back to as, according to the powers given me, rightly or wisely, in entireness spent, have been in sight of Mont Blanc, Monte Rosa, or the Jungfrau." (*Works*, XXXV, 474. *Cf.* Tolstoi's experience on seeing the Caucasus mountains for the first time, as described in the second chapter of his *Cossacks*.) Ruskin believed that the "color in the sky, the trees, flowers, and colored creatures round us, and in our own various arts massed under the one name of painting (has) a directly ethical influence" upon man, if he will give *himself* up to its appeals. "Color . . . is the purifying or sanctifying element of material beauty . . . It is just as divine and distinct in its power as music," and "more than all elements of art, the reward of veracity of purpose. . . . It is with still greater interest and reverence to be noted as a physical truth that in states of joyful and healthy excitement the eye becomes more highly sensitive to the beauty of color, and especially to the blue and red rays, while in depression and disease all color becomes dim to us, and the yellow rays prevail over the rest, even to the extremity of jaundice." The "love of beauty is an essential part of all human nature, and though it can long co-exist with states of life in many other respects unvirtuous, it is in itself wholly good;—the direct adversary of envy, avarice, mean wordly care, and especially of cruelty. It entirely perishes when these are wilfully indulged. . . . In the worst condition of sensuality there is yet some perception of the beautiful, so that man utterly depraved in principle and habits of thought, will yet admire beautiful things, and fair faces." (*Works*, XX, 210; VII, 417n.; XI, 218; VII, 418n; XXXIII, 386; XX, 90; IV, 320.)

soul of the artist. Great art is a noble spirit in the artist communicated to his material. Not in technique alone, not in a way of handling details, not in the facts of nature considered by themselves, indispensable as all these are, is to be found the secret of greatness in art. "Great art," Ruskin said, "is produced by men who feel acutely and nobly. . . . Great art is precisely that which never was, nor will be taught; it is pre-eminently and finally the expression of the spirits of great men." [1] An accomplished technician may paint with perfect accuracy a group of gamblers in their den, but no one but a truly refined artist will render the beauty of a fair countenance or the glory of an evening sky; for while a mean intellect will be occupied with mean objects, only a noble nature will correctly interpret noble objects. Objects, moreover, are not represented in the form of pure transcript from nature. "They invariably receive the reflection of the mind under whose shadow they have passed, and are modified or colored by its image."

These most Ruskinian of Ruskin's dogmas on art have been much misunderstood, and much ridiculed as the enthusiasms of a pious sentimentalist, who talked about pictures in the spirit of the preacher rather than of the critic. But Ruskin never advanced the fatuous notion that an ignoramus could be an artist merely because he might happen to be virtuous; nor did he confound a large and noble morality with a narrow and orthodox piety. No one could rate endowment higher than he. "Great men," he said,

[1] *Works*, II, 32, 69.

"always understand at once that the first morality of a painter, as of everybody else, is to know his business. . . . Art-gift and amiability of disposition are two different things; a good man is not necessarily a painter, nor does an eye for color necessarily imply an honest mind. But great art implies the union of both powers: it is the expression, by an art-gift, of a pure soul. If the gift is not there, we have no art at all; and if the soul—and a right soul too—is not there, the art is bad, however dexterous." [1] Goodness, it is to be noted, is nearly always identified by Ruskin with manhood, with a man's full humanity, and implies no particular creed or practice in religion or morals. "All art is great, and good, and true," he said, "only so far as it is distinctively the work of *manhood* in its entire and highest sense. . . . All great art is the work of the whole living creature, body and soul, and chiefly of the soul." An artist's greatness, he said further, in a striking passage, "is in his choice of things, in his analysis of them, and *his combining powers involve the totality of his knowledge in life. His methods of observation and abstraction are essential habits of his thought, conditions of his being.*" [2]

These laws, interpreting the relation between art and its creator, are just as true for the nation or the race, as for the individual. A national art is an accurate expression of the life and temper of the nation that produced it. From the least to the greatest, the arts spring from the whole humanity, debased

[1] *Works*, XX, 81; XIX, 392. Ruskin's position is stated many times over. *Cf.* XV, 416. The whole matter is most clearly and eloquently set forth in a long passage, from which the second quotation above is taken.
[2] *Ibid.*, XI, 201, 212; XIX, 34. The italics are mine.

by its vices, elevated by its virtues. "The art of a nation," said Ruskin, "much resembles the corolla of a flower; its brightness of color is dependent on the general health of the plant, and you can only command the hue, or modify the form of the blossom, by medicine or nourishment applied patiently to the root, not by manipulation of the petals." [1] The characteristics of a people, he contended, are written more legibly in its art than in any other expression of its activity. "You may read the characters of men, and of nations, in their art, as in a mirror. . . . The higher arts, which involve the action of the whole intellect, tell the story of the entire national character." [2] Find on the map of the world or in the history of the past a nation famous for its humanity as well as for its love of beauty, and if it has produced art at all, that art is a reflection of its national characteristics no less distinctly than the sculptures of Michael Angelo are a reflection of his superb power and dignity as a man. Wherever Ruskin turned to study the art of a people, he accordingly found an authentic record of its temper: he found written in stone or upon canvas the soldiership of early Greece, the sensuality of late Italy, the visionary religion of Tuscany, and the splendid human energy of Venice; for "all good art is the natural utterance of its own people in its own day." [3]

The fullest expression of this principle that Ruskin found was architecture,—"the beginning of arts" and "pre-eminently the art of the multitude," [4] not

---

[1] *Works*, XIX, 197.
[2] *Ibid.*, XIX, 389; 250.
[3] *Ibid.*, XIX, 418.
[4] *Ibid.*, VIII, 255; XI, 118.

only in its influence upon people in their daily life and interests, but as an expression of their common creative energy. In their buildings, domestic, civil, or ecclesiastical, they give visible evidence of their national spirit, their love of home, their civic pride, their religious aspiration. Unlike paintings or pieces of statuary, architecture cannot be withdrawn into the privacy of palace or mansion for the enjoyment of the few; and so, more richly than any other form of art, it expresses "to all the world the taste, and therefore the character, of the people by whom it has been created." Ruskin's two books on architecture were written with no other purpose than to set forth the closeness of relation between architecture and the spirit of the people that produced it. "The book I called *The Seven Lamps* was to show that certain right states of temper and moral feeling were the magic powers by which all good architecture, without exception, has been produced. *The Stones of Venice* had, from beginning to end, no other aim than to show that the Gothic architecture of Venice had arisen out of, and indicated in all its features, a state of pure national faith, and of domestic virtue; and that its Renaissance architecture had arisen out of, and in all its features indicated, a state of concealed national infidelity, and of domestic corruption." [1] Every national architecture that he saw or studied was to Ruskin an illustration of the principles thus clearly stated. The spirit of the Roman people was revealed in "the magnificent vaultings of the aqueduct and bath, and the colossal heaping of the rough

[1] *Works*, XVIII, 443.

stones in the arches of the amphitheatre; an architecture full of expression of gigantic power and strength of will." In the "extravagant foliation and exquisite refinement" of his pointed arches the Arab displayed unmistakably his intense love of excitement and his supple energy; just as the Lombard and the Norman gave evidence of their "savage but noble life gradually subjected to law" in the round arches and massive pillars of their buildings, ornamented with "endless imagery of active life and fantastic superstitions." Most expressive of all, because most truly and widely national, was Gothic architecture, the style that Ruskin loved best. In this "magnificently human" art, especially in the northern Gothic of France and England, he found the noble characteristics of multitudes of unnamed workmen legibly written upon the stones which they had shaped into infinite variations of pointed arch, grouped shaft, or intricate tracery. Here were visibly recorded their independence, fortitude, resolution, impatience, freedom, habitual tenderness, enthusiasm, and profound sympathy with the wealth of beauty in the material world. Gothic, too, was a democratic architecture, created not for knights and nobles, nor for baronial halls and sanctuaries, alone, but for the people, for their houses, their shops, and their places of commerce; it was good for all, enjoyed by all, and "had fellowship with all hearts, and was universal like nature." Then, because the people became money-loving and faithless, because they no longer delighted in art except as a minister to their pride and luxury, there grew up in Europe another architecture, called

the Renaissance. This, just as accurately as the
Gothic, was a witness of the character of its creators.
It was aristocratic and cold, a type of building made
for men of intellect and position, "for the academy
and the court;—princes delighted in it, and cour-
tiers." More and more it served the uses and the
interests of an aristocratic society, until in the
seventeenth and eighteenth centuries it became
associated with "the terraced and scented and grot-
toed garden, with its trickling fountains and slum-
brous shades," attaining "its utmost height" in the
palace of Versailles, the perfect symbol of a haughty
and degenerate nobility.

It is clear, then, that Ruskin found in architecture
the best possible illustration of his doctrine that the
art of a nation is the exponent of its social and
political life, and that a noble architecture, such as
the Gothic, sprang from a sound and noble national
existence. But his study of Gothic revealed to him
many supplementary lessons concerning the relation
of art to society, which he held and advocated with
increasing conviction as he grew older. It taught him
that to be truly great an art must be the flowering of
the creative effort of a whole people. Such an art
must be the product of many noble artists, small as
well as great, guided by a universal style, and working together towards certain large common ends.[1]
Gothic taught him, further, that a fully nationalized

[1] "The very essence of a Style, properly so called, is that it should be
practised *for ages*, and applied to all purposes; and that so long as any
given style is in practice, all that is left for individual imagination to
accomplish must be within the scope of that style, not in the invention of
a new one." (*Works*, XVI, 349.)

art comes only when the enjoyment of it is universal, and when the people who create it are living happily in an ordered and beautiful environment. "There is no way of getting good art," he said, "but one—at once the simplest and most difficult—to enjoy it." Ruskin did not believe in an art that was aristocratic and therefore exclusive, that was individual and therefore eccentric. "In all base schools of Art," he said, "the craftsman is dependent for his bread on originality; that is to say, on finding in himself some fragment of isolated faculty, by which his work may be recognized as different from that of other men. . . In all great schools of art these conditions are exactly reversed. An artist is praised in these, not for what is different from him in others, nor for solitary performance of singular work; but only for doing most strongly what all are endeavoring; and for contributing, in the measure of his strength, to some great achievement, to be completed by the unity of multitudes, and the sequence of ages." [1] Ruskin was engaged all his life, to use his own words, "in an ardent endeavor to spread the love and knowledge of art among all classes. . . . The end of my whole Professorship," he said, when speaking of his work as Slade Professor of Fine Arts at Oxford, "would be accomplished,—and far more than that,—if only the English nation could be made to understand that the beauty which is indeed to be a joy forever, must be a joy for *all*." [2]

[1] *Works*, III, 665; XXII, 212. *Cf.* "Not only sculpture, but all the other fine arts, must be for all the people." (XX, 299.) "All great art must be popular." (XXII, 317.)

[2] *Ibid.* XXII, 145.

But, in keeping with Ruskin's belief in the dependence of sound art upon sound life, his demand for an
art widely diffused over the whole of society im-
poses tremendous claims upon the people who are to
create it. They must first create beauty of surroundings and beauty of life. "Design is not the offspring
of idle fancy," said Ruskin, in one of his clearest·
utterances on this point; "it is the studied result
of accumulative observation and delightful habit.
Without observation and experience, no design—
without peace and pleasurableness in occupation, no
design—and all the lecturings, and teachings, and
prizes, and principles of art, in the world, are of no
use, so long as you don't surround your men with
happy influences and beautiful things. It is impossible
for them to have right ideas about color, unless they
see lovely colors in nature unspoiled; impossible for
them to supply beautiful incident and action in their
ornament, unless they see beautiful incident and
action in the world about them. Inform their minds,
refine their habits, and you form and refine their
designs. . . . The elements of character necessary
for the production of true formative art will be, first,
brightness of physical life, and the manly virtues
belonging to it; then the broad scope of reflection and
purpose; then the distinctive gift of imagination; the
innocent perception of beauty; to crown all, the perfect peace of an honest and living faith. All this is
needed in the nature of the artist himself; and yet it is
not enough. Endowed with all these attributes, or at
least capable of them, he may still be made helpless
by the lower conditions of persons and things around

him. For it is necessary to his healthy energy that
his subject should always be greater than himself.
He must not stoop to it, but be exalted by it, and
paint it with full strain of his force looking upward.
It is fatal to his strength, to his honor, if he is always
raising mean things and gilding defiled. He has
always the privilege, is often under the necessity, of
modifying, or choosing, or contracting his subject,
within assigned limitations of manners; but he must
always feel that the whole, out of which he has
chosen, could he have rendered it, was greater and
more beautiful than the part he chose, and that the
free fact was greater than his formalism. And therefore it is necessary that the living men round him
should be in an ethical state harmonious with his own,
and that there should be no continual discord nor
dishonor standing between him and the external
world. And thus a lovely and ordered unity of civil
life is necessary to fulfil the power of the men who are
raised above its level; such unity of life as expresses
itself palpably and always in the states capable of
formative design by their consenting adaptation of a
common style of architecture for their buildings, and
of more or less fixed standards of form in domestic
furniture and in dress. . . . We shall never make
our houses for the rich beautiful, till we have begun
by making our houses for the poor beautiful. As it is
a common and diffused pride, so it is a common and
diffused delight on which alone our future arts can be
founded." [1]

Common and diffused delights! Beautiful objects

[1] *Works*, XVI, 341; XIX, 184, 266.

and beautiful incidents! A lovely and ordered unity
of civil life! Artists with happy human creatures
round them in an ethical state harmonious with their
own! Ruskin's study of art had indeed led him far.
Passionate lover of the beautiful, passionate believer
in the dependence of beauty upon a right state of the
heart, passionate prophet of the contented craftsmanship that once throve in medieval communities of
cathedral builders, he clung with his whole intense
nature to the faith that art in its highest and health-
iest form could flourish only when happiness was the
possession not of the few, but of the many, the possession of a people living well-ordered lives in a beautiful
environment. His first sight of the Alps and of
Italian cities had come to him before the advent of
modern industrialism, when the skies were unsullied
with smoke-clouds and the marbles of Venice and
Verona yet shone with something of their ancient
luster, unspoiled by the hand of the restorer. Inspired poet rather than sober rationalist, he had seen
the splendors of nature and of art before his eyes were
troubled with the new order springing up about him.
He had grown accustomed to regard beauty, which
was to him a revelation of the glory and goodness of
God and which therefore was fully unveiled only to
the pure in heart, as the symbol of a peaceful and
contented society in the past, and as the promise
of a noble fellowship of men in the future. With
a mind full of such visions and faiths, with a
heart inflamed with hope, buoyant and sensitive
as a poet, he now turned to look upon the modern world that had grown up as if by miracle

while he was absorbed in following the footprints of Turner.

What Ruskin saw was a sight familiar enough to-day but wholly new to him, a sight that filled him with horror. He saw that however eloquently the heavens might declare the glory of God, the cities of men and their habitations were now subject to another power, the demon of disorder and ugliness, of grime and squalor and noise. "The vastness of the horror of this world's blindness and misery opens upon me," he wrote to C. E. Norton in 1862 from the little Alpine village of Mornex, where he was writing the essays that afterwards appeared as *Munera Pulveris*. The ugliness of this new era, which took beauty from the sky and clearness from the streams and which spread dreary acres of monotonous dwellings over the faces of cities, he described in his later books with the fierceness of Swift and the atrabiliar exaggeration of Carlyle, without, alas, Carlyle's Teufelsdröchkian humor. The language that he sometimes employed reminds one in its uncontrolled intensity and extravagance of the speech of Milton or Burke, in moments when their wrath overcame their reason. For Ruskin wrote, as he expressed it, with "a sense of indignation which burns in me continually, for all that men are doing and suffering." He wrote, too, with a discontent which he likened to that of Dante and Virgil. It seemed to him as if the peace and beauty, "the integrity and simplicity," of an older order was being trampled down by a people who lived in tenements instead of homes, and who substituted "mechanism for skill, photograph for

picture, cast-iron for sculpture." After a long drive
through the midland manufacturing districts of
England, he wrote: "The two most frightful things
I have ever yet seen in my life are the southeastern
suburb of Bradford (six miles long), and the scene
from Wakefield bridge, by the chapel." [1]   Could
beauty live in a pestilence like this? "I know perfectly," he said, "that to the general people, trained
in the midst of the ugliest objects that vice can design, in houses, mills, and machinery, *all* beautiful
form and color is as invisible as the seventh heaven.
. . . In literal and fatal instance of fact—think what
ruin it is for men of any sensitive faculty to live in
such a city as London is now! Take the highest
and lowest state of it: you have, typically, Grosvenor
Square,—an aggregation of bricks and railings, with
not so much architectural faculty expressed in the
whole cumber of them as there is in a wasp's nest or a
worm-hole;—and you have the rows of houses which
you look down into on the south side of the South-
Western line, between Vauxhall and Clapham Junc-
tion. Between these two ideals the London artist
must seek his own; and in the humanity, or the ver-
min, of them, worship the aristocratic and scientific
gods of living Israel. . . . Is this verily the end at
which we aim, and will the mission of the age have
been then only accomplished, when the last castle
has fallen from our rocks, the last cloisters faded from
our valleys, the last streets, in which the dead have
dwelt, been effaced from our cities, and regenerated
society is left in luxurious possession of towns com-

[1] *Works*, XXVIII, 267.

posed only of bright saloons, overlooking gay par-
terres? . . . Must this little Europe—this corner of
our globe, gilded with the blood of old battles, and
gray with the temples of all pieties—this narrow
piece of the world's pavement, worn down by so
many pilgrims' feet, be utterly swept and garnished
for the masque of the future?" [1] Readers familiar
with his later writings know how repeatedly Ruskin
drew these graphic pictures, for he could not dismiss
from his mind these scenes of a newer world which his
acute sensibilities were constantly impressing upon it
and which contradicted all his hopes for art.

It was not the ugliness of the industrialism only
that appalled him. Even more it was the luxury and
the misery, the lust of money and the injustice, which
went with the ugliness and were both cause and consequence. "The extremities of human degradation,"
Ruskin said, "are not owing to natural causes; but to
the habitual preying upon the labor of the poor by
the luxury of the rich." [2] In the severest language he
condemned the tendencies of the times that had their
root in these conditions,—the furious pursuit of

[1] *Works*, XXII, 473; XXXIII, 398; XII, 429.
[2] *Ibid.*, XXVIII, 374. Ruskin printed in *Fors* an extract from a contemporary paper (the *Builder* for August 25, 1877) in part to the following effect: "Five men own one-fourth of Scotland. One duke owns 96,000
acres in Derbyshire, besides vast estates in other parts of England and in
Ireland. Another, with estates all over the United Kingdom, has 40,000
acres in Sussex and 300,000 acres in Scotland. This nobleman's park is
fifteen miles in circumference! Another duke has estates which the
highroad divides for twenty-three miles! A marquis there is who can ride
a hundred miles in a straight line upon his own land! . . . One hundred
and fifty persons own half England, seventy-five persons own half Scotland, thirty-five persons own half Ireland; and all the lands of England,
Scotland, Wales, and Ireland are owned by less than 60,000 persons."
(*Works*, XXIX, 273.)

pleasure, the thirst for excitement and change, the criminal luxury and idleness of the rich, together with the discontent and unrest, the misery, dirt, and degradation of the poor. The overworked and the underworked were alike victims of prodigious social folly. "Our cities are a wilderness of spinning wheels instead of palaces; yet the people have not clothes. We have blackened every leaf of English greenwood with ashes, and the people die of cold; our harbors are a forest of merchant ships, and the people die of hunger." [1] In moods of anger and despair, Ruskin pictured the English people as a money-making mob, concentrating its soul upon pounds, shillings, and pence, and worshiping with all its heart the great Goddess of Getting-on, the Goddess, too, "not of everybody's getting on,—but only of somebody's getting on." The Crystal Palace, a gigantic toy-shop of glass, opened in London in 1854 to celebrate England's vast material expansion and "to exhibit the paltry arts of our fashionable luxury," was to him a perfect symbol of nineteenth-century life, its frivolity, its love of novelty, its immense and childish curiosity, its indifference or insensitiveness to beauty;—a supreme glorification indeed of an age of machinery and commercialism. Ruskin looked upon this age not merely with anger, but with genuine apprehension. Carlyle himself was not more troubled. Social changes and disturbances were in the air which threatened revolution. He saw with great clearness a coming struggle between a feudalistic and a democratic social order, for he knew that a society founded

[1] *Works*, XVIII, 502.

upon injustice could not endure. The upper classes were losing their power to govern, while the populace was losing respect for its rulers and was pressing blindly forward along a road that led it knew not where. "We are on the eve of a great political crisis, if not of political change," Ruskin wrote in 1869. "A struggle is approaching between the newly-risen power of democracy and the apparently departing power of feudalism; and another struggle, no less imminent, and far more dangerous, between wealth and pauperism." For eleven hundred years Europe has had kings to rule over it, but for the last fifty years the people "have begun to suspect, and of late they have many of them concluded, that they have been on the whole ill-governed, or mis-governed, by their kings. Whereupon they say, more and more widely, 'Let us henceforth have no kings; and no government at all.'" [1] In an article in the *Contemporary Review* for May, 1873, he stated "the causes and terms of the economical crisis of our own day" as follows: first, the growth of capitalism, by "occupation of land, usury, or taxation of labor"; second, the luxury and extravagance of capitalism, monopolizing "the music, the painting, the architecture, the hand-service, the horse-service, and the sparkling champagne of the world." In consequence, "it is gradually in these days becoming manifest to the tenants, borrowers, and laborers, that instead of paying these large sums into the hands of the landlords, lenders, and employers, for them to purchase music, painting, etc., with, the tenants,

[1] *Works*, XVIII, 494-5.

borrowers, and workers had better buy a little music
and painting for themselves. . . . These are views
which are gaining ground among the poor; and it is
entirely vain to repress them by equivocations. They
are founded on eternal laws." [1]

This system of things, as Ruskin saw it in the decades 1860 to 1880, continued to be upheld in the
main by the old individualistic economic creed of
Adam Smith and Bentham, Malthus, and Ricardo.
Its sacred principles—*laissez-faire*, competition, self-
interest—were yet regarded as the foundations of
national prosperity, the fixed laws by which men
were to get on in the world, although the thought and
influence of J. S. Mill showed clear tendencies in the
opposite direction. It was a political economy that
boasted of being a science. It professed to be impersonal and dispassionate. With infinite pains its high
priests had erected an image of wood and stone, which
they hailed as "the economic man," and which they
now called upon all the Philistines to bow down to
and worship, solemnly adjuring them to repeat all
the pious formulas by which men were to be economically saved: law of rent, law of population, law of
wages, and the other changeless dogmas of their
religion of Mammon. To Ruskin these doctrines
were as false as they were soulless. He therefore
attacked them as boldly as, twenty years before, he
had attacked the lifeless conventions of the contemporary schools of art. But his attack was not only
bold and brilliant; it was scornful, ironic, iconoclastic,
and irreverent. He opposed dogma with dogma. He

[1] *Works*, XVII, 564-5.

asked pertinent questions in a manner that must have seemed impertinent to the staid and stolid defenders of the orthodox creed. He flung challenge after challenge into the camp of the enemy, and, as Carlyle with grim pleasure declared, he plunged his rapier again and again up to the hilt into the belly of their pagan deity.

The science of modern political economy, said Ruskin, "is a Lie"; it is a "carnivorous political economy; it founds an ossifiant theory of progress on the negation of a soul. . . . All our hearts have been betrayed by the plausible impiety of the modern economist telling us that, 'To do the best for ourselves, is finally to do the best for others.' Friends, our great Master said not so; and most absolutely we shall find this world is not so made. Indeed, to do the best for others, is finally to do the best for ourselves; but it will not do to have our eyes fixed on that issue." [1] When J. S. Mill declared that moral considerations had nothing to do with political economy, Ruskin asked if questions of commerce and industry did not involve the justice and goodness of men. "Economy," he said, "does not depend merely on principles of 'demand and supply,' but primarily on what is demanded and what is supplied." [2] Against the statement of Jevons that pleasure and pain "are the ultimate objects of political economy," he loosed a shaft that might have come from Carlyle's quiver: "there is a swine's pleasure, and dove's; villain's pleasure and gentleman's, to be arranged." To Mill's aphorism that "labor is limited by capital," Ruskin

[1] *Works*, XVII, 26; XVIII, 455.   [2] *Ibid.*, XVII, 178.

replied: "in an ultimate, but entirely impractical sense, labor is limited by capital, as it is by matter— that is to say, where there is no material there can be no work,—but in the practical sense, labor is limited only by the great original capital of head, heart, and hand." [1] A follower of the economists had defended in orthodox fashion the extravagant expenditures of the rich on the ground that they benefited the poor. Ruskin drew from the experience of his father's wine-firm and their workers in Spain the apt and ironic rejoinder: "these laborers produced from the earth annually a certain number of bottles of wine. These productions were sold by my father and his partners, who kept nine-tenths, or thereabouts, of the price themselves, and gave one-tenth, or thereabouts, to the laborers. In which state of mutual beneficence my father and his partners naturally became rich, and the laborers as naturally remained poor." Again and again he opposed the stock English notion that it does not matter what a laborer produces, so long as he works and is paid for his work: "the real good," he contended, "of all work, and of all commerce, depends on the final intrinsic worth of the thing you make, or get by it." [2] Concerning the sacred laws of population and of wages, he asked embarrassing questions. "It is proposed to better the condition of the laborer by giving him higher wages. 'Nay,' say the economists,—'if you raise his wages, he will either people down to the same point of misery at which you found him, or drink your wages away.' He will. I know it. Who gave him this will? Sup-

[1] *Works*, XVII, 177.   [2] *Ibid*, XVIII, 391.

pose it were your own son of whom you spoke, declaring to me that you dared not take him into your firm, nor even give him his just laborer's wages, because if you did he would die of drunkenness, and leave half a score of children to the parish. 'Who gave your son these dispositions'—I should enquire. Has he them by inheritance or by education? By one or other they *must* come; and as in him, so also in the poor. . . . Ricardo defines what he calls the 'habitual rule of wages' as 'that which will maintain the laborer.' Maintain him! Yes; but how?"

Political economists, said Ruskin, call their science "the science of getting rich. But there are many sciences as well as many arts of getting rich. Poisoning people of large estates, was one employed largely in the Middle Ages; adulteration of food of people of small estates, is one employed largely now." Another method of acquiring wealth, as practiced by modern business, was pungently set forth by Ruskin in the form of parable, a means of illustration that he was fond of using: "Suppose that three men, instead of two, formed the little isolated republic, and found themselves obliged to separate, in order to farm different pieces of land at some distance from each other along the coast: each estate furnishing a distinct kind of produce, and each more or less in need of the material raised on the other. Suppose that the third man, in order to save the time of all three, undertakes simply to superintend the transference of commodities from one farm to the other; on condition of receiving some sufficiently remunerative share of every parcel of goods conveyed, or of some other parcel received in exchange for it. If this carrier or messenger always brings to each estate, from the other, what is chiefly wanted, at the right time, the operations of the two farmers will go on prosperously, and the largest possible result in produce, or wealth, will be attained by the little community. But suppose no intercourse between the landowners is possible, except through the travelling agent; and that, after a time, this agent, watching the course of each man's agriculture, keeps back the articles with which he has been entrusted until there comes a period of extreme necessity for them, on one side or other, and then exacts in exchange for them all that the distressed farmer can spare of other kinds of produce: it is easy to see that by ingeniously watching his opportunities, he might possess himself regularly of the greater part of the superfluous produce of the two estates, and at last, in some years of severest trial or scarcity, purchase both for himself and maintain the former proprietors thenceforward as his laborers or servants." [1]

These assaults, with scores of others, witty, ironical, trenchant, brought down upon Ruskin the jeers of the philistines, who vented their wrath by calling him a sentimentalist and a Don Quixote, a madman who

---

[1] *Works*, XVII, 106, 108, 61, 51. *Cf*. 138. "Ricardo's chapter on Rent and Adam Smith's eighth chapter on the wages of labor stand, to my mind, quite Sky High among the Monuments of Human Brutification; that is to say, of the paralysis of human intellect fed habitually on Grass, instead of Bread of God. . . . Nothing that I yet know of equals the saying of Bright, in the House, that 'in a common sense mercantile community the adulteration of food can only be considered a form of competition.'" (XXXVI, 416, 593.)

was attempting to explode established dogmas with mere heresies and paradoxes. It was in truth a many-headed monster that he set out to slay, when he put aside his drawing and his art-study to take up the problems of social reform. And when he forsook his art, he gave up his peace and happiness of heart, at least as he had known these in the old undisturbed days. Whoever will go through the mass of published letters and diaries for the decades 1860–1880, a most intimate record of Ruskin's mind for those years, will find there the tragic story of a brilliant and refined nature, goaded on and on by its own sense of the evil and injustice in the affairs of men, until it is obscured in the temporary eclipse of brain-fever, emerging again for a brief interval, only to pass at last into the lengthened twilight which preceded the end. *Fors Clavigera,* the collection of letters to workingmen, reads more like the outburst of a disillusioned and perplexed modern Hamlet than the sober attempt of a wise reformer to right the wrongs of the world about him. For after all Ruskin did not regard social reform as his proper field. "It is the 'first mild day of March,'" he wrote in 1867, "and by rights I ought to be out among the budding banks and hedges, outlining sprays of hawthorne and clusters of primrose. That is *my* right work." [1] In the years after 1860, he often referred to his vacillating temper, vacillating between desire for "quiet investigation of beautiful things," and duty to battle with the misery and folly of humanity.[2] As his biographer has said, the moral and active side of his soul was at strife with the artis-

[1] *Works,* XVII, 376. *Cf.* XVII, 415.   [2] *Cf.* XVIII, *intro.* XIX.

tic and contemplative. The contrast between the old
beautiful world that had burst upon him when he had
journeyed leisurely by stage-coach to the Alps or to
Italy, and the new world of industry, was more
tormenting each time that he revisited the continent.
"This first day of May, 1869," he said in his preface
to *The Queen of the Air*, "I am writing where my
work was begun thirty-five years ago, within sight of
the snow of the higher Alps. In that half of the permitted life of man, I have seen strange evil brought
upon every scene that I best loved, or tried to make
beloved by others. The light which once flushed
those pale summits with its rose at dawn, and purple
at sunset, is now umbered and faint; the air which
once inlaid the clefts of all their golden crags with
azure is now defiled with languid coils of smoke,
belched from worse than volcanic fires; their very
glacier waves are ebbing, and their snows fading, as if
Hell had breathed on them; the waters that once sank
at their feet into crystalline rest are now dimmed and
foul, from deep to deep, and shore to shore. These
are no careless words—they are accurately—horribly
—true. I know what the Swiss lakes were; no pool of
Alpine fountain at its source was clearer. This morning on the Lake of Geneva, at half a mile from the
beach, I could scarcely see my oar-blade a fathom
deep." [1] The acute disturbances that Ruskin's mind
suffered from time to time during these years is nowhere better suggested, perhaps, than in the bitter
comment upon his life as "a series of delights which

[1] *Works*, XIX, 293. *Cf.* XVI, 338; XXXVII, 204; also, travel by coach
as contrasted with travel by rail, XXV, 451.

are gone forever, and of griefs which remain forever." [1]

This conflict on the higher levels of his nature between the ethical and the æsthetic was inevitable, however, for, as we have seen, both passions had their rootage in a unity deeper down, and neither could be completely satisfied unless it was true to its source. Ruskin's interest in art demanded that the moral and social conditions of man should be improved as the foundation of art. It was futile to teach the dependence of art upon sound life, when society seemed to be rushing madly into everything that was unsound. "It is the vainest of affectations," he declared, "to try and put beauty into shadows, while all real things that cast them are in deformity and pain. . . . *You cannot have a landscape by Turner, without a country for him to paint; you cannot have a portrait by Titian, without a man to be portrayed. . . .* The beginning of art *is in getting our country clean, and our people beautiful. . . .* Beautiful art can only be produced by people who have beautiful things about them, and leisure to look at them." [2] Manifestly it was not a time for the entertainment of the arts, but for far weightier and more fundamental work. Ruskin therefore sternly resolved, as he said in *Fors*, to endure passively the present condition no longer, but to do his poor best to lead the way to better things. People had read his descriptions of nature and art and

[1] *Letters to Norton*, I, 184. Ruskin's letters to Norton are the best record of his mental condition from 1860 to 1880. It should be noted, however, that his love affair with Miss Rose LaTouche was in this period another important source of spiritual disturbance.

[2] *Works*, XVII, *intro.* XXIV; XX, 107; XVI, 338.

had pronounced them pretty, but they had heeded not his call to beauty. The day had come, therefore, for him to cease speaking and to begin doing. "My thoughts have changed also, as my words have; and whereas in earlier life, what little influence I obtained was due chiefly to the enthusiasm with which I was able to dwell on the beauty of the physical clouds, and of their colors in the sky; so all the influence I now desire to retain must be due to the earnestness with which I am endeavoring to trace the form and beauty of another kind of cloud than those; the bright cloud of which it is written—'What is your life?' " [1]

[1] *Works,* XVIII, 146.

CHAPTER VI

THE ART-IMPULSE IN INDUSTRY
AND THE NEW POLITICAL ECONOMY

"Life without industry is guilt, and industry without
art is brutality. . . . The real science of political economy, which has yet to be distinguished from the bastard
science, as medicine from witchcraft, and astronomy from
astrology, is that which teaches nations to desire and labor
for the things that lead to life."—*Ruskin*.

THE inspiration for social reform came to Ruskin
from art. His clue to the solution of social problems came also from art, and chiefly from architecture. In a concluding chapter of the last volume
of *Modern Painters*, he said: "Every principle of
painting which I have stated is traced to some vital
or spiritual fact; and in my works on architecture the
preference accorded finally to one school over another, is founded on a comparison of their influences
on the life of the workman—a question by all other
writers on the subject of architecture wholly forgotten
or despised." [1] The earliest suggestion of the precise
form which his social thought was to take may be
found in two or three passages in *Seven Lamps* (1849),
where he drew the attention of his readers to the bearing of architecture upon the condition of the workman: "I believe the right question to ask respecting
all ornament is simply this: was it done with enjoy-

[1] *Works*, VII, 257.

ment—was the carver happy while he was about it?"
Mere benevolent advice and instruction, he contends,
are futile as cures for the idleness and discontent of
the masses. What the men need is occupation, but,
he hastens to add, "I do not mean work in the sense of
bread,—I mean work in the sense of mental interest."[1]

This idea of mental interest in work, the alpha and
omega of Ruskin's social philosophy, was fully
developed for the first time in the famous chapter on
Gothic architecture in *The Stones of Venice* (1851–
1853),—one of the most convincing and most eloquent statements of the fundamental principles of
social reform written in the nineteenth century. "To
some of us when we first read it, now many years
ago," said William Morris, "it seemed to point out a
new road on which the world should travel." "It set
fire to his enthusiasm," says Professor Mackail,
Morris's biographer, "and kindled the belief of his
whole life." [2] Mr. Frederic Harrison, biographer and
friend of Ruskin, as well as himself a social reformer,
called the chapter "the creed, if it be not the origin,
of a new industrial school of thought." Ruskin himself attached great importance to this memorable
utterance for he called it "precisely and accurately
the most important chapter in the whole book"; and
he said that "of all that I have to bring forward
respecting architecture, this is the one I have most at

[1] *Works*, VIII, 218, 261.
[2] Morris, it will be recalled, printed the chapter at the Kelmscott Press
in 1892, writing for it an introduction from which the above remark of his
is taken. First distributed free, and afterwards sold in sixpenny pamphlet form, the chapter was used as the manifesto of the Working Men's
College, at its opening in 1854.

heart." We have seen how passionately he admired Gothic. From the multitudinous and fascinating diversity in the surface and form of those "perpendicular flights of aspiration," erected by the piety and enthusiasm of the communes of the twelfth and thirteenth centuries,—Chartres, Beauvais, Amiens, Rouen, and Rheims,—he discovered intimations of the true spirit of man, its freedom and fierceness, its fun and terror, its faith and longing, its ever haunting sense of mystery in the midst of the here and now. Upon their walls the poetry of the soul seemed to be written, not of the master builders only, but of multitudes of lesser workmen as well. In the shaping and placing of stone upon stone, in the creation of tower and arch, pinnacle, capital, and tracery, in the redundant and endlessly varied carving of leaf and vine, gargoyle and saint, Ruskin found perpetual evidence that the workman had realized, even though in humble manner often, the joy of creative effort. It was Gothic architecture, therefore, that revealed to him his way out of the wilderness of social problems which confronted him when he first looked upon the modern world. Gothic taught him that happiness in labor is the right of every worker, from gifted genius to humblest toiler. "It is, perhaps, the principal admirableness of the Gothic schools of architecture," he said, "that they receive the results of the labor of inferior minds." What we have to do with all our laborers is "to look for the *thoughtful* part of them, and get that out of them, whatever we lose for it, whatever faults and errors we are obliged to take with it."

Ruskin begins, in the chapter on the nature of Gothic, by condemning modern industry because it degrades men to machines. The trouble with labor to-day, he declared, is that men are "divided into mere segments of men—broken into small fragments and crumbs of life; so that all the little piece of intelligence that is left in a man is not enough to make a pin, or a nail, but exhausts itself in making the point of a pin or the head of a nail." It is this degradation, he continues, "which, more than any other evil of the times, is leading the masses of the nation everywhere into vain, incoherent, destructive struggling for a freedom of which they cannot explain the nature to themselves." What the worker must have is the opportunity for self-expression in his work, even though mechanical precision and perfection should be sacrificed. "You must either make a tool of the creature, or a man of him. You cannot make both. Men were not intended to work with the accuracy of tools, to be precise and perfect in all their actions. If you will have that precision out of them, and make their fingers measure degrees like cog-wheels, and their arms strike curves like compasses, you must unhumanize them. All the energy of their spirits must be given to make cogs and compasses of themselves. All their attention and strength must go to the accomplishment of the mean act. The eye of the soul must be bent upon the finger-point, and the soul's force must fill all the invisible nerves that guide it, ten hours a day, that it may not err from its steely precision, and so soul and sight be worn away, and the whole human being lost at last—a heap of sawdust, so far as its intellectual work in this world is concerned; saved only by its Heart, which cannot go into the form of cogs and compasses but expands, after the ten hours are over, into fireside humanity. On the other hand, if you will make a man of the working creature, you cannot make a tool. Let him but begin to imagine, to think, to try to do anything worth doing; and the engine-turned precision is lost at once. Out come all his roughness, all his dulness, all his incapability; shame upon shame, failure upon failure, pause after pause; but out comes the whole majesty of him also; and we know the height of it only, when we see the clouds settling upon him. And, whether the clouds be bright or dark, there will be transfiguration behind and within them. . . . Men may be beaten, chained, tormented, yoked like cattle, slaughtered like summer flies, and yet remain in one sense, and the best sense, free. But to smother their souls within them, to blight and hew into rotting pollards the suckling branches of their human intelligence, to make the flesh and skin which, after the worm's work on it, is to see God, into leathern thongs to yoke machinery with,—this it is to be slave-masters indeed; and there might be more freedom in England, though her feudal lords' lightest words were worth men's lives, and though the blood of the vexed husbandman dropped in the furrows of her fields, than there is while the animation of her multitudes is sent like fuel to feed the factory smoke, and the strength of them is given daily to be wasted into the fineness of a web, or racked into the exactness of a line. And, on the other hand, go forth again to gaze upon the old cathedral front, where you have smiled so often at the fantastic ignorance of the old sculptors: examine once more those ugly goblins, and formless monsters, and stern statues, anatomiless and rigid; but do not mock at them, for they are signs of the life and liberty of every workman who struck the stone; a freedom of thought, and rank in scale of being, such as no laws, no charters, no charities can secure; but which it must be the first aim of all Europe at this day to regain for her children." [1]

The gospel of joy in work was a new and strange gospel to Ruskin's contemporaries, and to many it is a very strange gospel still. The mill owners and the laborers of 1860, like the political economists of that day, looked upon work as something to be endured from necessity, something to be *done* and over with in the shortest time possible. It was a painful activity, falling chiefly upon the unfortunate, to be paid for by wages,—a disagreeable means to an unavoidable end. [2] "We do not pretend that these dingy toilers in mine or factory are happy, " said the captains of industry of that day; "but their toil keeps them alive; otherwise they and their children would starve to death like rats upon a deserted ship. We

[1] *Works*, X, 196, 194, 192-4.

[2] The difference between Ruskin's view of labor and the economists' is well shown in a remark that Ruskin wrote on the margin of Mill's *Principles of Political Economy;* in Mill's "first definition of labor he includes in the idea of it 'all feelings of a disagreeable kind connected with one's thoughts in a particular occupation.' True; but why not also, 'feelings of an agreeable kind'?" (*Works*, XVII, 67.) Mr. Frederic Harrison, in his *Memoirs* (I, 236), in speaking of Ruskin's vehement disapproval of Millet, the painter, quotes Ruskin: "no painter has any business to represent labor as gloomy. It is *not* gloomy, but blessed and cheerful."

do not even pretend that we ourselves enjoy our business, but we like to make money and we like the houses and lands and social position that our money provides. Moreover, behold the unexampled wealth and prosperity of England,—the richest nation on the globe!" Thus they argued. Whatever else these men were, they were not hypocritical. They suffered no delusions to distort the clear view they had of their own activities. Their convictions were reinforced, too, by a school of economic thought which, as we have seen, assumed that "the ruling passions of mankind were wealth and ease." But Ruskin, like Carlyle, took a different view. To him work was less a means than an end. It was not so much a necessity as an opportunity, and, if it yielded a livelihood, it should also develop a life. More than all else, therefore, Ruskin sought to put the art-motive into every possible form of human effort, into the crafts and industries, as it was already in the fine arts. He would broaden the definition of art and remove the rigid boundaries that existed between the lower kinds of art and the higher.

"There is not a definite separation between the two kinds," he said,—"a blacksmith may put soul into the making of a horseshoe, and an architect may put none into the building of a church. Only exactly in proportion as the Soul is thrown into it, the art becomes Fine. . . . Art is the operation of the hand and the intelligence of man together: there is an art of making machinery; there is an art of building ships; an art of making carriages; and so on. All these, properly called Arts, but not Fine Arts, are pursuits in which the hand of man and his head go together, working at the same instant." [1] The first principle of social reform and the last, Ruskin insisted, was that in labor hand and soul should be united, for if it was only by labor that thought could be made healthy, it was no less true that only by thought could labor be made happy. The primal eldest curse of modern industry was that it crushed the soul out of man and made work a torment. The one way to extirpate this root-calamity, therefore, was to establish as fast and as far as possible a condition of things wherein each worker should realize, according to his ability, and according to the nature of his work, that sense of life which comes in fullest measure to the creative artist, to him who bodies forth through one medium or another the forms of things unseen. The conservation of the individual through creative industry,—this was the star that Ruskin followed in his strange adventures upon the troubled waters of political economy and social reconstruction. [2]

---

[1] *Works*, XI, *intro.* XIX; XVI, 294. With perhaps mingled jest and earnest, because he was alluding to the much laughed-at Hinksey Diggers of Oxford (of whom more later), but with more earnest than jest, Ruskin included road-making as an occupation with something of "art" in it (XX, *intro.* XLIII.) "A true artist," he said, "is only a beautiful development of tailor or carpenter." (XXVII, 186.) Ruskin tried his hand at various "arts and crafts," including brick-laying, carpentering, house-painting, street-sweeping, and scrubbing. *Cf.* Cook, *Life*, I, 447; XXIII, 52; XXI, *intro.* XX.

[2] "I am myself more set on teaching healthful industry than anything else, as the beginning of all redemption," said Ruskin in *Fors*. (XXVII, 364.) "It matters little, ultimately, how much a laborer is paid for making anything; but it matters fearfully what the thing is, which he is compelled to make. . . . All professions should be liberal, and there should be less pride felt in peculiarity of employment, and more in excel-

It is well-nigh impossible to bring into connected form an account of these adventures, since Ruskin was the most irresponsible of voyagers, sometimes pursuing his course by the most devious of routes, and never weary of pushing his prow into various queer creeks and bays along the way. His writings on society and the laws by which men live are to be found not in one or two volumes, but in a dozen. They are, moreover, in the highest degree discursive,—"desultory talk," Ruskin once aptly called them,—"unprogressive inlets" of thought, he described them on another occasion. Just as in earlier days he had frequently been drawn away from art into the discussion of "irrelevant and Utopian topics" against which his friends had remonstrated in vain, so now he digressed at will from political economy and the guild of St. George into the fields of art, religion, mythology, and etymology. He concludes one of his chapters in *Munera Pulveris* with an extended exposition of the attitude of Dante, Homer, Plato, and Spenser on the use or the misuse of wealth; and in *Fors* he finds illustrations and lessons for modern conditions of society in Giotto's frescoes, Chaucer's *Romance of the Rose*, and other literary and art works all the way down to Lockhart's *Life of Scott*. So, too, in *Time and Tide*, brilliant suggestions for a new social order are freely interspersed with all manner of whimsical subjects, such as pantomime and Japanese jugglers, the four possible theories

lence of achievement."—In connection with his teaching at the Working Men's College, Ruskin testified before a parliamentary committee: "My efforts are directed not to making a carpenter an artist, but to making him happier as a carpenter." (*Works*, XVIII, 391; X, 201; XIII, 553.)

respecting the origin of the Bible, the use of music and dancing under the Jewish theocracy, and the like. Ruskin's fondness for verbal distinctions founded upon etymological principles involved him not only in futile digressions, but also at times in plain confusion of terms, as when in one work he distinguishes "labor" from "effort" (labor being that amount of effort which brings distress or loss of life), and then in subsequent books he drops the distinction, using the words in their ordinary meanings. Intermingled with these alien topics is an increasing amount of personalia, which in *Fors* is often little more than querulous egotism, interesting as the self-revelation of an extraordinarily sensitive man of genius during a prolonged period of mental disturbance, but irrelevant, if not impertinent, in a serious treatment of social ideals.[1] In *Fors* he made several attempts to bring together these scattered statements of social and economic doctrine, but gave up each time, finding, as he said, that his abstracts needed "further abstraction." In his later years, even more than in his earlier, his mind lacked what Arnold called "*ordo concatenatioque veri*," order and linked succession of truth.

But it is to be remembered, as regards any statement of fundamental principles, that Ruskin's plans were abruptly blocked by his publishers and the public. In their fragmentary state, *Unto This Last* and *Munera Pulveris*, the only works that were written to deal with political economy by itself, were never regarded as more than "prefaces" and "introduc-

[1] *E. g.*, "I rather enjoy talking about myself, even in my follies." (XXIX, 74.)

tory papers." Stung to anger by the hostile reception of *Unto This Last*, a book into which Ruskin thought he had put better work than into any of his former writings and "more important truths than all of them put together," he did intend, he says, after two more years of thinking, "to make it the central work of my life to write an exhaustive treatise on Political Economy." [1] But his purposes were a second time frustrated. And what we have, therefore, as the substance of his social philosophy, apart from its sources in his philosophy of art, are a few "broken statements of principle" in *Unto This Last* and *Munera Pulveris*, followed by many schemes and ideals of social reconstruction set forth mainly in the discursive form of letters in *Time and Tide* and *Fors Clavigera*, together with innumerable pregnant hints and suggestions scattered broadcast over all his later work and even here and there in some of the earlier volumes. Indeed the most casual efforts of his pen can scarcely be neglected, for in them the reader is likely to discover not a little of Ruskin's most luminous thought and happiest irony, without which the central doctrines would themselves lose much of their trenchant force.

The author of *Modern Painters* began by defining the aim of political economy to be "the multiplication of human life at the highest standard." [2] Certain things in the world are useful and lead to life; certain other things are useless or harmful and lead to death. Give a man corn and he will live; give him nightshade and he will die. It follows, therefore, that "the essential work of the political economist is to determine what are in reality useful or life-giving things, and by what degrees and kinds of labor they are attainable and distributable. This investigation divides itself under three great heads:—the studies, namely, of the phenomena, first, of Wealth; secondly, of Money; and thirdly, of Riches. . . . The study of Wealth is a province of natural science:—it deals with the essential properties of things. The study of Money is a province of commercial science:—it deals with conditions of engagement and exchange. The study of Riches is a province of moral science:—it deals with the due relations of men to each other in regard of material possessions; and with the just laws of their association for purposes of labor." [1] Although none of these divisions of inquiry in the field of economics proper was carried much beyond a statement of definitions, Ruskin had least of importance to say concerning the intricate subject of money, which we may therefore dismiss with his preliminary assertions. "Money," he said, "has been inaccurately spoken of as merely a means of exchange. But it is far more than this. It is a documentary expression of legal claim. It is not wealth, but a documentary claim to wealth, being the sign of the relative qualities of it, or of the labor producing it, to which, at a given time, persons, or societies, are entitled." [2]

Concerning wealth Ruskin regarded it as his first

[1] *Works*, XVII, 152.

[2] *Ibid.*, XVII, 157. Ruskin here and there had a good deal to say on the subject of money, but most of what he says is either too incomplete and detached or fantastic to be of much value. In the later *Fors* days especially, he wrote much on the subject of interest, which he condemned

object to give a "stable" definition, and "to show that the acquisition of wealth was finally possible only under certain moral conditions of society." [1] This statement of purpose reveals unmistakably the fact that the field of political economy in his hands was immensely broadened so as to include the larger questions of ethics and society. Wealth, he had said, deals with the properties of things; it "consists of things essentially valuable." Value, as the life-giving power of anything, is both intrinsic and effectual: intrinsic value is the absolute power of anything to support life"; effectual value is intrinsic value plus "acceptant capacity. *The production of effectual value, therefore, always involves two needs: first, the production of a thing essentially useful; then the production of the capacity to use it.*" [2] A strange gospel for a political economist! Wealth is, then, neither money nor accumulation of goods alone? An aristocrat with ten thousand acres of land, or a plutocrat with hundreds of old masters in his picture gallery is not to be called wealthy? Not at all necessarily, said Ruskin, since a thing is not wealth unless it is a useful thing in the possession of him who can use it for his own or his neighbor's good. The right thing in the right hands, the tools of a trade or the instruments of culture to him who can use them, —these only are wealth. [3]

as pillage and theft of the laborer, as increment to rich and decrement to poor, a tax by the idle and the rogue on the busy and honest, etc., etc. The reader may find a large number of references to the subject of money and interest listed in the *Index* to the Library Edition.

[1] *Works*, XVII, 19.
[2] *Ibid.*, XVII, 154.
[3] "*There is no wealth but life.* Life, including all its powers of love, of

A man's possessions, or his wealth, as wealth is ordinarily understood, Ruskin called his "riches." Riches are power over men, since no man can accumulate material possessions without being able to command the labor of others. This power is good or bad according as it is used justly or unjustly. Hence the problem of riches merges into a problem of wages, or just payment for labor,—a matter of capital importance, as Ruskin was well aware. In one way or another, it involved practically every large social question over which he was most disturbed,—relations between the employer and his men, conditions of employment and kind of work, and scores of other matters hardly less pressing to-day than they were in the decade 1860–1870. Like every other social reformer and idealist, Ruskin could point out far more difficulties than he could provide solutions for. But no other man of that day had a surer insight into the heart of the situation, or expressed his opinions with more startling audacity and more telling wit and irony. What he demanded above all things was justice. An unjust wage permitted concentration of riches into the hands of few and checked the advancement of the worker; while a just wage tended to the distribution of wealth into the hands of many, making it easier for each worker to rise in the social scale, if he chose to make the effort.[1] Clearly the application

joy, of admiration. That country is richest which nourishes the greatest number of noble and happy human beings; that man is richest who, having perfected the function of his own life to the utmost, has also the widest helpful influence, both personal, and by means of his possessions, over the lives of others." (*Works*, XVII, 105.)

[1] "The universal and constant action of justice in this matter is therefore to diminish the power of wealth, in the hands of one individual, over

of human values to the scheme of things in the economic world threatened to work havoc with sacred and immutable laws, and to frighten off the specter of the "economic man" as the bugaboo of a disordered imagination! In opposition to the dogma that wages were measured only by competition, Ruskin at the outset boldly advocated a fixed rate of wages for definite periods, irrespective of demand for labor. To provide against casual employment he further urged the maintenance of "constant numbers of workmen, whatever may be the accidental demand for the article they produce." [1] The complicated business of the world must in time be so adjusted, he thought, as that every willing worker shall have regularity of employment and contentment in it, a consummation only to be reached through an organization of labor of which most of the world at that time had no vision.

The first step, however, must be a just wage. But what is a just wage?—Ruskin asked. Reduced to its simplest terms, the law of justice respecting payment of labor is "time for time, strength for strength, and skill for skill. . . . I want a horseshoe for my horse. Twenty smiths, or twenty thousand smiths, may be ready to forge it; their number does not in one atom's weight affect the question of the equitable payment of the one who *does* forge it. It costs him a quarter of an hour of his life, and so much skill and strength of arm, to make that horseshoe for me. Then at some

masses of men, and to distribute it through a chain of men." (*Works*, XVII, 70.)

[1] *Works*, XVII, 35.

future time I am bound in equity to give a quarter of an hour, and some minutes more, of my time (or of some other person's at my disposal), and also as much strength of arm and skill, and a little more, in making or doing what the smith may have need of." [1] "Does not Ruskin, in such words, show himself blind to the plain facts of life?" we ask. Is *his* labor worth no more than the blacksmith's? Is one man's time as valuable as another's, regardless of natural gift or skill? Or, if this is not quite the correct conclusion (since a just wage includes payment of skill for skill), how much work shall a carpenter render for an hour's work of a trained surgeon? What shall a poet pay his plumber for a day's time? Both cost and price are of course inextricably bound up with these questions, since cost, or the quantity of labor required to produce a thing, and price, or the exchange value of a thing, must be calculated finally in terms of labor. Ruskin recognized the problem as one of "considerable complexity!" But he hopelessly complicated it by further qualifications and distinctions. He did not mean, he said, to confuse kinds, ranks, and quantities of labor with its qualities. "I never said that a colonel should have the same pay as a private, nor a bishop the same pay as a curate. Neither did I say that more work ought to be paid as less work." [2] He then introduced a distinction between "effort" and "labor,"—labor being "*suffering* in effort," whereas effort by itself was the joyful expenditure of human energy in results that were recreative. On the basis of these differences, "the 'cost' of the mere perfect-

[1] *Works*, XVII, 66.   [2] *Ibid.*, XVII, 70n.

ness of touch in a hammer-stroke of Donatello's, or
a pencil-touch of Correggio's, is inestimable by any
ordinary arithmetic."[1] But even at this point Ruskin
was not at the end of his difficulties. For when he
undertook to define a unit of "labor" in terms of an
hour's or a day's time, he was confronted with a
factor in the problem which he could not eliminate,
even though the orthodox economists could,—namely,
that "as some labor is more destructive of life than
other labor, the hour or day of the more destructive
toil is supposed to include proportionate rest."[2]
Any final determination of a just wage, therefore,
must have involved him in an elaborate analysis of
human variables and of conditions of toil of quite
infinite complexity.

Nevertheless Ruskin could not get rid of the notion
that although "the worth of work may not easily be
known, it *has* a worth just as fixed and real as the
specific gravity of a substance."[3] The platonism of
his youth still clung to him! He hoped to get back to
fixed values in political economy, just as he had gone
back to fixed potentialities of beauty in the data of
art. Passionately desiring to improve the conditions
of men, he allowed too much for the stability of class
differences and too little for the instability of human
tastes and the wide variations in human ability; and
he likewise left out of account the principles of evo-
lution as applied to human progress, whereby the
values of things change with the changing environment and ideals of man. On the lines he followed
there would seem to be no way of reducing to a com-

[1] *Works*, XVII, 184n.   [2] *Ibid.*, XVII, 184.   [3] *Ibid.*, XVII, 67.

mon denominator the various kinds of labor. The
cost of a surgeon's operation and the cost of a cob-
bler's repairing are incommensurables. Not until
mankind reaches the stage when an hour's work of
one person is considered the full equivalent in commercial value of an hour's work of any other person,
regardless of rank or skill, can wages be determined
on the basis of time alone,—the only ultimately just
basis, probably, and exactly the solution that Mr.
Bernard Shaw reached in his famous debate on
Equality!

But it is no doubt unfair to criticise "introductory
statements" as though they were final principles.
In connection with his social philosophy, the main
thing to note at this point is that Ruskin made a bold
frontal attack upon the accepted dogmas of political
economy, and led the fight for a recognition of the
human factor in industry, an element quite disre-
garded by the British manufacturer. As Professor
Hobson says, "Ruskin's first claim as a social reformer
is that he reformed Political Economy." Ruskin bent
all his efforts to cast the money-changers out of the
temple. He denied that any right scheme of social
action could be founded upon a faith in the immutable
selfishness of man, with cunning or violence thrown
into the scale, when necessary to obtain advantage.
He denied that the interests of masters and operatives
were antagonistic and that expediency was the only
guide in relations between them. With scornful
irony he ridiculed the notion, held by many, that the
luxury of the lord in his palace was a benefit to the
poor,—pointing out the inconsistency of upholding

the rich because they benefited society by drinking champagne out of bottles, while condemning the poor because they drank beer out of buckets! A strange world it was that occupied itself in piling up riches, whether they were accumulated at the cost of human life or in the conservation of it! To buy in the cheapest market might mean ruin to honest producers, and to sell in the dearest market, death to needy consumers. But what did it matter to John Bull, since commercial operations were founded not upon justice but upon legality?

The revolutionary character of Ruskin's attack upon such stock notions may be judged from a few of the questions which, at a meeting of the National Association for the Promotion of Social Science, he "thought should be put to eminent professors of political economy on behalf of the working men of England:"—

(1) "Supposing that, in the present state of England, capital is necessary, are capitalists so? In other words, is it needful for right operation of capital that it should be administered under the arbitrary power of one person?"

(2) "Whence is all capital first derived?"

(3) "If capital is spent in paying wages for labor or manufacture which brings no return (as the labor of an acrobat or manufacturer of fireworks), is such capital lost or not? and if lost, what is the effect of such loss on the future wages fund?"

(4) "If under such circumstances it is lost, and can only be recovered (much more recovered

with interest) when it has been spent in wages for productive labor or manufacture, what labors and manufactures are productive, and what are unproductive? Do all capitalists know the difference? and are they always desirous to employ men in productive labors and manufactures, and in these only?"

(5) "Considering the unemployed and purchasing public as a great capitalist, employing the workmen and their masters both, what results happen finally to this purchasing public if it employs all its manufacturers in unproductive labor? and what if it employs them all in productive labor?"

(6) "'If any man will not work, neither shall he eat.' Does this law apply to all classes of society?" [1]

Reviewers assailed Ruskin for the "effeminate sentimentality" of a political economy like this. He retorted that political economy was impossible except "under certain conditions of moral culture." The whole weight of his argument, consequently, rested upon a different set of premises, an unshakable conviction that every principle and practice of commercial and industrial activity must be subjected to the test of its effect upon life, and that human nature, at bottom not predatory but affectionate, "can be altered by human forethought." "All effort in social improvement is paralysed," he said, "because no one has been bold enough or clear-sighted enough to put and press home this radical question: 'What is indeed

[1] *Works*, XVII, 537-8.

the noblest tone and reach of life for men; and how can the possibility of it be extended to the greatest numbers?' It is answered, broadly and rashly, that wealth is good; that art is good; that luxury is good. Whereas some of them are good in the abstract, but good if only rightly received. Nor have any steps whatever been yet securely taken,—nor, otherwise than in the resultless rhapsody of moralists,—to ascertain what luxuries and what learning it is either kind to bestow, or wise to desire." [1] By insisting, therefore, that man is a creature with loyalties and affections that can be appealed to, and that the aim of political economy is the lifting of life to the highest standard, Ruskin rightly held that he builded upon fact and not upon sentiment. Assured of the solidity of his foundation, he went forward with plans that meant radical changes in the entire structure of economic thought. Political economy in the future must be regarded not merely as a science of *getting*, but also as a science of *spending;* since just distribution and right consumption are the real tests of production. Twenty people can gain money for one who can use it, and the vital question for individual and for nation is, never, " how much do they make?" but " to what purpose do they spend?" [2] And therefore the products of your industry can never be justly distributed or wisely consumed, Ruskin argued, if you do not all the while take into account the nature of the consumer as well as of the thing consumed; just as you must in production consider the effect of the thing produced upon the workman as well as its value

[1] *Works*, VII, 430.   [2] *Ibid.*, XVII, 98.

for the market. Otherwise your political economy remains a mere bandying of empty formulas and a piling up of useless statistics.

Ruskin was accordingly determined to let into this dismal science the light of ethical principles, to widen its scope, and to appeal first of all to men as individuals to obey the laws of justice and love. Of the worker he demanded honesty, industry, frugality. "Do good work, like a soldier at his post," he said in substance, "whether you live or die. Have an interest in *being* something as well as in *getting* something. Be less anxious to rise out of your station than to perfect yourself within it. Remember that no political arrangements nor privileges can lift up loafers and drunkards, lechers and brutes." He called upon the consumer to demand the products of healthy and ennobling labor, and to sacrifice "such convenience, or beauty, or cheapness as is to be got only by the degradation of the workman."[1] His appeal to the captains of industry was no less direct and concrete. On the one hand they must be faithful to their engagements,—the corner-stone of commerce,—and they must at all costs maintain "the perfection and purity" of their goods. On the other, as masters of large groups of men, they were to assume responsibility for the individual and associated life of these men while in their employ, seeing to it that employment was beneficial and not harmful. Ruskin's vision, like Carlyle's, carried him forward to a time when the merchant should be as honored as the soldier, when indeed it should be a more sacred calling to provide

[1] *Works*, X, 196.

for the life of a nation in peace than to imperil it with death in war. In that day the captains of industry, like the captains of war now, would be leaders, by reason of ability and self-sacrifice, not by reason of privilege and fortune; while the public would be prompt to bestow upon them a recognition and reward commensurate with their efforts.

A consummation like this, however, could not be realized by individual effort alone. The modern world was too complicated and too interrelated. Half the troubles, in fact, as matters already stood was that even good men were pulling in contrary directions. Patterns of unselfishness in their private relations, perhaps, they conducted their business on the maleficent principle of competition, whereby, each regarded his neighbor's interest as in collision with his own. To Ruskin this was wrong through and through. It meant that man was a beast of prey. It assumed the calculating cultivation of his worst instincts, and it meant the final triumph of anarchy over law. In the presence of the vast mutual dependencies of modern commerce, the self-centered utilitarianism of Adam Smith and Bentham, always false, now became even worse,—it became criminal folly, for it gave support to the most dangerous conditions in the social order, the extremes of wealth and poverty and the complete separation of masters and men. In reality, said Ruskin, the management of a great industry, or even of a great state, should rest upon exactly the same elementary principles as those which obtained in a household or upon a ship, where success was unthinkable without co-operation. Individual effort was indispensable, but it was far from enough. Big business meant the accumulation and concentration of wealth to such a degree, and involved the association of workmen to such an extent, that only through collective effort could economic and social reform be realized;—a conclusion recognized everywhere to-day, but regarded as revolutionary in 1864. Without knowing, therefore, how far or in what directions his gospel might be destined to go, Ruskin preached co-operation as a necessary basis of reconstruction, calling upon the masters of each industry "not to try to undersell each other, nor seek to get each other's business, but to form one society, selling to the public under a common law of severe penalty for unjust dealing, at an established price;" and calling upon the workers to cast their toil more and more "into social and communicative systems", somewhat after the fashion of the medieval guilds, for mutual support and protection. "Government and Co-operation," he said, "are in all things the Laws of Life; Anarchy and Competition the Laws of Death." [1]

At this point, accordingly, his political economy broadened out into social economy, or into a discussion of the varied problems of human welfare in a complex social order. After the forced interruptions of *Unto This Last* and *Munera Pulveris*, Ruskin gave up all attempt to set his economic theories into fixed order, and abandoned himself more than ever to a discursive treatment of all the questions that pressed upon him. No subject was henceforth treated extensively by itself. It was taken up, dropped, taken up

[1] *Works*, XVII, 317, 75.

again, and in the end perhaps left in a tentative and unfinished state. Economics, ethics, education, politics, schemes of social reconstruction, Utopian commonwealths, accounts of actual experiments jostle one another throughout *Time and Tide*, *Fors Clavigera*, and the later lectures. And yet in these discursive writings is to be found a large number of brilliant and pregnant suggestions for a new order, constituting on the whole the most fruitful side of Ruskin's social philosophy, apart from the fundamental principle with which we began the present chapter,—the conservation of the individual by means of the creative impulse. Without pretending to be exhaustive, we shall therefore in the next chapter endeavor to bring into connection these scattered schemes and suggestions of reform, concluding with a brief account of his adventures into Utopia.

CHAPTER VII

THE SWORD OF ST. GEORGE

"As we advance in our social knowledge, we shall endeavor to make our government paternal as well as judicial; that is, to establish such laws and authorities as may at once direct us in our occupations, protect us against our follies, and visit us in our distress: a government which shall repress dishonesty, as it now punishes theft; which shall show how the discipline of the masses may be brought to aid the toils of peace, as discipline of the masses has hitherto knit the sinews of battle; a government which shall have its soldiers of the ploughshare as well as its soldiers of the sword, and which shall distribute more proudly its golden crosses of industry—golden as the glow of the harvest,—than now it grants its bronze crosses of honor—bronzed with the crimson of blood."—*Ruskin.*

Part I—Social Ideals

To begin with, Ruskin insisted upon the right of every child to be well born. He looked to a future when nations would give "some of the attention to the conditions affecting the race of men, which it has hitherto bestowed only on those which may better its races of cattle." [1] To this end marriage must be regulated. Permission to marry should be a public attestation of the fact that youth and maid had lived rightly and had attained such skill "in their proper handicraft and in the arts of household economy," as to insure good hope that they would be able "to maintain and teach their children." Without

[1] *Works*, XVII, 420.

accepting in detail many of Ruskin's fantastic ideas upon this subject, most thoughtful persons to-day would agree with him in principle, namely, that the young couples who measure up to these standards should, where necessary, be kept in employment at the expense of the state during the years of stress, when they were finding their way in a complex social order. For upon purity of birth everything else must depend. Without it there could be no real elevation in the life of the state, whether corporate or individual.

Until communities saw to it that a child was well born they could not be certain that it would be well educated. And without education as its foundation Ruskin's structure of social reform would of course have nothing to stand upon. "There is only one cure of public distress," he said, "and that is a public education, directed to make men thoughtful, merciful, and just." [1] State regulation of education was therefore as important as state regulation of marriage. "I hold it for indisputable," he insisted, "that the first duty of a state is to see that every child therein shall be well housed, clothed, fed, and educated, till it attain years of discretion." [2] With an insight like that of Pestalozzi or Froebel, Ruskin understood the awakening potentialities of childhood, waiting upon guidance towards fine issues or base. "The human soul in youth," he wrote, "is *not* a machine of which you can polish the cogs with any kelp or brickdust near at hand; and, having got it into working order, and good, empty, and oiled serviceableness, start

[1] *Works*, XVIII, 107.   [2] *Ibid.*, XI, 263.

your immortal locomotive, at twenty-five years old or thirty, express from the Strait gate, on the Narrow Road. The whole period of youth is one essentially of formation, edification, instruction; I use the words with their weight in them; intaking of stores, establishment in vital habits, hopes, and faiths. There is not an hour of it but is trembling with destinies,—not a moment of which, once past, the appointed work can ever be done again, or the neglected blow struck on cold iron." [1] As this passage implies, education for Ruskin did not mean erudition. Pouring in facts, however well sifted and ordered, does not educate a mind, unless the facts are so related to the child's nature as to evoke from it right conduct. "You do not educate a man by telling him what he knew not, but my making him what he was not." [2] At every step of the process, from beginning to end, Ruskin would have the training of youth regulated by ethical ideals: getting knowledge should mean getting the right knowledge; reading books, the right books; learning a trade, learning to do something not only consistent with one's health and capacities but also "serviceable to other creatures." The sympathies and tastes of the child must be cultivated with as much attention as the knowing faculties, since a person's usefulness in life will depend upon his *attitude* towards society and towards his own work in it, no less than upon his intellectual capacity or technical skill taken by itself.[3] True

[1] *Works*, VI, 485.
[2] *Ibid.*, XVII, 232.
[3] Ruskin summarized the teaching and practice of his life in the brilliant

education must not only be moral, in this broad sense. It must also sift men according to their capacities and the work they are to do; the differences among all men being "eternal and irreconcilable, between one individual and another, born under absolutely the same circumstances." Ruskin carried these general principles yet one step further and insisted that individual training must in the end be so ordered as that men shall find *contentment* in the lower callings when they are without capacity for the higher,—a consummation which could be realized (as Ruskin knew) only as a result of changes in the social consciousness towards certain kinds of labor. Let the chance of advancement in station be extended to all, as a matter of course, but let it be understood that education is itself advancement in life, that it should be rather a means of getting on with one's work than of climbing up in the world, and that it is better to train a man to be more expert in his trade than to inspire him with discontent, because, by reason of natural ability, he must remain there.

Ruskin of course made no attempt to propose anything so definite as a curriculum for the realization of these principles. And yet with characteristic audacity he threw out a great number of suggestions, remarkable on the whole for their wisdom, and still more remarkable in the decades 1860–1880 as bril-

aphorism on education quoted in a previous chapter: "The entire object of true education is to make people not merely *do* the right things, but *enjoy* the right things:—not merely industrious, but to love industry—not merely learned, but to love knowledge—not merely pure, but to love purity—not merely just, but to hunger and thirst after justice." (*Works*, XVIII, 435.)

liant anticipations of the future—Ruskin's future
and ours. "There are, indeed," he said, "certain
elements of education which are alike necessary to
the inhabitants of every spot of earth. Cleanliness,
obedience, the first laws of music, mechanics, and
geometry, the primary facts of geography and astronomy, and the outlines of history, should evidently be
taught alike to poor and rich, to sailor and shepherd,
to laborer and shopboy. But for the rest, the efficiency of any school will be found to increase exactly
in the ratio of its direct adaptation to the circumstances of the children it receives; and the quantity of
knowledge to be attained in a given time being equal,
its value will depend on the possibilities of its instant
application. You need not teach botany to sons of
fishermen, architecture to shepherds, or painting to
colliers; still less the elegances of grammar to children
who throughout the probable course of their total
lives will have, or ought to have, little to say, and
nothing to write." [1]   The program thus outlined
includes the elements of both liberal and technical
training, and is elsewhere described in detail. The
laws of health came first. The schools of St. George
were to be built in the country, in the midst of large
spaces of land, where children should have plenty of
fresh air and room for all kinds of healthful exercises.
Children next were to be taught reverence, compassion, and truth: reverence for what was most worthy
"in human deeds and human passion"; compassion,
so that "it shall be held as shameful to have done a
cruel thing as a cowardly one"; truth, so that a boy

[1] *Works*, XXIX, 495.

shall have as intense a purpose "to *think* of things as they truly are, as to *see* them as they truly are," so far as in him lies.[1] Ruskin would also require music and dancing of all,—music to include the learning of the best poetry by heart. It was of course consistent with his social philosophy that he should attach the highest importance to the æsthetic training of the child. He wished to see bare and bleak schoolhouses transformed into attractive centers of study by means of beautiful surroundings, without and within.[2] "We shall not succeed," he said, "in making a peasant's opinion good evidence on the merits of the Elgin marbles; yet I believe we may make art a means of giving him helpful and happy pleasure, and of gaining for him serviceable knowledge." [3]

With these elements, physical, ethical, and æsthetic, as foundations, every boy and girl should be taught manual training, politics, religion, mathematics, natural science, and history. Respecting the last three branches, Ruskin made a curious and suggestive provision: "Your schools," he said, "will require to be divided into three groups: one for children who will probably have to live in cities, one for those who will live in the country, and one for those who will live at sea; the schools for these last, of course, being always placed on the coast. And for

[1] *Works*, XVII, 398-9.

[2] Ruskin had definite ideas on the socialization of art. He advocated not only the collection of art in public galleries and in all private homes, "as a means of refining the habits and touching the hearts of the masses of the nation in their domestic life" (*Works*, XVI, 81), but urged the use of art for school rooms, guild-halls, almshouses and hospitals.

[3] *Works*, XVI, 144.

children whose life is to be in cities, the subjects of
study should be, as far as their disposition will allow
of it, mathematics and the arts; for children who are
to live in the country, natural history of birds, insects,
and plants, together with agriculture taught practically; and for children who are to be seamen, physical
geography, astronomy, and the natural history of sea
fish and sea birds." [1]   General training was thus
always to be followed by special training, in obedience
to the principle that youths are to be placed "according to their capacities in the occupations for which
they are fitted." Government, therefore, should provide schools for every trade; and in order to discover
what youths in given localities possess special skill in
one or another of the arts and crafts, "schools of
trial" should be established in these communities
at state expense. Ruskin's whole conception of education was thus shot through with the conviction
that training must have constant regard for social
ends. This was a pioneer and iconoclastic conception for the England of his time. He contended that
a boy was not educated merely because he "could
write Latin verses and construe a Greek chorus."
He contended that science for schools (and science
was just being introduced into the higher curricula)
should have less to do with theories and more with
realities: botany should deal with the plant life
around the students, and chemistry should teach
them "to find out whether the water is wholesome in
the back-kitchen cistern, or whether the seven acre
field wants sand or chalk." [2]   In short he demanded

[1] *Works*, XVII, 400.   [2] *Ibid.*, XVI, 112.

for every youth a full and harmonious co-ordination of his life with the life of the community in which he was destined to live, such as no system of education has realized even to the present day.[1]

Ruskin was fully alive to the effects of such an educational program upon position in life and upon the problem of debasing labor. He faced the issues more squarely than reformers of his type are wont to do. Will a boy, he asked, who has been educated according to the foregoing program wish to be a tailor or a coalheaver? Some of his readers and correspondents argued that among well-educated boys there would remain a percentage "constitutionally inclined to be cobblers, or looking forward with

[1] Ruskin's ideas on education are a chapter by themselves. Various writers have called attention to the richness of his suggestions and to their connection with the aims and principles of educational reformers. Ruskin, it will be remembered, was anything but a closet theorist. He was always interested in the practical work of the schoolroom, as shown in his frequent visits to the school at Coniston, and in his relations with a school for girls at Winnington Hall, Cheshire, and with the Whitlands Training College for Girls at Chelsea, where he made many visits and did much to encourage the pupils in various activities, such as dancing, drawing, and festival-making. Then, of course, he was Slade Professor of Fine Arts at Oxford for many years, and for four or five years taught drawing classes at the Working Men's College, London.

Ruskin was always very strongly opposed to the examination system in schools. "The madness of the modern cram and examination system arises principally out of the struggle to get lucrative places; but partly also out of the radical block-headism of supposing that all men are naturally equal, and can only make their way by elbowing;—the facts being that every child is born with an accurately defined and absolutely limited capacity; that he is naturally (if able at all) able for some things and unable for others; that no effort and no teaching can add one particle to the granted ounces of his available brains; that by competition he may paralyse or pervert his faculties, but cannot stretch them a line; and that the entire grace, happiness, and virtue of his life depend on his contentment in doing what he can, dutifully, and in staying where he is, peaceably." (*Works*, XXIX, 496.)

unction to establishment in the oil or tallow line, or fretting themselves for a flunkey's uniform." [1] But Ruskin did not read man's life in this way, although few writers have more emphatically declared their fixed faith in the unconquerable differences in the clay of the human creature. The effect of an educational system that reached down to the masses and touched every life there would be, he thought, to reduce the wide differences in bodily and mental capacity, so that "in a few generations, if the poor were cared for, their marriages looked after, and sanitary law enforced," the old gin-drinking, criminal type would begin to disappear, while a new type would emerge, healthy, progressive, and with no disposition to be fettered like slaves to a life of monotonous toil.[2] Although brought up in the lap of luxury himself, Ruskin well knew the effect of rough work upon a man. "The man," he said, "who has been heaving clay out of a ditch all day, or driving an express train against the north wind all night, or holding a collier's helm in a gale on a lee shore, or whirling white-hot iron at a furnace mouth, is not the same man at the end of his day, or night, as one who has been sitting in a quiet room, with everything comfortable about him, reading books, or classing butterflies, or painting pictures." [3] How shall these

[1] *Works*, XVII, 405.

[2] "Crime can only be truly hindered by letting no man grow up a criminal—by taking away the *will* to commit sin; not by mere punishment of its commission. Crime, great and small, can only be truly stayed by education—not the education of the intellect only, which is, on some men, wasted, and for others mischievous; but education of the heart, which is alike good and necessary for all." (*Works*, XVII, 392.)

[3] *Works*, XVIII, 417.

lower jobs be done when men are better educated and desire time to sit in a quiet room for the cultivation of intellectual and æsthetic interests? After all, should not education be denied to some people in order that they may be kept in slavery for the lowest work, in accordance with Plato's scheme in his *Republic?* This has been the traditional faith and the traditional solution among the conservative and aristocratic classes in all ages, including our own. Ruskin was himself a Tory, and medievalism ran in his blood, but he could not endure a system that kept men, capable of better things, in involuntary servitude. Accordingly he attacked the labor problem from several different angles, and especially from the point of view of one who profoundly believed in education for all.

As we shall see again in connection with his guild-idea, he believed in fixed wages, for fixed periods, settled not by the law of competition, but by the law of justice; and he believed in an eight-hour day for all workers as a minimum. These principles were fundamental and should, he thought, be universal. But it was possible to go much further. Let the demand for foolish luxuries and for the products of debasing employment be greatly diminished. Repeatedly Ruskin pointed out that luxuries must be paid for by labor withdrawn from the production of useful things, such as food and clothing. Society should curb its extravagance, at least until "all the poor are comfortably housed and fed." Foul and mechanical work, too, could actually be lowered to a minimum, if people would consistently refuse to demand its products. "It is the duty of all persons in higher stations of life by every means in their power," he said, "to diminish their demand for work of such kind, *and to live with as little aid from the lower trades*, as they can possibly contrive." [1]   In this connection he never neglected an opportunity to urge people, when buying objects of art, to buy only those which were the creations of *thoughtful*, and not of *mechanical*, labor.   It is safe to say that Ruskin himself could not enjoy a beautiful thing when he knew that it was the product of debasing toil.   On the other hand, he loved so much the evidence of a free, happy mind in work that he no doubt often overestimated the values of what in reality was often crude and unlovely.   But his principle was sound. Get the happy workman first, he argued, and you will get better art in the end if not in the beginning.   "Let us remember, that every farthing we spend on objects of art has influence over men's minds and spirits, far more than over their bodies.   By the purchase of every print which hangs on your walls, of every cup out of which you drink, and every table off which you eat your bread, you are educating a mass of men in one way or another.   You are either employing them healthily or unwholesomely; you are making them lead happy or unhappy lives; you are leading them to took at Nature, and to love her—to think, to feel, to enjoy,—or you are blinding them to Nature, and keeping them bound, like beasts of burden, in mechanical and monotonous employments." [2]

[1] *Works*, XVII, 423.

[2] *Ibid.*, XII, 68.   It may be worth noting that Ruskin recognized certain kinds of work as debasing and "mechanical":—"*simply* or *totally* manual work; that, alone, *is* degrading" (XVII, 423): forging, "unclean,

Ruskin would not only substitute so far as possible the products of happy labor for the products of servile labor,—he would, by a change of attitude in the entire social consciousness, elevate many kinds of work to positions of dignity. Any necessary work is noble, if we only *think* it so and rightly honor the loyal worker. The toil of the miner or stoker would be lightened if he received recognition from a grateful public, not merely in a just wage, but in some badge of service that should give him a place in the hearts of people, like that of the brave sailor or soldier. We dishonor the worker when we dishonor his work. Ruskin knew that the art-motive could not be put into every kind of employment, but he saw the possibility of offsetting the influence of education upon lower callings by a change of mind toward these callings. With cunning irony yet with an undercurrent of serious intention, he argued that servile work if undertaken in a serious spirit might be the holiest of all and that therefore evangelicals and ritualists might perform such work as evidence of the sincerity of their Christianity! "Let the market have its martyrdoms as well as the pulpit, and the trade its heroisms as well as war!" Ruskin indeed proposed that the merchant's work should be made a liberal profession like the lawyer's and physician's, demanding like them its peculiar sacrifices and

noisome, or paltry manufactures, various kinds of transport,—and the conditions of menial service" (XVII, 428): "all work with fire is more or less harmful and degrading; so also mine, or machine labor" (VII, 427n.): "a great number of quite necessary employments are, in the accuratest sense, 'Servile'; that is, they sink a man to the condition of a serf, or unthinking worker, the proper state of an animal, but more or less unworthy of men." (XVII, 406.)

receiving its special rewards. He not only proposed, he pointed out a way of realization. The first thing was to remove the stigma of vulgarity and degradation attached to the business of the retail merchant. This could be done, he maintained, "by making all retail dealers merely salaried officers in the employ of the trade guilds," thus taking away the temptations to profit and the various other tendencies to selfishness usually recognized as part of the business. To all objections that might be raised against such a system, Ruskin was content to answer that if a soldier could be trained to offer himself fearlessly to the chance of being shot, then "assuredly, *if you make it also a point of honor with him*," [1] a merchant, or a "dealer," could also be sufficiently trained in self-denial to look "you out with care such a piece of cheese or bacon as you have asked for."

It was necessary only to change the consciousness of society toward various kinds of employment, so that there should be less concern among workers about what work they were doing, and far more about how they were doing it. Suppose the different trades were taken up in this spirit, with a consequent enormous rise in the standards of achievement, until by the rules of the craft no man were permitted to have independent use of any material until he knew how to make the best of it? What would be the result? "The arts of working in wood, clay, stone, and metal," said Ruskin, "would all be *fine* arts (working in iron for machinery becoming an entirely distinct business). There would be no joiner's work,

[1] The italics are mine.

no smith's, no pottery nor stone-cutting, so debased
in character as to be entirely unconnected with the
finer branches of the same art; and to at least one of
these finer branches (generally in metal-work) every
painter and sculptor would be necessarily apprenticed
during some years of his education. There would be
room, in these four trades alone, for nearly every
grade of practical intelligence and productive imagination."[1] Consistent with his ideals of education and
of art, as well as with his schemes for the elevation of
many kinds of work, he would go yet further with the
crafts. "It would be a part of my scheme of physical
education," he said, "that every youth in the state—
from king's son downwards,—should learn to do
something thoroughly and finely with his hand, so as
to let him know what *touch* meant; and what stout
craftsmanship meant; and to inform him of many
things besides, which no man can learn but by some
severely accurate discipline in doing. Let him once
learn to take a straight shaving off a plank, or draw a
fine curve without faltering, or lay a brick level in its
mortar; and he has learned a multitude of other
matters which no lips of man could ever teach him.
He might choose his craft, but whatever it was, he
should learn it to some sufficient degree of true
dexterity: and the result would be, in after life, that
among the middle classes a good deal of their house
furniture would be made, and a good deal of rough
work, more or less clumsily, but not ineffectively,
got through, by the master himself and his sons,
with much furtherance of their general health and

[1] *Works*, XVII, 426.

peace of mind, and increase of innocent domestic pride and pleasure, and to the extinction of a great deal of vulgar upholstery and other mean handicraft." [1]

With the increase of handicrafts there should follow a reduction of machine-labor to the minimum. Ruskin's attitude toward machinery has often been misunderstood and his antagonism exaggerated. He was first and last opposed to machine-labor because he regarded it as servile, invariably degrading the man who became a slave to it, grinding out his soul and reducing his body to the level of an automaton. He was opposed to it in the arts because it put mechanism in the place of skill, destroyed sensibility to artistic values, and substituted mere agreeable form for evidence of human care and thought and love: "so that the eye loses its sense of this very evidence, and no more perceives the difference between the blind accuracy of the engine, and the bright, strange play of the living stroke." [2] He opposed machinery on economic grounds also; arguing that it was wrong to use machines so long as men starved for want of employment. But even Ruskin's medieval enthusiasm for handwork never prompted him to urge the complete abandonment of machinery. Where they could effectively shorten human labor or accomplish what unaided human hands could not otherwise accomplish, machines were to be used; as, for example, "on a colossal scale in mighty and useful works," such as reclaiming waste lands, irrigating deserts, deepening river channels, and otherwise

[1] *Works*, XVII, 426.   [2] *Ibid.*, XII, 173.

recovering earth's resources for man's use.[1] Machinery moved by steam, manufactories "needing the help of fire," he would have reduced to the lowest limit, "so that nothing may ever be made of iron that can as effectively be made of wood or stone; and nothing moved by steam that can be as effectively moved by natural forces." He would use all vital muscular power first, all natural mechanical power next (wind, water and electricity), and all artificially mechanical power last.[2] The whole problem of servile employment, to summarize, would thus be solved in these various ways:—by a reduction in the demand for the product of servile work and for senseless luxuries; by the elevation of many kinds of work, now regarded as vulgar and menial, to a position of honor in the public mind; by a raising of the standard of the crafts and a union of these with the arts through guilds or companies of workers, together with an immense extension of craft-interest and skill into all kinds of domestic manual work; and, finally, by a reduction of machine-labor to the minimum, and all possible increase of hand-labor to the maximum.

But even if society applied these remedies, there

[1] Ruskin's panegyric on the locomotive is one of his most wonderful passages of prose; in the *Cestus of Aglaia*, XIX, 60.

[2] *Works*, XX, 113. Ruskin raged against the noise and dirt of railroads, but he traveled on them and admitted their necessity: *e. g.*, "Steam, or any modes of heat-power, may only be employed justifiably under extreme or special conditions of need; as for speed on main lines of communication, and for raising water from great depths, or other such work beyond human strength." (XXVIII, 655.) He believed in a far more extensive use of wind and water power than was realized anywhere in his day or is realized even to-day. He suggested, for example, the use of reservoirs filled by the tides, to furnish power for mills.

would remain rough work to be done. With all his dreaming, Ruskin did not expect to see a state of society in which all disagreeable or debasing toil should be completely eliminated. This should be given, first, to all persons willing to work but out of employment. Every such man, woman, and child should be received at the nearest government agency or school and put to the work they were fit for "at a fixed rate of wages determinable every year." Should they object, they were then to be compelled to perform the more painful and degrading tasks, especially those "in mines and other places of danger (such danger being, however, diminished to the utmost by careful regulation and discipline)." [1] Criminals and idlers, Ruskin believed, should likewise be rigorously conscripted for the more dangerous work, such "mechanical and foul employment" taking the form of punishment or probation. Indeed forced employment for these classes should be made a means of reformation even more than of punishment. All three classes—the poor, the indolent, the vicious—might under proper governmental supervision be organized into groups for the performance of various enterprises to be carried on by the state, such as road-making, reclamation of waste land, harbor-making, all kinds of porterage, repair of buildings, and even certain kinds of arts and crafts, like dress-making, pottery, and metal work. For the rough work that might yet remain to be done, especially agricultural and other out-door work, not a little of it should be done by workers recruited from the upper classes!

[1] *Works*, XVII, 22.

Ruskin looked with disgust upon an aristocracy that
consumed enormous amounts of time in wasteful, or
destructive field sports, particularly hunting, shooting, and horse-racing. Were this exertion put to
serviceable use on the farm, the gain would be incal-
culable all round. "It would be far better, for instance, that a gentleman should mow his own fields,
than ride over other people's." [1] As for that portion
of the rough work still untouched, notably manufacture, it would fall to the lot of a large class incapaci-
tated by nature for anything higher. Like Carlyle,
Ruskin held to the belief that some people are born to
do the lower work such as was performed by serfs in
medieval times; intellectually they are the inferiors,
whom education can make little of and to whom
should fall the lot of doing the "common mechanical
business" of the world. He of course felt that the
status of these workers would be determined in great
part by the kind of masters they served. His ideal
for them, however, was essentially medieval; whether
domestic or civil servants they should be attached by
loyalty to a benevolent superior, who would have
authority to compel them to work when they refused
to serve willingly. In truth Ruskin believed in
slavery, if by slavery is meant that there is a governing power somewhere which can, when necessary,
force men to work. "I am prepared," he said, "if
the need be clear to my own mind, and if the power is
in my hands, to throw men into prison, or any other

[1] *Works*, VII, 429. *Cf.* XVII, 234. While Ruskin all his life vigorously
condemned destructive field sports, he no less vigorously encouraged all
forms of athletic exercise, such as boxing, wrestling, cricketing, rowing,
etc. *Cf.* VII, 340.

captivity—to bind them or to beat them—and force them, for such periods as I may judge necessary, to any kind of irksome labor: and, on occasion of desperate resistance, to hang or shoot them. But I will not *sell* them." [1]

It is clear that Ruskin was not a sentimentalist in his treatment of the labor problem. His ideals imply, throughout, the rigors of work, but also its sacredness and necessity. As an accomplished draughtsman, as an intense student of technique, he knew what precision of hand meant and what prolonged effort, patience, and uprightness of character it cost the masters. He knew, too, by observation, if not by experience, that the vast resources of earth could not be made available for mankind without continuous and wearing toil. His convictions were undoubtedly intensified by the influence of Carlyle; for in his later writings he returned repeatedly to the idea of nobleness in work, and he preached a gospel of labor that often has the unmistakable accent of his master. "All education," he said, for example, "begins in work. What we think, or what we know, or what we believe, is in the end, of little consequence. The only thing of consequence is what we *do*." [2] Like Carlyle, also, he made much of the ideal of soldiership in work, a new chivalry of labor. Again and again he appealed to the British people to lift the worker to the level of the fighter, to make the business of maintaining life at least as honorable as destroying it, to band the workers together in companies to do some of the hard and servile jobs, performing them with all the *esprit de*

[1] *Works*, XVII, 438.   [2] *Ibid.*, XVIII, 507.

corps and *élan* of an army going into battle! Soldiers themselves, in the first place, when not fighting should be working. "Our whole system of work," he said, "must be based on the nobleness of soldiership—so that we shall all be soldiers of either ploughshare or sword; and literally all our actual and professed soldiers, whether professed for a time only, or for life, must be kept to hard work of hand, when not in actual war; their honor consisting in being set to service of more pain and danger than others; to lifeboat service; to redeeming of ground from furious rivers or sea—or mountain ruin; to subduing wild and unhealthy land, and extending the confines of colonies in the front of miasm and famine, and savage races." [1] In the second place, not only should trained soldiers be employed when not fighting, but also civilians should be enlisted for the purpose of doing some of the hard work. Society had only to make up its mind that way and it would find that the virtues of loyalty and obedience and industry could be developed as well for manufacture as for massacre; that men could serve their country with the spade even better than with the sword; and that the builders were as worthy of honors and pensions in old age or disability, as the destroyers. A rational and fruitful ideal! An ideal which future generations of mankind will have the wisdom to adopt, if they shall keep the world safe for growth in the arts of peace.[2]

The problem of servile labor, however, is a problem that in the main and for the present involved only the lower orders of society. Ruskin was no less concerned

[1] *Works*, XVII, 463.   [2] *Ibid.*, XVIII, 419, 449.

with the position and function of the higher orders, and he had much to say, first and last, regarding their part in the social scheme and the complex questions involved therein. The aristocracy of a nation he regarded as composed of (a) landed proprietors and soldiers, (b) captains of industry, (c) and professional classes and masters in science, art, and literature.[1] From the landed aristocracy should be chosen "the captains and judges of England, its advocates, and generally its State officers, all such functions being held for fixed pay." Looking forward to ideal conditions, Ruskin would set apart certain state officers who were to be "charged with the direction of public agency in matters of public utility,"—anticipating in this pregnant phrase a vast extension of government control.[2] His ideas of control for the future were further suggested in his conception of the proper duties of bishops: "Over every hundred (more or less) of the families composing a Christian State, there should be appointed an overseer, or bishop, to render account, to the State, of the life of every individual in those families; and to have care both of their interest and conduct to such an extent as they may be willing to admit, or as their faults may jus-tify: so that it may be impossible for any person, however humble, to suffer from unknown want, or live in unrecognized crime;—such help and observance being rendered without officiousness either of

[1] I omit a discussion of the soldier and professional classes, since Ruskin said nothing concerning them sufficiently new or striking to deserve special treatment. The reader may consult the general Index under "Soldiers" and "Professions" for a good deal of discursive comment.

[2] *Works*, XVII, 440, 441.

interference or inquisition (the limits of both being determined by national law), but with the patient and gentle watchfulness which true Christian pastors now exercise over their flocks; only with a higher legal authority. . . . of interference on due occasion." [1] Instead of continuing to be parasites on society, living in epicurean seclusion, bishops were thus to be real *overseers*, and were to inform themselves as to the material condition of their flocks even before they attempted to minister to their spiritual welfare.[2]

It was impossible for Ruskin to discuss the landed aristocracy without reference to the land question. He was deeply dissatisfied with actual conditions of land tenure, and signs of disturbance, in his opinion, were as plain here as in the world of industry. The holders of land were largely mere rent-receivers, gathering the products of others' labors and spending them for luxuries; "able-bodied paupers," he called them, reaping where they had not sowed. Unwilling to endure this situation forever, the poor were already showing signs of revolt. Unless reforms in land tenure were brought about soon, Ruskin urged, speaking to English landlords, "You will find your-selves in Parliament in front of a majority resolved on the establishment of a Republic, and the division

[1] *Works*, XVII, 378.
[2] Ruskin spoke out boldly and often against the comfortable and com-placent professionalism of English bishops,—"with its pride, privilege, and more or less roseate repose of domestic felicity. The present Bishops of the English Church," he said, "have forfeited and fallen from their Bishoprics by transgression; and betrayal of their Lord, first by simony, and secondly, and chiefly, by lying for God with one mouth, and contend-ing for their own personal interests as a professional body, as if these were the cause of Christ." (*Works*, XXVIII, 364, 514.)

of lands." [1]   As to fundamental economic principles governing tenure, his program was simple and not extreme. One of the essential forms of wealth, land should not only supply food and mechanical power for the use of man; but it should also supply beauty for his spirit, exercise for his body, and means for the support of animal life, for which uses sufficient mountains and moorland should be set apart by direction of the state. Since, however, the land is limited in quantity, it ought not to be monopolized by a favorite few,—"hereditarily sacred persons to whom the earth, air, and water of the world belong, as personal property." The state must secure "various portions" of it to those who can use it properly, for the most part leaving them free in the management,—"interfering in cases of gross mismanagement or abuse of power," and enforcing upon the holders due conditions of possession, such as prevention of waste and pollution. "The land to those who can use it," was thus Ruskin's ideal, precisely as he had said that wealth of all kinds must be dependent upon the capacity of its possessor to use it for his own or for society's good. Possession of land, therefore, was to imply the duty of living upon it and by it, if there were enough; and if there were more than enough, the duty of making it fruitful and beautiful for as many more as it could support. "The owner of land, necessarily and justly left in great measure by the State to do what he will with his own, is nevertheless entirely responsible to the State for the generally beneficial management of his territory." [2]   In the

[1] *Works*, XXVIII, 152.   [2] *Ibid.*, XXIX, 495.

ideal state Ruskin thought that landlords would be paid a fixed salary for superintendence, all the income derived from the land going back to the tenants or for improvements. Under such ideal conditions wherein each person possessed only the land he could *use*, tenure should be hereditary, the property passing from father to son strictly in accordance with the law of primogeniture; for Ruskin desired to see the agricultural classes bound to the land as the artisans were bound to the guild, bound by ties of tradition and group-pride, as well as by personal interest. Land nationalization was, therefore, to him nonsense. He held for private ownership, albeit private ownership under severe responsibilities to the state and under the state's constant control.

Turning from ideal to actual conditions, however, Ruskin declared expressly for fixity of rent and security for tenants' improvements. He protested against the practice of squeezing the tenant for increased rent as often as the tenant raised the productivity of the land or improved the buildings, thus keeping him down to a uniform level of poverty and servitude. The landlord should voluntarily fix his income, live well within it, and put his whole soul "into the right employment of the rest for the bettering of (his) estates, in ways which the farmers for their own use could not or would not." [1] Though Ruskin, as we have just seen, favored an extension of state control over land, under ideal conditions, he was slow to advocate by law either immediate redistribution of land or limitation of income in the case of

[1] *Works*, XXVIII, 155.

the landed aristocracy. He much preferred that the present holders should not be arbitrarily dispossessed, but rather put under further state control; and he urged workers of every description to buy land (having got it "by the law of labor, working for it, saving for it, and buying it:—but buying never to let go"), and to become landowners on their own account,— "diminutive squires." He urged the trade-unions and co-operative societies to acquire land and to make the most of it for the common purpose of their organizations, subject always to the laws of the state.[1] A gradual redistribution of land by peaceful means under law was thus what Ruskin hoped for. A sudden and forced redistribution could not be effected "without grave and prolonged civil disturbance," and would in itself be of little advantage, besides being an unjust arrangement,—a consummation devoutly to be avoided. But sure to come, he believed, if abuses of landlordism were allowed to continue unchecked.

The great merchants constituted another order of the aristocracy. As we have already noticed in a previous connection, Ruskin believed that the office of merchant should be immensely elevated. It was his duty to *provide* for the people, a duty as sacred and as honorable as that of the soldier whose duty it was to defend them, or that of the physician and lawyer, who must maintain health and enforce justice. The merchant was a master producer and organizer,

---

[1] "A certain quantity of public land must be set aside for public uses and pleasure, and especially for purposes of education." (*Works*, XXIX, 495.)

exercising vast power and therefore bound by equally vast responsibilities. Upon him rested the sacred obligation of supplying goods to the public the quality of which he could guarantee, if need be, with his life; and of caring for his workers (their whole status of life both in the shop and at home) with a painstaking care that Ruskin could only liken to the care of a father for his children. In this function of providing for his men, the master should indeed be "invested with a distinctly paternal authority and responsibility." Here, as everywhere else in Ruskin's social philosophy, high ethical ideals must control industrial relations. Conditions of mutual trust and regard should so much prevail as to give the workers "permanent interest in the establishment with which they are connected, like that of the domestic servants in an old family, or an *esprit de corps*, like that of the soldiers in a crack regiment." [1]   Instead of a system of profit-sharing, on the one hand, or the current wage-system on the other, working under the pressure of competition, Ruskin favored an "intermediate method, by which every subordinate shall be paid sufficient and regular wages, according to his rank; by which due provision shall be made out of the profits of the business for sick and superannuated workers; and by which the master, *being held responsible, as a minor king or governor, for the conduct as well as the comfort of all those under his rule*, shall, on that condition, be permitted to retain to his own use the surplus profits of the business which the fact of his being its master may be assumed to prove that he

[1] *Works*, XVII, 33.

has organized by superior intellect and energy." [1] It is clear from this statement that Ruskin wished to see the captains of industry free to make fortunes and to reap the rewards of their higher abilities and virtues. But as in the case of the landlords, he thought that the merchants should voluntarily fix their incomes and refuse increase of business beyond defined limits, thus "obtaining due freedom of time for better thoughts." The maker of fortune should also be the spender of it; it should be his aim not to die rich, but to live "rich" and die poor, using his wealth, during his life, for the well-being of himself and his fellows.

In an ideal social state, in Ruskin's Utopia, he would have the incomes of captains of industry, like the incomes of landlords, fixed by law, and he would have both classes paid, not for ownership of capital, but for stewardship of property and superintendence of labor. Thus, he contended, the temptation to consume energy in the heaping up of wealth would be removed; and when the older men of these upper classes, having attained the "prescribed limits of wealth from commercial competition," should be withdrawn in favor of younger leaders, these older men should be induced to serve the state, unselfishly, either in parliament, in the superintendence of public enterprise, or in the furtherance of the public interest wherever their ripe experience would be of service. [2] Captains of industry would therefore round out their career in the most honorable toil and with the highest

---

[1] *Works*, XVII, 319.

[2] The narrow-mindedness and greed of the capitalists of his time Ruskin condemned as severely as he did the faults of the landlords and the bishops. (*E. g.* XXVII, 127; XVI, 343n.; XVIII, 415.)

reward. What of the retail merchants, meantime, the distributors of commodities, the middlemen? These, as we have already pointed out in connection with the problem of servile labor, Ruskin would, under ideal social conditions, make "salaried officers in the employ of the trade guilds; the stewards, that is to say, of the saleable properties of those guilds, and purveyors of such and such articles to a given number of families." [1] But at this point we come to the third and last group in the social order, to the skilled and classified workers, to the operatives and craftsmen, and to their organization into independent communities, or guilds. We here touch upon one of the most suggestive and fruitful aspects of Ruskin's social philosophy.

In *The Political Economy of Art* (1857) he had defined political economy as the wise management of labor. He made this view of it the central theme of *Unto This Last*, where he declared that the supreme need of the time was the organization of the workers. And in an unpublished epilogue to *Fors* (1884), interesting as a kind of farewell to his work in the field of social reconstruction, he returned to the problem with the old insistence, lamenting the absence of constructive reform in the thing that mattered most, the daily toil of the worker. Isolated, enslaved to commercialism, the modern operative worked for a wage without interest in his labor and without a voice in the control of the industry in which he was an impersonal unit. Ruskin's social ideals were of course impossible of realization in a

[1] *Works*, XVII, 427.

scheme like this. What he wished to see was the organization of workers into *communities* for the effective control of their own lives and occupations. How far he would go in the way of such community control Ruskin did not say; and he probably had not fully thought out. Did he look for an eventual disappearance of capitalism and an ultimate ownership, or control, of the tools of all industry by the workers? There are indications here and there that he did, as for example in a resolution which he proposed at a meeting of The National Association for the Promotion of Social Science (1868), running as follows: "That, in the opinion of this meeting, the interests of workmen and their employers are at present opposed, and can only become identical when all are equally employed in defined labor and recognized duty, and all, from the highest to the lowest, are paid fixed salaries, proportional to the value of their services and sufficient for their honorable maintenance in the situations of life properly occupied by them." [1] But in the writings published during his lifetime, there is nowhere a completely coherent plan of labor organization, such as might be operated in an actual community of workers. In the important matter of the relation of such communities to the state, Ruskin appears to have been of divided mind; for at one time he advocated voluntary organizations, wholly independent of the state, while, at another, he set forth a plan of workshops that were to be under government direction.

[1] *Works*, XVII, 539. Similar ideas found expression in the Guild of St. George, of which more later.

Many of his ideals of industrial organization go back for their inspiration to the medieval guilds, especially to the craft-guilds of thirteenth-century Florence. The thirteenth century was to Ruskin, as it has been to so many other lovers of the beautiful, not merely the century of Dante, Giotto, and St. Francis, of the Nibelungen Lied and the Holy Grail, but the century also of the cathedral builders and the guilds, when art had its roots in industry and when industry flowered into the lovliest art of the world. "A great age in all ways," said Ruskin; "but most notably so in the correspondence it presented, up to a just and honorable point, with the utilitarian energy of our own days." [1] No other city was so fair a representative of this period as Florence. The view from Fiesole was, he thought, the view of all the world, and the baptistery "the center of the arts of the world"; while the bell-tower of Giotto, whose "spiral shafts and fairy traceries, so white, so faint, so crystalline," were a perpetual delight to his eyes, was "the model and mirror of perfect architecture." This magnificence of art, both civil and ecclesiastical, was the creation of a company of artists whose patrons were *the public*. Side by side with this finer art, there flourished an extensive and highly developed domestic art, the work of "a vast body of craftsmen," the artisan class. They were the hand-workers, associated together for the production of "a staple of excellent, or perhaps inimitable, quality,"—the weavers, ironsmiths, goldsmiths, carpenters, and stonecutters, upon whose occupations "the more refined

[1] *Works*, XXIII, 47.

arts were wholesomely based." The artists and craftsmen were thus brought together in the same workshops and initiated into fellowships in the same guilds; the artist never ceased to be a craftsman, while, under the guidance and inspiration of his masters, the craftsman might one day become an artist. In these companies of Florentine guildsmen Ruskin found his ideals of art and society in a high degree realized. "No distinction," he said of them, "exists between artist and artisan except that of higher genius or better conduct; the best artist is assuredly also the best artisan; and the simplest workman uses his invention and emotion as well as his fingers." [1] With common traditions and with common pride in hereditary skill, industry and art flourished together in these guilds under the judicious patronage of a public intent upon engaging great creative energies for the common service. Studio art and dilettante craftsmanship, turning out bizarre products for aristocratic patrons, were unknown. Even the humblest worker lived in an atmosphere congenial to the expression of whatever spark of creative impulse might be awakened to life within him.

It was no doubt mainly because of this close association of the arts and crafts in the medieval guilds, such as existed in thirteenth-century Florence, that the guild-idea as applicable to modern conditions of industry came to Ruskin. From his earliest references to the re-establishment of guilds upon a new basis, in the lectures called *The Political Economy*

[1] *Works*, XXIII, 52.

of Art (1857), and in his *Cambridge Inaugural Address* in the following year, it is evident that he first thought of them in connection with a better production and distribution of art. "I believe it to be wholly impossible," he said, "to teach special application of Art principles to various trades in a single school. That special application can be only learned rightly by the experience of years in the particular work required. The power of each material, and the difficulties connected with its treatment, are not so much to be taught as to be felt; it is only by repeated touch and continued trial before the forge or the furnace, that the goldsmith can find out how to govern his gold, or the glass-worker his crystal; and it is only by watching and assisting the actual practice of a master in the business, that the apprentice can learn the efficient secrets of manipulation, or perceive the true limits of the involved conditions of design. . . . All specific Art-teaching must be given in schools established by each trade for itself. . . . Therefore, I believe most firmly, that as the laws of national prosperity get familiar to us, we shall more and more cast our toil into social and communicative systems; and that one of the first means of our doing so, will be the re-establishing guilds of every important trade in a vital, not formal, condition;—that there will be a great council or government house for the members of every trade, built in whatever town of the kingdom occupies itself principally in such trade, with minor council-halls in other cities; and to each council-hall, officers attached, whose first business may be to examine into the circumstances of every operative, in that trade, who chooses to report himself to them when out of work, and to set him to work, if he is indeed able and willing, at a fixed rate of wages, determined at regular periods in the council-meetings; and whose next duty may be to bring reports before the council of all improvements made in the business, and means of its extension: not allowing private patents of any kind, but making all improvements available to every member of the guild, only allotting, after successful trial of them, a certain reward to the inventors." [1]

Ruskin here brings into clear light the principles of medieval craftsmanship as a basis for the modern reconstructed workshop, in opposition to private schools of design and philanthropic institutes, where art is taught not to apprentices but to amateurs, by teachers who know nothing of the practical and associated craftsmanship of the workshop. But even in 1857 he went beyond a statement of principles and offered practical suggestions. He proposed the establishment by government of a paper manufactory for the purpose of producing for artists' use a paper of guaranteed quality, purchasable at an extra shilling above the commercial price. He proposed, also, "government establishments for every trade, in which all youths who desired it should be received as apprentices on their leaving school; and men thrown out of work received at all times." [2] A little later, in 1862, the idea of government workshops—essentially guilds under state control—had become more definite and inclusive: "manufactories and workshops for the

[1] *Works*, XVI, 178, 97.   [2] *Ibid*, XVI, 112.

production and sale of every necessary of life, and for the exercise of every useful art. And, interfering no whit with private enterprise, nor setting any restraints or tax on private trade, but leaving both to do their best, and beat the Government if they could, —there should, at these Government manufactories and shops, be authoritatively good and exemplary work done, and pure and true substance sold; so that a man could be sure, if he chose to pay the Government price, that he got for his money bread that was bread, ale that was ale, and work that was work." [1] Later still (1867 and after) Ruskin's ideas expanded in all directions, in favor of *voluntary* organizations of labor into self-governing communities, or guilds, for co-operative effort. "The magnitude of the social change hereby involved," he said, "and the consequent differences in the moral relations between individuals, have not as yet been thought of,—much less estimated,—by any of your writers on commercial subjects." The master bakers in a town, for example, instead of destroying one another's business by competition, should "form one society, selling to the public under a common law of severe penalty for unjust dealing, and at an established price." Similarly "all bankers should be members of a great national body, answerable as a society for all deposits." Ruskin called upon the workingmen of England likewise to band together for the furtherance of their own interests by the establishment of a council with regular meetings to "deliberate upon the possible modes of the regulation of industry, and

[1] *Works*, XVII, 22.

advisablest schemes for helpful discipline of life." [1]
Now and again he suggested, tentatively and without
complete formulation, that the trade unions should
take over many of the functions of the old guilds; at
all events that through them the guild idea might be
adapted to modern industry, the natural and essential
divisions of labor furnishing a proper basis on which
to start the new groups. [2] Get these thoroughly
organized, he said to the workers, "and the world
is yours, and all the pleasures of it." A necessary
part of such a voluntary enterprise, he believed, was
the possession of land, purchased by the thrift and
toil of the laborers, proportioned to their numbers,
and owned by them as a corporate body, according to
the principles of community tenure practiced by the
monks in medieval times.

The trade guilds having once been established upon
such a foundation, their life should go on in obedience
to certain ideals to be regarded as sacred. First, last,
and always there must be *sound work*. The knave
who should turn out a product that was sham, or
light in weight, or adulterated, or otherwise dishonest,
should instantly be dismissed from the guild under
severe penalties. Ruskin believed, however, that
when such penalties were backed up by a right public
opinion, demanding good work and rejecting bad,
"sham articles would become speedily as rare as

[1] *Works*, XVII, 317, 327. "The Trade Union Congress, often described
as 'The Parliament of Labor,' first assembled in the year after this passage was written (at Manchester in 1868)."

[2] Ruskin named eighteen classes of work "assuredly essential" (the
various trades necessary for the production of food, buildings, and
clothing), and three "not superfluous" (the musicians, painters, goldsmiths). (XXIX, 410.)

sound ones are now." To secure these ends a fixed
standard of product should be established. "This
would have to be done by the guild of every trade in
its own manner, and within easily recognizable limits,
and this fixing of standard would necessitate much
simplicity in the forms and kinds of articles sold.
You could only warrant a certain kind of glazing or
painting in china, a certain quality of leather or cloth,
bricks of a certain clay, loaves of a defined mixture of
meal. Advisable improvements or varieties in manufacture would have to be examined and accepted by
the trade guild: when so accepted, they would be
announced in public reports; and all puffery and self-
proclamation, on the part of tradesmen, absolutely
forbidden, as much as the making of any other kind
of noise or disturbance." [1] But this was not to be all.
The prices of standard or warranted articles "should
be fixed annually for the trade throughout the kingdom." The wages of workmen were likewise to be
fixed, as also the profits of the masters,—all within
such limits as the state of the trade would allow.
Every firm belonging to a guild, moreover, should be
free to produce other than the warranted class of
articles, *above* the standard quality, "whether by skill
of applied handicraft, or fineness of material above
the standard of the guild." Finally, the affairs of
every corporate member should be reported annually

---

[1] *Works*, XVII, 384. Merchants and traders outside the guild, said
Ruskin, should have leave to puff and advertise and to gull the public as
much as they could. If people wished to buy of those who refused to
belong to an honest society, they might do so "at their own pleasure and
peril." Guilds should also have the stimulus of "erratic external in-
genuity."

to the guild and the books laid open to inspection "for guidance in the regulation of prices in the subsequent year; and any firm whose liabilities exceeded its assets by a hundred pounds should be forthwith declared bankrupt." [1]

With these ideals for the organization of labor upon the lines of the reconstructed guild, Ruskin's account breaks off. It is much to be regretted that he did not find time to work out his brilliant suggestions to greater fulness and coherence, since no phase of his social philosophy is richer in promise and no part springs so naturally out of the general soil of his thought. The guild in some form, indeed, would seem to be the only fit means for the realization of the ideals of social reconstruction for which Ruskin stood; a plan, in other words, for the co-operation of the workers within collectively controlled groups, each doing his appointed task in an environment that both materially and socially aroused him to his best efforts, and each finding his task a natural outlet for his instinct for public service and his instinct for self-expression.[2] But it was left for others who came after to develop the guild-idea in fuller detail as a basis for the reorganization of the present industrial order, and even to put it to practical test in the form of the "reconstructed workshop," an experiment which Ruskin would have regarded as full of hope for the future. Meantime his restless mind was drawn

---

[1] *Works*, XVII, 387.

[2] Ruskin did not overlook, in his guild-ideas, the importance of environment for the worker. His guild halls, or social centers, were to be made beautiful by paintings and decorations, so as to help establish the worth and honorableness of the trades represented.

aside to still other plans and projects, substantially all of which, at least in general outline, have been set before the reader. An account of Ruskin's social philosophy would be incomplete, however, without some separate consideration of his ideas of the state and state control.

Part II—The Function of the State

In his visions of a new order Ruskin turned to the state as the central source of control. The state, as we have seen, should regulate marriage, should supply a universal and democratic system of education, and should provide employment for those out of work, including forced labor for the idle and criminal classes. It should set apart mountain and moorland for beauty, for exercise, and for support of animal life, and thus assure healthy diversions for its people. It should accomplish in the course of time a revolution in land tenure, with extended control over landholders; it should in the long run fix the incomes of landlords and of captains of industry, making both classes virtually salaried superintendents. It should establish and direct workshops for the manufacture and sale of every necessary of life, in rivalry with private producers and for the express purpose of setting up a just standard of quality and price to all consumers. Still other forms of state control were suggested or discussed from time to time by Ruskin in his writings. He advocated old age pensions in 1857; and at the same time made it plain that he favored extensive changes by law in the accepted modes of accumulation and distribution of property.

In 1863 he urged government ownership of railroads. "Neither the roads nor the railroads should belong to any private persons," he said; and they should not pay dividends, but working expenses only. "Had the money spent in local mistakes and vain private litigation, on the railroads of England, been laid out, instead, under proper government restraint, on really useful railroad work, and had no absurd expense been incurred in ornamenting stations, we might already have had,—what ultimately it will be found we must have,—quadruple rails, two for passengers, and two for traffic, on every great line; and we might have been carried in swift safety, and watched and warded by well-paid pointsmen for half the present fares." [1]

There are evidences also of Ruskin's belief that not railroads only, but all public utilities should be "under government administration and security," if not under direct state ownership.[2] Very early in his literary career he conceived of state control on the broadest lines, and from these he never departed.[3] To a program calling upon the state to make sure that its people were properly fed, clothed, and housed he often returned, describing in more detailed manner than he had in earlier accounts his notion of the state's responsibilities. Many of his declarations are alike bold and prophetic, as for example certain of those in the concluding paragraphs of his lecture on

[1] *Works*, XVII, 252.

[2] See, for example, his reprinting in *Fors* for September, 1877, a report of the Bread-winner's League in New York. He gave unmistakable assent to government ownership of the following: postroads, railroads, gasworks, waterworks, mining operations, canals, post-offices, telegraphs, expresses, medical assistance. (*Works*, XXIX, 218; XXVII, 471.)

[3] *Works*, XI, 263.

The Mystery of Life and Its Arts (1868),—a lecture into which, he said, he had put all that he knew and which Sir Leslie Stephen regarded as "the most perfect of his essays." After driving home the scriptural truth that if any man will not work neither shall he eat, he speaks of governmental control of food as follows: "the first thing is to be sure that you have the food to give; and, therefore, to enforce the organization of vast activities in agriculture and in commerce, for the production of the wholesomest food, and proper storing and distribution of it, so that no famine shall any more be possible among civilized beings." He next takes up the housing problem. Providing lodging for the people, he says, "means a great deal of vigorous legislature, and cutting down of vested interests that stand in the way, and after that, or before that, so far as we can get it, thorough sanitary and remedial action in the houses that we have; and then the building of more, strongly, beautifully, and in groups of limited extent, kept in proportion to their streams, and walled round, so that there may be no festering and wretched suburb anywhere, but clean and busy street within, and the open country without, with a belt of beautiful garden and orchard round the walls, so that from any part of the city perfectly fresh air and grass, and sight of far horizon, might be reachable in a few minutes' walk. This is the final aim; but in immediate action every minor and possible good to be instantly done, when, and as, we can; roofs mended that have holes in them—fences patched that have gaps in them—walls buttressed that totter—and floors propped that shake; cleanliness and order enforced with our own hands and eyes, till we are breathless every day. And all the fine arts will healthily follow." [1]

Ruskin knew that such suggestions, plain and practical to him, must have appeared chimerical to the British business man, whose normal vision of the world was that of a vast mob scrambling for wealth and trampling down the weak who cumbered his way. But he knew, too, that such a man was in truth a self-centered pessimist, who opposed all kinds of government interference on principle; and who, knowing well both past and present abuses of the state, refused to believe that they ever could be fewer or his fellow men wiser. To Ruskin, however, the "notion of Discipline and Interference" lay "at the very root of all human progress or power." [2] His whole idea of the state, reiterated a hundred times, was the idea of a centralized authority, directing, guiding, watching, and rewarding its people. In his later years he liked to do nothing so much as to draw a picture of society in which the energies of man were spent, not in the destruction of his fellows, in war, but in the conquest of his old-time enemies,—disease, want, and ignorance,—and of his ancient and still unsubdued environment, the vast waste places of earth and the yet vaster forces of nature. For the function of government, as he interpreted it, was paternalistic. Such a view to him was the most natural and the simplest possible. Its principles were no more and no less than the principles of the house, the farm, or the ship, written large. The French,

[1] *Works*, XVIII, 183.   [2] *Ibid.*, XVI, 26.

said he, in their efforts to work out a new social system hit upon one true principle, that of brotherhood; but in their disastrous experiments they forgot that the fact of brotherhood implied also the fact of fatherhood: "that is to say, if they were to regard the nation as one family, the condition of unity in that family consisted no less in their having a head, or a father, than in their being faithful and affectionate members, or brothers." [1]

It may be said that Ruskin's paternalistic government is state socialism pure and simple. In the sense that he regarded society as an organic whole, composed of mutually dependent units, acting together in harmony for common ends, under state control, he was a socialist. He was a socialist, also, in his burning protests against the senseless extravagance and irresponsibility of the upper classes; and in his demand for a reduction of the inequalities of wealth, upon the principle that property and land and tools alike belong to those who can use them.[2] Moreover his stern insistence that economists in the future should give the same attention to problems of distribution as, in the past, they had given to problems of production, was through and through socialistic, a cardinal principle of all progressive thinkers from his day to ours. But he was not a Christian Socialist after the manner of Kingsley and Maurice, who relied more upon sentiment than upon law as a means of securing

[1] *Works*, XVI, 24.
[2] Ruskin had no very definite program for the orderly reduction of inequalities of wealth. He relied mostly upon three methods, abolition of interest and profits on capital, taxation (including income, property, and excise tax on luxuries), and voluntary action.

social justice. He was a good deal nearer to the revolutionary socialists of the Marxian stripe, not only in his occasional prophecy that the crimes and follies of the capitalistic classes might precipitate power into the hands of the lower orders, but also in his bold denunciation of the whole competitive system of industry. Like the Marxists, Ruskin demanded the right to work for all, and theoretically adopted, as we have seen, the Marxian principle that quantity of labor should determine the price of commodities. More than all else he was socialistic in the *spirit* and *tendency* of much of his program for social reform. Every principle for which he contended and every practical remedy which he urged was inspired, as the best socialistic thought has been inspired, by a profound sense of the injustice in the present industrial order, and an equally profound conviction that justice could come only when the work of the world should be organized upon such a co-operative basis as to secure to every human being, obedient to the higher laws of his nature, that opportunity for self-development in labor which is the intuitive craving of mankind everywhere.

But Ruskin was not a leveler. Although he believed that "the fortunes of private persons should be small," and that large fortunes could "not honestly be made by the work of any *one* man's hands or head," [1] he had a vivid sense of the natural inequalities of men and of the consequent inevitable inequality in their material possessions. He therefore indignantly repudiated the suggestion that his social teaching

[1] *Works*, XXVII, 121; XVII, 388.

implied an equalitarian socialism. "If there be any one point insisted on throughout my works more frequently than another," he said, "that one point is the impossibility of Equality." [1] He agreed with all reformers, of whatever creed or race, that the educational system must reach down to every child in the state; but he had no sympathy with the desire on the part of the lower orders to secure education for the purpose of making themselves the upper orders. "They will be mightily astonished," he said, "when they really get it, to find that it is the fatallest of all discerners and enforcers of distinction; piercing, even to the division of the joints and marrow, to find out wherein your body and soul are less, or greater, than other bodies and souls, and to sign deed of separation with unequivocal zeal." [2] It was no less a fundamental tenet in his social creed that within certain limits the industrial and economic independence of each individual should be guaranteed by the state. The freedom of the worker must imply a right to the economic advantages resulting from his work. It will no doubt be a very complex difficulty in the national economy to adjust the laws so as to secure both a maximum of co-operation and a maximum of individual initiative. Nevertheless the creation of such laws seemed to Ruskin imperative; laws "which, marking the due limits of independent agency, may enable it to exist in full energy, not only without becoming injurious, but so as more variously and perfectly to promote the entire interests of the commonwealth." [3] With these foundations to stand

[1] *Works*, XVII, 74.   [2] *Ibid.*, XVII, 456.   [3] *Ibid.*, XVII, 375.

upon, therefore, he disapproved of land nationalization and the equal division of property. He was a communist, he said, but a "Communist of the old school, reddest of the red," which meant that everybody should work in common for his living; but not that everybody should own lands, houses, and personal property in common. "Any attempts to communize these," he said, "have always ended, and will always end, in ruin and shame."[1]

It was Ruskin's distrust of popular government, however, that separated him furthest from socialistic or radical thought of all kinds. Like Carlyle, he had a deep-rooted disbelief in the ability of the people to exercise political power. Democracy meant the overthrow of government and the rule of the mob, with everybody scrambling to be uppermost; it meant the vast upheaval of an untamed populace, believing in magnitude instead of nobleness, and totally ignorant of the higher arts and amenities of life. Ruskin

[1] *Works*, XVII, 487. *Cf. ibid.*, 266, 192–3, *intro.* CIX. Ruskin never attempted to say how far the independence and superior ability of an individual should be permitted to go in the accumulation of private property. He was no doubt wise in this, since the problem taken theoretically seems hopeless. Time and education and actual conditions must bring the solution nearer from generation to generation. On two points, moreover, he was clear and consistent: the right of a person, within limits, to what he earned; and the necessity for limitation of large incomes. As to whether such limitation should be compulsory or voluntary, he wavered, now favoring the one method, now the other. In either case he recognized the difficulty: "no action can be taken in redistribution of land or in limitation of the incomes of the upper classes, without grave and prolonged civil disturbance." (*Works*, XVII, 436.) What he undoubtedly hoped for was a gradual change in the social consciousness toward riches, together with a tax on incomes and a tax on luxuries, so that in the end superior ability would be paid a reasonable salary for superintendence, but would not wish to, nor be permitted to, have its reward in large personal property.

identified political liberty with licence, or the abandonment of illiterate masses to their appetites. For the machinery of popular government,—the party system, elections, parliaments,—he had almost nothing but scorn and derision. "If you have read any of my late works (any of my political works at all, lately or long since written)," he wrote to a correspondent in 1869, "you must have seen that they all speak with supreme contempt of the 'British Constitution,' of elections and popular opinion, and, above all, of 'Liberty.' . . . The wisest system of voting that human brains could devise would be of no use as long as the majority of the voters were fools, which is manifestly as yet the fact." [1] All these instrumentalities of democracy were to him synonymous with popular disturbances, with hypocrisies, with endless balancing of conflicting personal interests, and with bribery and corruption on a wide scale. At the moment when Disraeli was introducing the Reform Bill of 1867 into Parliament, Ruskin challenged the workingmen of England to say if they had intelligent convictions upon the great questions of labor and national policy: "your voices are not worth a rat's squeak, either in Parliament or out of it, till you have some ideas to utter with them." [2] He accepted universal suffrage as inevitable, but he believed that the electors of a nation should have votes proportional to their education, age, wealth, and position, so that the populace could be kept in its place. [3]

[1] *Works*, XVII, 326n.
[2] *Ibid.*, XVII, 326.
[3] "I should be very glad if it were possible to keep the common people from thinking about government, but, since the invention of printing, it

His outlook upon the political movements of his day thus corresponded exactly with Carlyle's. By gross misgovernment the aristocracy had deservedly lost the respect of the lower orders, who were now threatening to overthrow the constitution and to substitute a republic, which Ruskin could only look upon as political anarchy. As he read the signs of the times, if this movement went on unchecked, with increasing extravagance among the upper classes and with increased license among the lower, the only way out, after the populace had had its day of democracy, was to set up, for a time, a military despotism as the forerunner of genuine reconstruction,—a Carlylean interpretation of events through and through.[1] Ruskin's distrust of the capacity of the people for political power, therefore, implies the same curious paradox that we found in Carlyle,—a bold and pioneer championship of the workers against oppression of every kind and a well-nigh fanatical opposition to all their efforts to secure political freedom as a basis and guarantee of social reform. Despite his belief in universal education, when he came to consider the larger matters of state administration and control, he could not conquer the conviction that for

is not—of all impossibilities that is now the most so; the only question is how to make them of exactly the proper weight in the State, and no more." (*Works*, XII, *intro.* LXXXIII.) *Cf.* XVII, 253; XXXIV, 499, 674.

[1] "A nation once utterly corrupt can only be redeemed by despotism—never by talking, nor by its free effort. . . . The British Constitution is breaking fast. . . . The gipsy hunt is up also; . . . and the hue and cry loud against your land and you; your tenure of it is in dispute before a multiplying mob." (*Works*, XVIII, 484; XXVIII, 152, 151; *Cf.* XVII, 264; XVIII, 497; XXVIII, 152.)

these higher responsibilities the masses of mankind would remain unfit.[1]

Politically speaking, Ruskin could see an ordered society only as made up of two classes,—the lordly and the servile, those born to rule and those born to be ruled; and "the whole health of the state," he said, "depends on the manifest separation of these two elements."[2] Every man in the kingdom should be "equally well educated" with every other; yet the result would only bring into clearer light the eternal differences among men. There was not a sentence in his writings, Ruskin declared in 1884, "implying that the education of all should be alike, or that there is to be no distinction of master from servant, or of scholar from clown."[3] In 1860 he appeared before a parliamentary committee to testify as to his teaching in the Working Men's College, and when asked if he did not think that the desire to rise out of their class was almost inseparable from the instruction that the men received from him, he replied: "I should think not; I think that the moment a man desires to rise

---

[1] The agreement of Ruskin with Carlyle on political principles is shown in the following strongly Carlylean passages: "The essential thing for all creatures is to be made to do right; how they are made to do it—by pleasant promises, or hard necessities, pathetic oratory, or the whip—is comparatively immaterial." (XVII, 255.) "Religion, primarily, means 'Obedience'—bending to something, or some one." (XXVIII, 156.) "The wise man knows his master. Less or more wise, he perceives lower or higher masters; but always some creature larger than himself—some law holier than his own." (XXVIII, 343.) "Of all the puppet-shows in the Satanic carnival of the earth, the most contemptible puppet-show is a Parliament with a mob pulling the strings." (XII, 552.) "In the modern Liberal there is a new and wonderful form of misguidance." (XXVII, 179.) Cf. passage on the fly as a type of liberty,—XIX, 123.

[2] Works, XVII, 236. Cf. ibid., 228.

[3] Ibid., XXIX, 499.

out of his own class, he does his work badly in it; he ought to desire to rise in his own class, and not out of it." [1]   It was the duty of such men—the workers, the servers—to stick to their appointed tasks like good soldiers, and not to meddle with politics and problems of government. It was their duty to render to their superiors obedience and reverence; for Ruskin, like Carlyle, regarded these virtues as the rocks upon which all sound politics must forever rest. Just as the elements of the universe, the stars, the earth in its revolutions, the waters of the sea, act in obedience to law, so, too, should inferior men respect the authority of superior men, venerate the good in them, be faithful to them in appointed duties,—in a word be utterly loyal in all the relations of life.

In politics it is clear that Ruskin was an aristocrat and conservative, bred in the bone, dyed in the blood. He called himself "a violent Illiberal"; "I am, and my father was before me, a violent Tory of the old school (Walter Scott's school, that is to say, and Homer's)," [2]   From Scott and Homer in boyhood, just as from Plato and Carlyle in maturity, he imbibed eternal fidelity to conservatism and "strange ideas about kings." [3]   His long study of art, moreover, taught him the significance of distinctions, the immense superiority of a Turner, for example, over a

---

[1] *Works*, XVI, 474. *Cf.* XVII, 397.

[2] *Ibid.*, XXVII, 167.

[3] Although Ruskin's sober convictions were undoubtedly in favor of a governing aristocracy of intellect, he retained to the end of his days a romantic and æsthetic reverence for old castles and for the distinctions of a more or less feudalistic social order. "I hate republicans, as I do all other manner of fools," he once said in whimsical irritation. "I love Lords and Ladies; and Earls and Countesses, and Marquises and Mar-

Stanfield. It was thus inevitable for him to look to the aristocracy to be the rulers and lawgivers of the state. "To them," he said, "be they few or many, we English people call for help to the wretchedness, and for rule over the baseness, of multitudes desolate and deceived, shrieking to one another this new gospel of their new religion: 'let the weak do as they can, and the wicked as they will'. . . . The office of the upper classes, as a body, is to keep order among their inferiors, and raise them always to the nearest level with themselves of which these inferiors are capable. So far as they are thus occupied, they are invariably loved and reverenced intensely by all beneath them, and reach, themselves, the highest types of human power and beauty." [1]

Apart from the condition that the rulers, at peril of their places, were to *rule* the people wisely, and were not to represent them, Ruskin was not much concerned about the form of government. The central authority might be vested in king, council, or parliament, according to the genius and tradition of the nation concerned. "The stuff of which the nation is made is developed by the effort and the fate of ages," he declared; "according to that material, such

chionesses, and Honorables, and Sirs" (*Works*, XXVIII, 547.) He showed the violence of his toryism more than once in his championship of strong authority, as well as in his contempt of popular struggles for liberty, such as were going on in America 1861–1865.

[1] *Works*, XVIII, 499; XVII, 430. In his lecture on *The Future of England* (1869) Ruskin pointed out that no answer had come to the question put by the *Saturday Review*, "What is to become of the House of Lords?"; and therefore "it seems thus to become needful for all men to tell them, as our one quite clear-sighted teacher, Carlyle, has been telling us for many a year, that the use of the Lords of a country is to *govern* the country," (XVIII, 498.)

and such government becomes possible to it, or impossible." [1] His view is characteristically British at this point; for he conceived of the forms of government as of slow growth. The structure of a state might be blown up, like a ship, in the twinkling of an eye; but to build up a code of laws, to appoint means for their execution, to stabilize the vast mechanism of a state,—this could not be done in an instant, by beat of drum. Let particular forms of government, however, be what they might, any form would work provided its purpose was "*the production and recognition of human worth*, and the detection and extinction of human unworthiness." [2]

But how is the state to accomplish this great purpose, so as to effect progress? Where are the leaders to be found who will lead, and how are the "people" to be induced to follow them obediently and reverently? What is to give society its initial push in the right direction, so that it can begin its upward march out of the slough into which it has fallen? These are the final challenging questions that we must put to Ruskin, as we did to Carlyle. No man saw the social injustice in the work about him with clearer vision than Ruskin, and no man, not even Carlyle, hurled against it stronger attacks, sustained year after year, with blow upon blow. "The people," he said, "have begun to suspect that one particular form of misgovernment has been that their masters have set them to do all the work and have themselves taken all the wages. In a word, that what was called governing them meant only wearing fine clothes and

[1] *Works*, XXVII, 235.   [2] *Ibid.*, XVII, 446.

living on good fare at their expense. And I am sorry to say, the people are quite right in this opinion too. If you enquire into the vital fact of the matter, this you will find to be the constant structure of European society for the thousand years of the feudal system; it was divided into peasants who lived by digging; priests who lived by begging; and knights who lived by pillaging; and as the luminous public mind becomes fully cognizant of these facts, it will assuredly not suffer things to be altogether arranged that way any more." [1] So spoke the prophet, and so he spoke with increasing vehemence in his later years. In the spirit of a prophet, too, he turned from the democratic movements of the day as a means of carrying out his elaborate and far sighted plans of industrial reconstruction, and called upon a wayward people "to repent." In other words, industrial reform was really to be set going not by political changes first of all, nor by a collective sanction of *legal* means, but by a voluntary reformation of the individual. As Professor Hobson justly points out, Ruskin thus found "the spring of progress in the individual will." "All effectual advancement towards this true felicity of the human race," said Ruskin, "must be by individual effort. Certain general measures may aid, certain revised laws guide, such advancement; but the measure and law which have first to be determined are those of each man's home." [2]

He, therefore, first appealed to the aristocracy to change their ways before the rising floods of anarchic democracy overwhelmed them. To the rich every-

[1] *Works*, XVIII, 496.   [2] *Ibid.*, XVII, III.

where he said in effect: "see for yourselves what degradation your extravagance is bringing upon multitudes of mankind who toil in filthy factories and swarm in crowded tenements; and seeing, be strong enough to sacrifice all convenience, beauty, or cheapness that you get through such degradation, and to *live with as little aid from the lower trades* as you possibly can contrive." As an interesting illustration of what could be done through individual initiative of this kind, Ruskin instanced the way in which he believed that the misery in the crowded suburbs of so vast a city as London might be relieved: "any man of influence who had the sense and courage to refuse himself and his family one London season—to stay on his estate, and employ the shopkeepers in his own village, instead of those in Bond Street—would be practically dealing with, and conquering, this evil, so far as in him lay; and contributing with his whole might to the thorough and final conquest of it." [1] He called upon the landlords, as we have seen, voluntarily to fix their rents upon a just basis and to guarantee to their tenants a fair compensation for improvements. He called upon them, also, voluntarily to fix their incomes within reasonable limits, setting aside all surplus for the benefit of land and tenants. His demand upon the captains of industry was of like character. "Treat your ordinary workmen," he said to them, "exactly as you would treat your son if he were in their position": "this is the only effective, true, or practical *rule* which can be given on this point of political economy." Addressing the students of

[1] *Works*, XXVII, 175.

the Royal Military Academy in 1869—young men of the upper classes,—he told them in vivid language of the evil times on which they had fallen. "Whose fault is it?" he asked. "Yours, gentlemen, yours only. You alone can feed (the people), and clothe, and bring into their right minds, for you only can govern." He thereupon appealed to these aristocratic youths to lead in all reform—in education, in social betterment,—and to begin by showing the masses how to spend. Through such leadership must England be saved: "so and no otherwise can we meet existent distress." [1]

Ruskin's last word to the workers was likewise an appeal to the individual. "If you will have the upper classes do *their* duty," he said, "see that you also do yours. See that you can obey good laws, and good lords, or law-wards, if you once get them— that you believe in goodness enough to know what a good law is. A good law is one that holds, whether you recognize or pronounce it or not; a bad law is one that cannot hold, however much you ordain and pronounce it. That is the mighty truth which Carlyle has been telling you for a quarter of a century." [2] He appealed to the lower classes to make the three-fold promise: to do their work well, whether for life or death, to help others at their work and to seek to avenge no injury, and to obey good laws before trying to alter bad ones. Such was all the law and all the prophets. Political salvation for the workers, therefore, was summed in the command, "Find your true superiors, reverence their worth, obey

[1] *Works*, XVIII, 502, 508.   [2] *Ibid.*, XXVII, 178.

their word, and stick to your task";—a truly astonishing conclusion to a social program of which much was and still remains so splendidly idealistic and revolutionary.

Part III—Utopia

But the prophet believed in his message to the uttermost, and through many years and in various ways he strove to show to the world his faith by his works. Nothing angered him more than the reproach of sentimentality or the insinuation that all his ideals and schemes were at best no better than beautiful dreams. Of his burning sensitiveness to the miseries and follies of mankind, we have had abundant evidence in the preceding pages; his "pervivacity" of temperament, as he called it, is conspicuous everywhere. [1] He was fairly maddened, therefore, to find his visions of a better social order regarded as insubstantial as a mirage, and to have his political economy dismissed contemptuously as "effeminate sentimentality."

Against such insinuations Ruskin insisted upon his "intensely practical and matter-of-fact" nature. Above all things he wished that the public should not consider him a mere theorist and doctrinaire, painting word-pictures lovely to read, but with no real message to men. Readers of *Modern Painters* will recall that in the prefaces to the first and third vol-

[1] The heart of Dean Swift was not more swept by the fires of indignation. "I have been reading Dean Swift's Life," he wrote to his mother in 1869, "and *Gulliver's Travels* again. Putting the delight in dirt, which is a mere disease, aside, Swift is very like me, in most things, in opinions exactly the same." (Cook, *Life*, II, 547.)

umes he seemed to anticipate Whistler's sneer about a man's talking for forty years of what he has never done, when he referred to his long study of practical art and pointed out his share in the drawings and illustrations for the work. It was the same with the crafts and the rougher forms of labor. "Half my power of ascertaining facts of any kind connected with the arts," he said, "is my stern habit of doing the thing with my own hands till I know its difficulty; and though I have no time nor wish to acquire showy skill in anything, I make myself clear as to what the skill means, and is. Thus, when I had to direct road-making at Oxford, I sate, myself, with an iron-masked stone-breaker, on his heap, to break stones beside the London road, just under Iffley Hill, till I knew how to advise my too impetuous pupils to effect their purpose in that matter, instead of breaking the heads of their hammers off (a serious item in our daily expenses). I learned from an Irish street crossing-sweeper what he could teach me of sweeping; but found myself in that matter nearly his match, from my boy-gardening; and again and again I swept bits of St. Giles' foot-pavements, showing my corps of subordinates how to finish into depths of gutter. I worked with a carpenter until I could take an even shaving six feet long off a board; and painted enough with properly and delightfully soppy green paint to feel the master's superiority in the use of a blunt brush. But among all these and other such student-ships, the reader will be surprised, I think, to hear, seriously, that the instrument I finally decided to be the most difficult of management was the trowel.

For accumulated months of my boy's life I watched bricklaying and paving; but when I took the trowel into my own hand, abandoned at once all hope of attaining the least real skill with it, unless I gave up all thoughts of any future literary or political career." [1] Ruskin's life is filled with what his biographer calls his "passion for practice," from the planting and pruning and cultivating of trees at Coniston, from his treatment of domestic servants and his numberless private benefactions in money and books and pictures, to his active interest in the educational life of various institutions, including his establishment of the Ruskin drawing school at Oxford, with its fine collection of specimens. It was the same with his social experiments. He was not content *to state* what must be done. He wished to demonstrate a method of realization. He disclaimed any intention of setting himself up "either for a champion or a leader," but he believed that some example of what he knew to be necessary might convince others, better qualified to lead, of the feasibility of his ideals. And so it came about during the active period of his life that Ruskin, "the Don Quixote of Denmark Hill," as he playfully called himself, was occupied with various experiments in social reform, some undertaken independently, some in co-operation with others, but all in the ardent effort to point out to a perverse generation what might be effected toward the realization of beauty and love and justice in an actual world.

One of the earliest movements with which he was associated was the Working Men's College, started

[1] *Works*, XXXV, 427.

by F. D. Maurice in 1854, for the laboring classes in East London. Established at a time when education (except in the most elementary form) did not reach the common people, it was the aim of the college to bring to a segment of the masses at least the same kind of education that the upper classes enjoyed. Dr. F. J. Furnivall, "a humble disciple and friend" of Ruskin, sent him a prospectus of the enterprise, and Ruskin responded with an offer to Maurice to take the classes in art. His chapter on "The Nature of Gothic," through Furnivall's initiative, was distributed as a manifesto to all who came to the opening meeting on October 31. Inspired by Ruskin's example, Rossetti, Burne-Jones, Ford Madox Brown, and others volunteered their services for longer or shorter periods. With the exception of summer terms, when his attendance was irregular, Ruskin taught drawing classes in the college from 1854 until May, 1858, returning again for a term in the spring of 1860. He was from the first an enthusiastic and successful teacher, if we may judge from such accounts as have come to us,—"wildly popular with the men" and an "eloquent" talker, as Ford Madox Brown declared. To his classroom he brought a wealth of illustrative material from the Denmark Hill home,—precious stones, bird-plumage, drawings, missals, even some of the treasured Turners, and always liberal supplies of the best drawing paper. In suitable weather sketching expeditions to the open country around Denmark Hill were frequent, concluding with luncheon there or at some convenient inn. It needs scarcely to be said that Ruskin under-

took this work, not in the spirit of the aristocratic
trifler, carried away by a whim of fashion, but in the
spirit of a reformer, who saw in the Working Men's
College an organized effort to offset the crushing
results of competitive industry, by bringing to the
men who could not rise out of their class a means of
being happier within it. In spite of this interpretation of purpose, however, many of Ruskin's pupils
won for themselves no little distinction in fields of
work to which they felt called as a result of his
inspiration.[1] It is interesting to know that out of his
intimate personal contact with his students there
came to him an idea, which he called his "Protestant
Convent Plan," of establishing a community of craftsmen. Although nothing came of the scheme, one
seems to catch from it a glimpse of the guild idea,
which was first mentioned in a lecture in 1857, at a
time when his teaching at the college was a fresh and
vivid experience.

Another famous instance of the fascination which
Ruskin exercised over young men (how different from
the East London group!) was the quixotic experiment
in road mending at Oxford by a company of undergraduates, since known to all the world as the Hinksey Diggers. As Slade Professor he was a familiar
and notable figure at the University for many years,
lecturing ostensibly upon art, but more often digres-

---

[1] "George Allen as a mezzotint engraver," says Collingwood, "Arthur
Burgess as a draughtsman and woodcutter, John Bunney as a painter of
architectural detail, W. Jeffrey as an artistic photographer, E. Cooke as a
teacher, William Ward as a facsimile copyist, have all done work whose
value deserves acknowledgment, all the more because it was not aimed at
popular effect." (*Works*, V, *intro.*, XLI.)

sing in whimsical fashion into all manner of unconventional subjects, chiefly social and economic. It was these digressions that had the most telling effect upon the undergraduate mind. On one occasion, according to an account by one of the "diggers," Ruskin dropped some remarks "about the waste of time he noticed in the Oxford world of athletics. He could not but believe that the same training of muscles might be turned to better account, if only the young men, as they labored to increase the muscles of their biceps and forearms, would try to help others round them to a happier life. . . . He instanced the need of good roads in a neighboring village." [1] He instanced a further purpose. He wished that these Oxford young men, who lived in a world so different, might understand for themselves, however faintly, the meaning of a life of toil. The suggestion awoke a response. A group of twelve Balliol men met the Professor at breakfasts in his college rooms, where arrangements were completed and allegiance was sworn. There was a stretch of green near Ferry Hinksey, two miles out of Oxford, much damaged by the ruts of carts that went over it for lack of road. Ruskin obtained permission to build a road through this green,—"a Human Pathway," it was to be, "rightly made through a lovely country, and rightly adorned." Thither, in the first summer term of 1874, the young disciples went, "sixty men, in relays of twenties, on two days each week," handling pick and barrow and spade in obedience to the Master, who

---

[1] *Atlantic Monthly*, V. 85, p. 573. The unsigned article was probably written by Canon Rawnsley.

was then absent in Italy. Later, Ruskin often joined them, directing and applauding their efforts with the zeal of one who was conscious of trying to break something far harder than a new road,—the rigid crust of Oxford tradition. The experiment was of course the butt of jokers and cartoonists. Dons came to scoff, and village loafers to jeer. "A mile or so of road was laid out," says Dean Kitchin; "it led to nowhere in particular, unless it had been intended to lead to a comely farm on the hillside; and even that it did not reach. When I saw the road, about a year or so after, it showed obvious signs of decay. No prudent farmer would have brought his carts over it; he would have stuck to the turf of the open meadow." [1] Ruskin himself was heard to admit that his road was "about the worst in the three kingdoms."

But the Hinksey digging had results that were far from ridiculous. It brought a number of promising undergraduates into intimate touch with Ruskin, who on the walks to and from Hinksey and at the breakfasts in his rooms at Corpus Christi unfolded to them, as master to disciples, his hopes and fears for the future. The talk was free and plenteous and brilliant upon all manner of questions relating to art and society. Among the undergraduate followers was Arnold Toynbee, a foreman among the diggers, a young man of gifted mind and rarely beautiful character, whose passion for social service among the people was quickened through his contact with Ruskin. Described by those who knew him best as one who combined the mystical ardor of a medieval

[1] *Ruskin in Oxford,* 45.

saint with the desire to serve his fellow men in his own time, Toynbee was just the man upon whom Ruskin's influence might fall with most effect. And it is indeed difficult not to believe that his later work both among the East London poor and as a lecturer on economic questions owed much to the inspiration of the "digging-parties," where, as Ruskin's biographer says, "the seeds were sown, or watered, of that practical interest in social questions which was to be the next Oxford Movement." [1] For Ruskin was a dreamer of Utopias among his Oxford students, even as he had been a dreamer twenty years before among the Londoners who gathered about him at the Working Men's College; and in a letter to one of the Hinksey Diggers he gave expression to one of his dreams. It was a hope that some of them might "band themselves together, one day, and go out in a kind of Benedictine brotherhood to cultivate waste places and make life tolerable in our great cities for the children of the poor." [2]

To show what could be done for the poor in great cities he made three experiments in the crowded districts of London. One was street-cleaning. Ruskin secured permission from the local authorities "in the pleasant environs of Church Lane, St. Giles's," to exhibit to the populace for a quarter of a mile square, "without leaving so much as a bit of orange peel in the footway, or an egg shell in the gutters." In January, 1872, he assembled a small troupe of sweepers, including his faithful gardener as foreman,

[1] Cook, *Life of Ruskin*, II, 190.
[2] *Atlantic Monthly*, V. 85, pp. 572-6.

and himself led off on the job, broom in hand. The enterprise appears to have collapsed early. "I failed," said Ruskin, "partly because I chose too difficult a district to begin with (the contributions of transitional mud being constant, and the inhabitants passive), but chiefly because I could no more be on the spot myself, to give spirit to the men, when I left Denmark Hill for Coniston." [1] The next experiment was a tea-shop in Paddington, St. Marylebone. Ruskin's purpose, he said, was "to supply the poor in that neighborhood with pure tea, in packets as small as they chose to buy, without making a profit on the subdivision." [2] Over the door was placed a sign, "Mr. Ruskin's Tea-Shop" (painted by Mr. Arthur Severn), the window was ornamented with old china "bought at Siena," and two of his mother's old servants were put in charge. The business ran, with diminishing returns, for two years (1874–76), and was then given up after the death of one of the keepers. But long before the shop was closed Ruskin had come to the conclusion that he could not successfully compete with the other more brilliantly lighted shops or with the increasing consumption in the neighborhood of less innocent liquids than tea.

A far wiser effort in social welfare was an experiment in "model landlordism" in the worst part of London, carried out under the management of Miss Octavia Hill, a young woman whose passion for service found its opportunity through her early enthusiasm for Ruskin. He had long felt that the rents exacted from the ignorant and necessitous poor were

[1] *Works*, XXVIII, 204. [2] *Ibid*.

outrageous. "The most wretched houses of the poor in London," he said, "often pay ten or fifteen per cent to the landlord; and I have known an instance of sanitary legislation being hindered, to the loss of many hundreds of lives, in order that the rents of a nobleman, derived from the necessities of the poor, might not be diminished." [1] Ruskin had inherited from his father some small tenements, and he now bought still others. These he intrusted to the stewardship of Miss Hill, in order to try what change in the comforts and habits of the tenants he could effect "by taking only a just rent, but that firmly." [2] If the idea was his, the successful realization of it was due to Miss Hill. She worked without pay and she made it her business to keep in personal touch with her tenants. To them the benefits were almost immediate. Profits were spent in improvements, overcrowding was much reduced, decency and cleanliness were made possible, and the people themselves began to rise in self-respect and independence. Miss Hill managed these tenements for Ruskin during many years, but finally he sold them to her, after an estrangement between them, because she had spoken of him as "unpractical," an epithet which, of all that she might have applied to a disappointed and tormented spirit, "was the fatalest." In spite of this unfortunate experience, he was highly and justly gratified with the experiment, and hoped that other landlords would follow his example. But he was under no illusion concerning its temporary character. "The best that can be done in this way,"

[1] *Works*, XVII, 437.
[2] The leasehold property paid him five per cent; the freehold, three.

he said, "will be useless ultimately, unless the deep source of the misery be cut off."

But the attacks upon competitive commercialism went on, regardless of the shouts of ridicule that rose from the philistines. While he had strength to fight Ruskin delivered one assault after another upon the strongholds of modern business, always hoping, with a kind of forlorn hope, that others, stronger and wiser, would enlist in the struggle until the enemy would be compelled to capitulate. Like the experiment in model housing, and contrary to expectation, his next undertaking proved highly successful. When *Fors Clavigera* was started in 1871, it was to be a protest against the ways of the modern world of commerce; for one thing, against advertising (puffery), discounts, and credits. These evils, it seemed to Ruskin, were concentrated in the book business, with consequent injustice alike to authors and public. He therefore decided to issue *Fors* (which was to appear monthly at seven pence per copy) at a fixed price both to trade and consumers, allowing no discounts and no credit even for purchases in quantity. "This absolute refusal of credit, or abatement," said he, "is only the carrying out of a part of any general method of political economy; and I adopt this system of sale because I think authors ought not to be too proud to sell their own books any more than painters to sell their own pictures." [1] The plan, begun for *Fors*, was gradually expanded to include all of Ruskin's works. At first his old publishers, Smith, Elder, and Co., with the co-operation of George Allen, one of the students

[1] *Works*, XXVII, 257.

in the drawing classes at the Working Men's College, undertook to carry out the enterprise. In 1873 the entire management was turned over to Mr. Allen, who set up the publishing business at Orpington, Kent, twelve miles out of London, in his cottage "Sunny-side,"—"standing in its own grounds, which slope down into one of the prettiest vales of Kent." The printing was likewise done in the country, at Ayles-bury, by Messrs. Hazell, Watson, and Viney, who had, says Mr. Allen, "quite an ideal printing-office— with light and cheerful buildings, allotment gardens, recreation-ground, clubs, a magazine, and all the other machinery for 'mutual improvement.'" Rus-kin's ideal was the establishment of a happy village industry, wherefrom the middleman should be eliminated, and where books should be supplied at fixed prices to all purchasers,—the producer answer-ing to the best of his power for the quality of the product, "paper, binding, eloquence, and all"; and the retail dealer charging "what he ought to charge, openly." [1] On this basis the plan was so bitterly opposed by the booksellers, resulting in a boycott of his books, that in 1882 Ruskin agreed to a modifica-tion. For the fixed price to all purchasers, leaving the booksellers to add their own profit if they chose, he now substituted a fixed price at which the books should be retailed to the public, and allowed the trade a fixed discount. He thus became the pioneer of the "net book system." Under the wise control of Mr. Allen the business prospered. [2] One of his greatest

[1] *Works*, XXVII, 100.
[2] "Last year (1886) I was able to pay over to Mr. Ruskin, as his

achievements in Ruskin's lifetime was the 1888 edition of *Modern Painters* (actually issued in May, 1889), from which it was estimated that Ruskin's share in the profits was not less than £6,000. The enterprise was carried out in a way that must have delighted its originator (then too feeble in health to take an active part in it),—under the best of working conditions, without stint in labor or cost of material, and with the sole purpose of delivering to the public a guaranteed article. "I need not add," says Mr. Allen, "that (there) was no machine-stitching about it, but only honest hand-work." [1]

profit, £4,000." For many years the profits were as much as this.

[1] Carlyle once visited the publishing plant at Orpington, and afterwards wrote to Emerson of Ruskin's "strange ways towards the bibliopolic world."

As a result of his frequent visits to the Alps and Italy, Ruskin became greatly absorbed for a time in an irrigation project. He noted with dismay the constant waste and destruction caused by floods from Alpine torrents, such as the Arve, the Adige, the Ticino, the Rhone, and even the Tiber. In 1869 he was full of a scheme for building reservoirs on the upper reaches for use in prevention of floods and for irrigation. He tried to interest the Alpine Club. On his visits to Carlyle he poured out his plans. "One day," said Carlyle to Froude, "by express desire on both sides, I had Ruskin for some hours, really interesting and entertaining. He is full of projects, of generous prospective activities, some of which I opined to him would prove chimerical." Ruskin wrote to the public press on the subject, and his letter was translated into Italian. In answer to further inquiries, he unfolded his ideas more fully. "The simplest and surest beginning," he said, "would be the purchase, either by the government or by a small company formed in Rome, of a few plots of highland in the Apennines, now barren for want of water, and valueless; and the showing what could be made of them by terraced irrigation such as English officers have already introduced in many parts of India. The Agricultural College at Cirencester ought, I think, to be able to send out two or three superintendents, who would direct rightly the first processes of cultivation, choosing for purchase good soil in good exposures. . . . And the entire mountain side may be made one garden of orange and vine and olive beneath; and a wide blossoming orchard above; and a green

None of these experiments, however, not even this successful venture into the publishing business, had for Ruskin anything like the significance of St. George's Guild, a scheme of social reform about which he thought and planned down to his last working years, and out of which he evoked some of his most glowing visions of a better order. It was to be his last stand against the advancing tide of modern life, a final effort to slay the dragon of nineteenth-century industrialism. To his eyes the evil forces of modern civilization—everywhere assembled in strength— were sweeping onward, while the good forces were withdrawing from the turmoil and the foulness, eager to seek shelter in quiet retreats scattered over the land. With small beginnings but with clear purposes, Ruskin hoped to show how the sound elements of society might unite in a crusade against the common enemy. More particularly he wished to draw people away from the corruption and congestion of modern cities to the free, healthy life of the country. He had hoped, he said, that by 1871 the "earnest adjuration of Carlyle" in *Past and Present*, and his own analysis of "the economical laws on which the real prosperity of a nation depends," to which he had given his best thought between 1860 and 1870, would draw attention to what might be done by landlords who should devote their interests to the welfare of

---

highest pasture for cattle, and flowers for bees—up to the edge of the snows of spring." (*Works*, XVII, 549, 552.) Ruskin always thus became quickly enthusiastic over his latest scheme. "If I had followed the true bent of my mind," he once said to a friend, "I should have been a civil engineer. I should have found more pleasure in planning bridges and sea breakwaters than in praising modern painters." (XXXVII, 699.)

the peasantry as a primary and not as a secondary object. Disappointed in this expectation, he now determined to invite any who had yet stout hearts to draw together and initiate a true and wholesome way of life, in defiance of the world. He resolved to see what might be done by a company of persons pledged to devote a portion of their income to "the purchase of land in healthy districts, and the employment of laborers on that land, under the carefullest supervision, and with every proper means of mental instruction." Ruskin stated his purposes more fully in the following words: "This Guild was originally founded with the intention of showing how much food-producing land might be recovered by well-applied labor from the barren or neglected districts of nominally cultivated countries. With this primary aim, two ultimate objects of wider aim were connected: the leading one, to show what tone and degree of refined education could be given to persons maintaining themselves by agricultural labor; and the last, to convince some portion of the upper classes of society that such occupation was more honorable, and consistent with higher thoughts and nobler pleasures, than their at present favorite profession of war; and that the course of social movements must ultimately compel many to adopt it;—if willingly, then happily, both for themselves and their dependents,— if resistingly, through much distress, and disturbance of all healthy relations between the master and paid laborer." [1] The St. George's Guild was thus an effort to demonstrate on a small scale what could be done

[1] *Works*, XXX, 17, 45.

in rational organization of country life. It was an effort also, Ruskin confessed, to draw the peasantry away from socialism and to reduce to practice "Carlyle's nobler exhortation in *Past and Present*." Should fortune deign to smile upon humble beginnings, no man could predict what beneficent revolutions might be effected in the lives of English men and women!

On December 23, 1871, Ruskin set aside £7,000, or a tenth of his fortune, as the St. George's Fund, and he called for volunteers to join him in giving a tenth of their incomes or whatever they could afford for general charity. They were to be organized into a company for the purchase of land. They were to be under the control of a master, elected by a majority of the members and liable to instant deposal, but while in office exercising autocratic power. Trustees were appointed to take charge of the funds. Ruskin's appeal, however, met with little or no response. After many months of waiting, he wrote in *Fors* (May, 1872): "Not one human creature, except a personal friend or two, for mere love of me, has answered." Only £236, 13s. came in at the end of three years. It was not until October, 1878, after endless trouble with the law, that a license was at last granted to the Guild to hold lands.

The immediate practical plan of the organization was the establishment of agricultural communities. Land was to be bought (or given) for cultivation, "with humble and simple cottage dwellings under faultless sanitary regulation." Existing timber was to be preserved and streams kept unpolluted. Tenants were to be under overseers, appointed by the trustees. They were to occupy the land under long lease, at a fixed rent, with the privilege of purchasing their holding if they could save the price of it. Meantime the rents were to be lowered in proportion to every improvement by the tenant; and all money accumulated by the Guild was to be put back into the land that most needed it. The size of the allotment of land to each family was in some undefined way to be proportional to the family's reasonable needs,—it always being understood that no man should have more than he could cultivate with his own and his children's efforts. There were to be no machines moved by steam-power. All work was to be done by hand, or with the help of wind and water, and perhaps electricity. Everything that the farmers could make for themselves they were to make. They might build their cottages to their own minds, except "under certain conditions as to materials and strength." [1] There was to be as little trade or importation of goods from outside as possible. The middleman must go. Goods, or imported foods, were to be sold at fixed prices, and according to a fixed standard of quality, by salaried tradesmen, whose books "must always be open on the Master's order, and not only

[1] *Works*, XXVIII, 20. As to the tenants' making everything for themselves, Ruskin replied to a woman who objected to working at the loom while raising children that "if on those terms I find sufficient clothing cannot be provided, I will use factories for them,—only moved by water, not steam." The members of St. George were not asked to abjure machinery or travel on railroads, but "they should never do with a machine what can be done with hands and arms, while hands and arms are idle." (*Ibid.*, 248.) Ruskin also consented to the use of the sewing-machine, though he preferred hand-work.

(their) business position entirely known but (their) profits known to the public: the prices of all articles of general manufacture being printed with the percentages to every person employed in their production or sale." [1] Complete publicity of all commercial transactions was to be the law, all accounts of the masters and overseers, for example, being open for inspection at any time.

Not only the economic foundations, but the educational also, were to be strictly Ruskinian. Schools and museums, "always small and instantly serviceable," would be established in the villages. Children were to be taught "compulsorily" on the basis of such principles as Ruskin had long advocated. Tenants should have libraries in their homes, paid for out of the general fund, and made up of books selected from an authorized list. Newspapers were prohibited. "What final relations," said Ruskin, "may take place between masters and servants, laborers and employers, old people and young, useful people and useless, in such a society, only experience can conclude; nor is there any reason to anticipate the conclusion." Meantime all members of the landowning company—the proprietors—must subscribe to the following eight articles of St. George's Creed:

I. "I trust in the Living God, Father Almighty, Maker of heaven and earth, and of all things and creatures visible and invisible.

I trust in the kindness of His law, and the goodness of His work.

[1] *Works*, XXIX, 113.

And I will strive to love Him, and keep His law, and see His work, while I live.

II. I trust in the nobleness of human nature, in the majesty of its faculties, the fulness of its mercy, and the joy of its love.

And I will strive to love my neighbor as myself, and, even when I cannot, will act as if I did.

III. I will labor, with such strength and opportunity as God gives me, for my own daily bread; and all that my hand finds to do, I will do with my might.

IV. I will not deceive, or cause to be deceived, any human being for my gain or pleasure; nor hurt, or cause to be hurt, any human being for my gain or pleasure; nor rob, or cause to be robbed, any human being for my gain or pleasure.

V. I will not kill nor hurt any living creature needlessly, nor destroy any beautiful thing, but will strive to save and comfort all gentle life, and guard and perfect all natural beauty, upon the earth.

VI. I will strive to raise my own body and soul daily into higher powers of duty and happiness; not in rivalship or contention with others, but for the help, delight, and honor of others, and for the joy and peace of my own life.

VII. I will obey all the laws of my country faithfully; and the orders of its monarch, and of all persons appointed to be in authority under its monarch, so far as such laws or commands are consistent with what I suppose to be the law of God; and when they are not, or seem in anywise to need change, I will oppose them loyally and deliberately, not with malicious, concealed, or disorderly violence.

VIII. And with the same faithfulness, and under the limits of the same obedience, which I render to the laws of my country, and the commands of its rulers, I will obey the laws of the Society called St. George, into which I am this day received; and the orders of its masters, and of all persons appointed to be in authority under its masters, so long as I remain a Companion, called of St. George." [1]

Such were the hopes and plans for a better society. "The actual realization," to quote Ruskin's biographer, "was a Master who, when wanted to discuss legal deeds, was often drawing leaves of anagallis tenella; a society of Companions, few and uninfluential; some cottages in Wales; twenty acres of partly cleared woodland in Worcestershire; a few bleak acres in Yorkshire; [2] and a single museum. The large schemes for the reclamation of waste land and the novel use on a great scale of tides and streams shrunk into some minute gardening experiments at Brant-

[1] *Works*, XXVIII, 419.

[2] Cook is evidently in error here, since the "few bleak acres" can only mean a plot of thirteen acres at Totley, in *Derbyshire*. There was a "small plot" in Yorkshire, but (to quote Cook) only of "about three-quarters of an acre."

wood." [1]   The cottages in Wales, eight in number, were the first gift to St. George. They were situated on the high cliffs at Barmouth, overlooking Cardigan Bay. The owner, Mrs. Talbot, offered them to Ruskin in 1874, and he accepted them "at once with very glad thanks. . . . No cottagers," he wrote, "shall be disturbed, but in quiet and slow ways assisted, as each may deserve or wish to better their own houses in sanitary and comfortable points. My principle is to work with the minutest possible touches, but with steady end in view, and by developing as I can the energy of the people I want to help." [2]   Ruskin was as good as his word. He demanded punctual payments of rents but never changed the rate, and he kept up the property out of funds from the Guild. As a result the tenants lived out their lives in contentment, regarding their cottages as homes rather than as temporary dwellings. No doubt much of the success of the enterprise was due to the devoted and direct management of Mrs. Talbot, who was in charge as late as 1900, according to an account by Miss Blanche Atkinson. "Year by year, any little improvement which can add to the comfort of the cottagers is carried out under her orders," says Miss Atkinson; "a larger window here, a new fireplace there, an extra room contrived, as the children begin to grow up. But the chief aim is to keep the cottages at the original low rentals, so that the poor may be able to stay in their old homes; and nothing is done to change the entirely cottage character of the dwellings.

[1] *Life of Ruskin*, II, 335.
[2] *Works*, XXX, intro., XXIX.

Of course, no tenant would be accepted unless of good character; and the knowledge that rent must be paid punctually, that no real discomfort or inconvenience will be overlooked—if it can be remedied—and that each one is personally known, cared for in sickness, and helped in any difficulty, is an immense incentive to good conduct." [1] The second gift to St. George was twenty acres of woodland in Worcestershire, the donation of Mr. George Baker, a member of the Guild and at that time (1876–1877) mayor of Birmingham. "The ground is in copse-wood," said Ruskin, "but good for fruit trees; and shall be cleared and brought into bearing." A beginning was made. Ruskin even thought at one time of building a museum upon the property. But his plans came to nothing. "The Guild," says Cook (1907), "has recently built a good farm-cottage on the land, for the purpose of letting it as a fruit farm." Another experiment in land-holding by the Guild met with much the same fate. "A few of the Sheffield workingmen," said Ruskin, "who admit the possibility of St. George's notions being just, have asked me to let them rent some ground from the Company, whereupon to spend what spare hours they have, of morning or evening, in useful labor." He responded to this appeal by the purchase in 1877 of thirteen acres of "waste" ground some six miles out of Sheffield, at Totley, in Derbyshire. He knew little of the plans of these Sheffield workers, some of whom were shoemakers; but he determined not to interfere, at least until he saw developments. St. George would

[1] *Ruskin's Social Experiment at Barmouth*, 24.

require of them the observance only of "bare first principles—good work, and no moving of machinery by fire." Details of what happened are wanting, but the scheme appears to have fallen through very early as a result of disagreements or misunderstandings. "The proposed allotments," says Cook, who should know, if anyone, "had a short and, I believe, somewhat stormy career, and Ruskin fell back upon a favorite resource on occasions of this kind; that is to say, he called his old gardener, David Downs, to the rescue." Ruskin hoped that the land might be made available for raising fruit trees, and for the cultivation, under glass, of rare European plants. But the climate was inhospitable, and so finally the ground was "brought unto heart" to furnish strawberries, currants, and gooseberries to the Sheffield markets "at a price both moderate and fixed." The master soon lost interest in these waste Derbyshire acres, however, and they were subsequently let to a tenant.[1]

Although these agricultural schemes were of all his experiments in social reconstruction nearest the Master's heart, he found that he could not escape failure, unsupported and alone. He confessed his incapacity to manage the intricate affairs of business,

[1] Ruskin purchased a small parcel of land ("two acres and a few odd yards," he said; "about three-quarters of an acre," said Cook) at Cloughton, near Scarborough, for the use of a member of the Guild, Mr. John Guy. Ruskin looked to this "brave and gentle companion" to show what could be done in "practical and patient country economy." But Mr. Guy withdrew after five years' stay, and the property was rented to another tenant, who was occupying it in 1907. "Of other property," says Cook, "the Guild holds some investments, now (1907) bringing in about £75 per annum."

just as he was in the "midst of the twelfth century divinity of the mosaics of St. Mark's," or some other equally rapturous investigation in the field of art or nature; and he could find no one to assume leadership in his place. But his own special aptitudes found at last a proper expression in the museum of St. George at Sheffield, an enterprise in the best sense successful. One of Ruskin's former students at the Working Men's College, Mr. Henry Swan, had invited him to meet a company of workmen at Walkley, a mile or so from Sheffield. As a result of this visit, he decided in 1875 to establish there the first museum of St. George, and to appoint Mr. Swan as curator. The site selected was the top of a hill "in the midst of green fields," commanding an extensive view over the surrounding country, including the valley of the Don and the woods of Wharncliffe Crags. The building was a small stone cottage, which had to accommodate both the specimens and the curator. To this modest shrine of the muses lovers of beauty came in numbers and from distant lands for many years. Finally the collection became too large for the Walkley cottage, and a new location had to be found. For some years Ruskin cherished the hope of building a marble museum, according to his own ideas, on the St. George land in Worcestershire, but the dream had to remain unrealized for lack of funds. In 1889 he accepted the offer of the Sheffield Corporation of an estate of forty acres known as Meersbrook Park, where the museum might find a permanent home. The Corporation agreed to furnish the land, the house, and the maintenance, while the Guild loaned its treasures for a period of years, which would no doubt be extended indefinitely.

Upon this foundation the Ruskin Museum, as it came to be called, has had a notable record, both as a center for visitors and for students. It became at once the concrete expression for Ruskin of what art might do for the people. It was conceived as a *local* Museum, intended especially for the "laboring multitude," who, in times to come "when none but useful work is done and when all classes are compelled to share in it," will devote their leisure hours no more to the alehouse, but "to the contemplation and study of the works of God, and the learning that complete code of natural history which, beginning with the life and death of the Hyssop on the wall, rises to the knowledge of the life and death of the recorded generations of mankind, and of the visible starry Dynasties of Heaven." [1] It was thus a place for re-creative study, not for idle amusement. And it embodied Ruskin's ideal of what such a place should be,—small, accessible, containing "nothing crowded, nothing unnecessary, nothing puzzling," but only what was good and beautiful of its kind and that fully explained. With characteristic energy and enthusiasm, the Master of St. George devoted much time, down to the end of his working days, collecting and arranging materials for the museum. Illuminated manuscripts, minerals, precious stones, coins, casts, drawings he gave liberally from his own treasures or purchased with funds of the Guild. He engaged a company of young artists to make photographs or

[1] *Works*, XXVIII, 451.

copies of French and Italian art before the ravages of
time or the hand of the restorer had done their irrep-
arable damage. Not until his shattered health
compelled him to put aside every task did he pause in
his efforts to realize his ideal. "Every house of the
Muses," he said, "is an Interpreter's by the wayside,
or rather, a place of oracle and interpretation in one.
And the right function of every museum, to simple
persons, is the manifestation to them of what is lovely
in the life of Nature, and heroic in the life of
Man."

With the museum the work of St. George culmi-
nated but did not end. Its history would not be complete without at least a brief mention of two or three
industrial experiments, all of them visible, though
feeble, realizations of Ruskin's hopes of a new social
order. He had said in *Fors Clavigera* that in St.
George's Society the girls were to learn "to spin,
weave, and sew, and at the proper age to cook all
ordinary food exquisitely." He had expressed more
than once the craftsman's interest in needlework and
in all the art of creating fabrics;—"the true nature of
thread and needle, the structure first of wool and
cotton, of fur and hair and down, hemp, flax, and
silk. . . . The phase of its dyeing. What azures and
emeralds and Tyrian scarlets can be got into fibres of
thread! Then the phase of its spinning. The mystery of that divine spiral, from finest to firmest, which
renders lace possible at Valenciennes;—anchorage
possible, after Trafalgar. Then the mystery of weaving. The eternal harmony of warp and woof; of all
manner of knotting, knitting, and reticulation. . . .

And, finally, the accomplished phase of needlework." [1] Undoubtedly Ruskin would have been happy could he have enlisted the co-operation of women over the countrysides in a revival of domestic arts,—women who should "secure the delivery on demand," he said, "for one price, over at least some one counter in the nearest country town, of entirely good fabric of linen, woollen, and silk; and consider *that* task, for the present, their first duty to Heaven and Earth. . . . I believe myself that they will find the only way is the slow, but simple and sure one, of teaching any girls they have influence or authority over, to spin and weave; and appointing an honest and religious woman for their merchant." [2]

Through the co-operation of two companions of St. George he found opportunity to carry out this interest in the domestic crafts. In 1876 Mr. Rydings of Laxey, Isle of Man, wrote to Ruskin that wool-spinning was still a healthy industry among the women there, although remuneration was so small that the aged and infirm were frequently obliged to leave their spinning-wheels for work in the mills. Ruskin's sympathy was at once aroused and, with the help of Mr. Rydings, he determined to revive spinning and weaving at Laxey. Accordingly a water mill was erected "for the manufacture of the honest thread into honest cloth—dyed indelibly." Farmers brought their wool to the mill and were paid in finished cloth or yarn for home knitting. Much cloth, besides, was made for the outside market. Ruskin never saw the mill. He loaned the Guild's

[1] *Works*, XXIX, 510. [1] *Ibid.*, XXIX, 118.

money to Mr. Rydings for support of the industry, which he hoped to see continued as it began. In the course of time, however, it was found impossible to keep up the enterprise on the basis of hand-spinning and hand-weaving; and so it was given over to the manufacture of woollen cloths. The debt having now been paid, the Guild of St. George had no further connection with the business, and "Laxey homespun" became a thing of the past.

Meantime, through the enthusiasm of another disciple and companion of St. George, Ruskin was to realize his "vision of thread and needlework." It came through the Langdale linen industry, revived by Mr. Albert Fleming among the cottagers of the Westmoreland hills around Coniston. The romantic story is best told in Mr. Fleming's own words, written in 1890: "Scattered about on the fell side were many old women, too blind to sew and too old for hand work, but able to sit by the fireside and spin, if any one would show them how, and buy their yarn. . . . I got myself taught spinning, and then set to work to teach others. I tried my experiment here, in the Langdale Valley, in Westmoreland, half-way between Mr. Ruskin's home at Coniston and Wordsworth's at Rydal. Sixty years ago every cottage here had its wheel, and every larger village its weaver. . ." After much difficulty wheels were made, flax imported from Ireland, and a cottage school of spinning begun. . . . "When a woman could spin a good thread I let her take a wheel home, and gave her the flax, buying it back from her when spun, at the rate of 2s. 6d. per pound of thread. . . . Next came the weaving. In a cellar of Kendal we discovered a loom; it was in twenty pieces, and when we got it home not all the collective wisdom of the village knew how to set it up. Luckily we had a photograph of Giotto's Campanile, and by the help of that the various parts were rightly put together. We then secured an old weaver, and one bright Easter morning saw our first piece of linen woven—the first purely hand-spun and hand-woven linen produced in all broad England in our generation. . . . The next process was to bleach it. . . . As Giotto fixed our loom for us, Homer taught us the true principle of bleaching. . . . Sun, air, and dew were our only chemicals." [1] Mr. Fleming found that people bought the product of his loom, and so the work prospered. "It has spread in many directions," said Cook in 1907, "and there are branches in London and in many parts of the country; but the original industry still flourishes" now at Coniston. [2]

So ends the story of the activities of St. George's Guild. It is generally said that nothing came of them, that they were the dreams of a medieval dreamer, "born out of due time," who longed to revive a thir-

[1] *Works*, XXX, 328–330.

[2] *Ibid*, XXX, *intro.*, XXXVII. Another industry that owed its reorganization to the inspiration of Ruskin was the woollen firm of George Thomson & Co. at Huddersfield. Mr. Thomson was a disciple of Ruskin, was one of the trustees of St. George, and in 1911 was its Master. The new plan rested upon co-partnership. It provided "a sick pay and pension fund"; and adopted the eight-hour day, with fixed wages for all. Half of the net profits went to the workers, half to the consumers. Gradually the workers were to buy the shares of the capital and own the concern. In 1886 Ruskin wrote to Mr. Thomson of the experiment as "the momentous and absolutely foundational step taken by you in all that is just and wise, in the establishment of these relations with your workmen." (*Works*, XXX, 333.)

teenth-century society a little after the pattern of the
fellowship of St. Francis; or, worse still, that they
were the grotesque efforts of a modern Don Quixote,
rushing madly at imaginary evils and making himself
ridiculous before the world. Even Carlyle at first
thought the whole thing a joke. It is true that Ruskin's fancy at times played fast and loose with the
idea of a new society, with the result that his sober
plans, as he confessed, were too much colored with
romance. He thought of a system that should be
fit "for wide European work," and under the name
of Monte Rosa it was to "number its members
ultimately by myriads." He wrote out a fantastic
scheme of government, a kind of feudal hierarchy
beginning with the master, as absolute lord, including
various ranks of companions, and ending at the bottom of the scale with the tenant farmers and hired
workers. And for this society, each class with its
distinguishing costume, he was to devise a medieval
Florentine coinage! But all this was rather the
whimsical amusement of Ruskin than his serious
purpose. Medievalist he was and a disciple of St.
Francis, but he never seriously thought of setting up
pure medievalism in the nineteenth century, as the
actual experiments of St. George abundantly showed.
He disclaimed any idea of founding a colony, or
separate society, after a medieval or communistic
pattern. There was nothing *new* in the laws of St.
George, he protested, "not a single object which had
not been aimed at by good men since the world
began." Undoubtedly what he had most at heart in
all his thinking about the Guild was a fellowship of

workers sworn to live out the gospel of work as it had been preached by Carlyle and himself, and was even then being preached by William Morris. He wanted to see a company of people pledged to a certain individual and social conduct in the places where they already were; pledged to honesty; pledged to earn their living with their own hands and heads; and pledged to use their leisure in the cultivation of their souls. "You are to work," he said, "so far as circumstances admit of your doing so, with your own hands in the production of substantial means of life—food, clothes, house, or fire. . . . What you have done in fishing, fowling, digging, sowing, watering, reaping, milling, shepherding, shearing, spinning, weaving, building, carpentering, slating, coal-carrying, cooking, coster-mongering, and the like,—that is St. George's *work*, and means of power. . . . And the main message St. George brings to you is that *you* will not be degraded by this work nor saddened by it."[1] Surely a dream of restoring honesty and health and happiness to our modern world of workers is not after all such a "frantic" dream!

[1] *Works*, XXIX, 472.

CHAPTER VIII

HERALDS OF THE BETTER ORDER

"There must be a new world, if there is to be any world at all. . . . In the course of long strenuous centuries, I can see the State become what it is actually bound to be, the keystone of a most real 'Organization of Labor,'— and on this Earth a world of some veracity, and some heroism, once more worth living in!"—*Carlyle*.

"Whatever our station in life may be, at this crisis, those of us who mean to fulfil our duty ought first to live on as little as we can; and, secondly, to do all the wholesome work for it we can, and to spend all we can spare in doing all the sure good we can. And sure good is, first in feeding people, then in dressing people, then in lodging people, and lastly in rightly pleasing people, with arts, or sciences, or any other subject of thought."—*Ruskin*.

IT is one of the glories of English literature that it has remained close to the life of the English people. Men of letters in every age of England's history have taken the substance of their art, as well as its inspiration, directly from the traditions, the struggles, the hopes and fears of the men and women who have made up its national life, whether on its political, economic, social, or religious side. Dilettanti and critics from time to time have found fault with a literary art that was (as they thought) everything but literary, that sometimes espoused ethics and eschewed æsthetics, and that often seemed to care at least as much for the welfare of society as for its entertainment. But the creators of art have thought differently. Poets and prosemen alike, to a degree hardly paralleled in any other country of modern times, have been unable or unwilling to alienate their art from the social life about them; or where their more purely imaginative interests have conflicted with the duties of the hour they have been ready, like Milton, to give their pen to the services of the state, even though the voice of the muse should for the while be silenced. No age of English literature is more conspicuous in this respect than the Victorian, for the very good reason, no doubt, that in this age more than in any other, the problems of society became suddenly complex and urgent, threatening disturbances, both material and spiritual, of a kind undreamed of by generations that had gone before. Consequently the greater writers of this period, with few exceptions, turned their attention to the "condition of England question," not with the purpose of exciting the curiosity of a sophisticated public with unusual, out-of-the-way matters, nor with the latter-day notion of exploiting a segment of society in the interest of imaginative literature. The great Victorians turned to the world around them, because, seeing that it was a world disturbed to its center by new and ominous social phenomena, they saw also that unless something were done to awaken the public heart and mind to a sense of the vast evils and the vast injustice in the changed industrial order, nothing might save England from a catastrophic disaster such as an earlier generation had witnessed across the Channel. And so literature became a handmaid of reform. The social ideals of a great epoch were

touched, and, to a degree beyond any man's comput-
ing, were transformed by the magic of art. Let any
one who doubts the truth of this assertion, contrast
the public conscience of England during the last
twenty years of the nineteenth century with the
public conscience during the period stretching for
fifty years back of 1880; and then let him consider
the content as well as the immense vogue and force
of English letters during the same period, and he will
be a dull inquirer if he be not convinced that for the
higher standards of social justice which the people of
the later decades possessed over those of the earlier
period they owed a large debt to the Victorian writers
who had already passed from the stage, or whose
work was practically done. The novels of Dickens,
Thackeray, and George Eliot, of Mrs. Gaskell,
Disraeli, Kingsley, and Charles Reade, the poetry of
Tennyson, the essays of Arnold, each and all in their
various ways, told powerfully in the direction of fuller
knowledge of social abuses or problems, and of more
humane ideals in the work of suppression or solution.
Of all the forces in Victorian letters that affected the
great currents of industrial and social life, however,
the writings of Carlyle and Ruskin were probably the
most potent in their own time and most influential
upon leaders who came after them.

Their challenge and their program have been
reviewed in detail in the preceding chapters, with
some reference to the circumstances out of which
their message arose. It will be necessary in conclusion to sketch the broader outlines only of their
work, for the sake of comparison and contrast, and as

a background against which to set down some aspects of their influence upon their time and ours. The comparisons are more numerous, if not more striking, than the contrasts. It is not to be forgotten in this connection that Ruskin, when referring to his social philosophy, always regarded himself as the pupil and disciple of Carlyle. He spoke the truth when in 1880 he wrote to a correspondent of himself and his master as follows: "We feel so much alike, that you may often mistake one for the other now." Their attacks upon their time were indeed in many essentials identical. Both looked upon the era in which they lived as one of transition from an older settled feudalistic order to one whose ultimate form no man could predict, but which all the signs of the times seemed to declare was likely to be in some sense democratic. To Carlyle and Ruskin, looking out upon a world in which the masses were almost to a man unenlightened, democracy was synonymous with anarchy and must be put down; for so they interpreted the popular movements around them in the light of the revolutions of 1789, 1830, 1848, and 1871. But the threatened upheaval of roaring Demos from below nevertheless meant that something was rotten in the state of affairs and that steps must be taken, and taken quickly, to remove the cause of disease in the body politic. And so they attacked the extravagance, the indifference, the cupidity of the rich,—the Mammon worshipers and all their breed, who clothed themselves in purple and fine linen and doffed the world aside. They attacked the notion that human labor was a commodity and that workmen were only so many "hands." They held up before their contemporaries the misery and ignorance of the poor, and all the evils of an industrial system erected upon the foundations of *laissez-faire*. Radical and conservative in mingled strains, at once communistic and Tory, in economics reddest of the red, in politics often more reactionary than the House of Lords, they yet broke into the smug and detached circles of Victorian society as with the force of thunderbolts, clearing the air for wiser thinking and healthier living.

And into this clearer atmosphere they projected proposals of reform in most cases alike in principle and, underneath all the impetuous force of the challenge, supported by a spirit essentially and typically British in its conservatism; for they knew that thoroughgoing social reconstruction could be effected, if at all, only gradually, a little to-day, a little to-morrow, and yet more in the years to come. Carlyle would have entirely agreed with Ruskin, who said that "all useful change must be slow and by progressive and visibly secure stages. The evils of centuries cannot be defied and conquered in a day." [1] All the more were they conservative, because they believed that reform to be effectual must reach down to men and not be content with legislative adjustments. And so we hear, from *Sartor Resartus* to *Fors Clavigera*, a reiterated declaration of the rights and dignities and possibilities of the soul of man irrespective of station in life, better than all machinery, bigger than all theories, richer than all the wealth of the British

[1] *Works*, XXIX, 548.

Isles. The whole message of Carlyle and Ruskin was in effect a challenge,—a challenge to the leaders of their time to realize that infinitely the most important element in industry was the human factor, and that what the worker wanted more than all else was justice and freedom, the indefeasible rights of his spiritual nature. This was first and fundamental, but always with the implication of an unchanging status in the workers as a class. What the workers needed next was guidance rather than political power. In a time when the world was "becoming dismantled" and when the destinies were spinning new "organic filaments," Carlyle and Ruskin looked to an aristocracy for leadership, an aristocracy of talents to be regenerated under pressure of the immense responsibilities of the new era. They looked to the *aristoi* to express through the state,—that is to say, through constitutional government,—a control over social forces far more complete than most people then dreamed of, and to be exercised in accordance with the findings of a wide investigation as to the conditions and needs of the people. A wise and just centralized authority would accomplish many things. It would throw out the policy of *laissez-faire*, root and branch. It would organize labor, gradually admitting it to some form of partnership with industry. It would extend education to the masses. And in this guidance of labor to a better organization both Carlyle and Ruskin believed that leaders would find suggestions and inspiration from medieval times; for in those days there were association and freedom in work, and the various classes in the social order were held together not by cash-nexus alone, but by ties of human fellowship.

Their combined program of reform was thus socialistic rather than socialist. Its worth and power are obvious, and of these qualities we shall say more presently. But its weakness is no less obvious. It was at once too individualistic and, especially in the case of Ruskin, too paternalistic. Both Carlyle and Ruskin regarded the masses too much as individual units when it came to *moral* reform, and they regarded the leaders too much as an independent controlling class when it came to *political* reform. This is a criticism which suggests the whole force of Mazzini's vigorous attack upon Carlyle (an attack that might with equal justice have been made upon Ruskin), to the effect that Carlyle wholly overlooked the true conception of modern democracy as a movement in which "the *collective* thought was seeking to supplant the individual thought in the social organism." [1] To Carlyle as to Ruskin the sins of society were fundamentally the sins of individual men and women far more than they were the evil fruits of a vicious system. And on the political side, they could not see, as did John Stuart Mill, that political freedom might educate the masses for increased responsibility and that the cure for democracy might be more democracy.

It is easier from the vantage point of our time, however, to find fault with the ultra-aristocratic

[1] *The Writings of Thomas Carlyle*, in Mazzini's *Essays*, 21. *Cf.* "Mr. Carlyle comprehends only the *individual;* the true sense of the unity of the human race escapes him. He sympathizes with all men, but it is with the separate life of each, and not with their collective life." (*ibid.*, 124.)

politics of these great Victorians than it would have been in theirs, sixty and seventy years ago, when individualism was still a rampant creed, and when any form of collectivism as a political force was practically unheard of. Carlyle and Ruskin were by no means alone in their fear of what might happen if political power should suddenly be transferred to the masses. Elections were notoriously corrupt. Bribery was open and unabashed. The populace was densely ignorant, and was ever and anon boiling with discontent and threatening to explode. Irresponsible crowds, many of them hardly more than hoodlums, were likely to be set off by popular firebrands like the Chartist, Feargus O'Connor, who talked wildly about "physical force without cease," and who in a speech at Manchester in 1838 said: "If peace giveth not law, I am for war to the knife." [1] General Sir Charles Napier, who saw the starved and desperate poor in the manufacturing towns of Lancashire in 1839, declared that it looked to him as if "the falling of an Empire were beginning."[2] Popular uprisings in Europe in 1848 were put down only by strong military power, sometimes with terrible cost of life, as in the street fighting in Paris, June 23–26. Events were so portentous in those years that even so rationalistic an observer as John Stuart Mill, reflecting upon the questions which the progress of democracy was pressing forward, remarked in a letter (1852) to a friend: "It is to be decided whether Europe shall

[1] Carlyle once told Lecky, the historian, that two great curses seemed to him to be eating away the heart and worth of the English people,—drink and "stump oratory." (Lecky, *Historical and Political Essays*, 112.)

[2] Hovell, *The Chartist Movement*, 136.

enter peacefully and prosperously into a better order
of things, or whether the new ideas will be inaugu-
rated by a century of war and violence like that which
followed the Reformation of Luther." [1] Was it safe to
place the ballot into the hands of ignorant and pro-
pertyless men, capable of mob violence? Macaulay,
Lord John Russell, and Sir Robert Peel did not think
so, for in the debate in the House of Commons on the
famous Chartist petition of 1842, they led in an
attack upon universal manhood suffrage and carried
the day by an overwhelming vote. Opposition of
course subsided with the years, but it was very much
alive even after the Reform Act of 1867, as is shown
in the political writings of Herbert Spencer, Maine,
Fitzjames Stephen, and Bagehot.[2] No man was
more liberal in his political thought than Mill and yet
to the end of his days Mill feared the ignorance and
inferiority of the working classes; and to check their

[1] *Letters of John Stuart Mill*, I, 170. *Cf.* Rose, *The Rise of Democracy*,
Ch. IX. *e. g.*—"When Louis Philippe, King of the French, escaped out of
Paris in a cab; when Metternich, after controlling the destines of Central
and Southern Europe, was fain to flee from Vienna in a washerwoman's
cart; when Italian Dukes and German translucencies hastily granted
democratic constitutions, to petition for which had recently been a sure
passport to the dungeon, could not a monster demonstration of the men
of London force the Charter on a trembling and penitent Parliament?"
(137). *Cf.* also, Mazzini, *Europe: Its Condition* (1862), *e. g.*—"For sixty
years Europe has been convulsed by a series of political struggles which
have assumed all aspects by turns; which have raised every conceivable
flag, from that of pure despotism to that of anarchy; from the organization of the *bourgeoise* in France and elsewhere as the dominant caste, to
the *jacqueries* of the peasants of Gallicia. Thirty revolutions have taken
place. Two or three royal dynasties have been engulfed in the abyss of
popular fury," etc. (*Essays*, 265.)

[2] In his introduction to the second edition (1872) to his *English Constitution* (1867), Bagehot shows throughout a fear of political power in the
hands of workingmen. He feared subservience to them on the part of
politicians, and he feared combinations among themselves as a class

power he favored plurality of votes for the better qualified citizens, the kind of thing (at least in principle) which Ruskin endorsed and which there is no reason to suppose Carlyle also would not have supported could he have once seen its effective establishment.[1] It should be understood, moreover, in a consideration of the suffrage situation in those days, that among the ultra-radical thinkers there was still a good deal of equalitarian philosophy in the air, a philosophy that went back to Bentham and Adam Smith and beyond them to the French Revolution and Rousseau, saying that men were by nature equal in capacity and different only because their environment had differed.   To Carlyle and Ruskin such thinking gave the lie to the plainest facts of life, and was full of peril to the state.   Something of the fierce scorn which they at times let loose upon prison reformers and sentimental prophets of humanitarianism must therefore be attributed to their fear of the spread of this dangerous heresy concerning equality.[2]

against the other classes,—"an evil," he says, "of the first magnitude. . . . I am exceedingly afraid of the ignorant multitudes of the new constituencies."

[1] See Ruskin's proposed second letter (1852) to the *Times* on election, *Works*, XII, 600.   The letters were suppressed by Ruskin's father.

[2] The severest criticism that can be directed against the *political* thought of Carlyle and Ruskin is not that they would have thrown out the ballot, for they would not; nor that they believed in despotism rather than in constitutional government (a travesty of their creed).   It is that they had no faith that the responsibility of the ballot (with education) would raise the standard of life among the masses.   They would first raise the standard of life and *then* bestow the ballot.   The paradox remains, therefore, that the prophets who habitually championed the cause of the workers and who eloquently preached the gospel of the worth of the individual *soul*, always distrusted the capacity of the masses for political power. They did not believe that their contentment depended upon their voting.

Admitting the paradox, the critics of Carlyle (for he has been more

Enough has been said, however, to indicate their position among their contemporaries on a great political question of the day, and it is time to turn from comparisons to certain striking contrasts. Ruskin came to the study of industry and society from art, and from art he brought with him a gospel of work, not more powerful nor more sane than Carlyle's, but richer and with more promise in it for the future. Both stood for self-expression in work, but for Carlyle it was the expression of duty, of grim fidelity to a task, a task generally unpleasant but needing to be done, and done without whimpering. Carlyle felt that toil kept men out of sin, and that toil, manfully accomplished, added immensely to the nobility of a man's nature. Ruskin believed all this as an antidote to laziness or dissipation and as a way of getting the rough work of the world done. But he went further, at least for wise men in a wisely ordered society. He preached the gospel of joy in creative effort. He taught that it was *right* work only that made men happy. In art, the symbol of man's highest felicity in self-expression, he read the significance of work on a wider scale. A man must find in his appointed task something more than an expression of duty; he must find in it an outlet for his

assailed on this point than Ruskin) are not justified in saying that he provides no machinery for the discovery of his hero-governor. It is true that he disclaims any responsibility for inventing machinery, and that he is vague and general as to methods of political reform; but he everywhere assumes that the established ways (ballot, public meetings, representative assemblies) will be used by those who have the capacity to use them. The able men will be placed in power, and kept there, by those who can recognize ability when they see it, be they toilworn craftsmen or titled aristocrats.

creative capacities, his loyalties to society, his crav-
ings for fellowship, and even for his spirit of play.
And along with this newer gospel of work Ruskin
brought from art his hatred of the ugliness in modern
life. Hence he preached far more than did Carlyle
(who in fact only touched on the subject here and
there) against the dirt and noise that industrialism
had brought in its train. Accordingly, one of his
favorite remedies for social regeneration was increased
beauty in our daily life, in our cities, and in our
homes.

For the reason that he came to industry by the
pathway of art, Ruskin had a truer appreciation than
Carlyle of the grinding slavery of machine labor.
Mechanism for Carlyle was, as we have seen, a broad
term to cover all the manifestations of materialism in
the nineteenth century, and as such he laid upon it
titanian blows, such as the hands of Ruskin could not
deliver. Mechanism for Ruskin meant division of
labor and a worse than serfdom, in the factory system. It meant the negation of his whole gospel of
joy in work. Consequently his attack upon it, while
less powerful and dramatic than Carlyle's, was far
more reasoned and carried with it far more hope for
the future. Ruskin's entire social program, in fact,
although nowhere supported by so impressive a
personality as Carlyle's, was far more detailed and
went much further in the right directions. Carlyle
never pretended to write political economy and he
suggested specific economic remedies hesitatingly.
Ruskin marched straight into the camp of the enemy,
striking about him, to the right and to the left, and

sometimes making a sad spectacle of himself. But he did good service,—most of all, probably, in socializing economics; for he showed that man cannot be economically considered without being educationally, ethically, and even religiously considered also. He developed, indeed, much further than did Carlyle the idea of a man's work in the world as a *social* service, and he understood better than his master the possibility of a changed attitude in the social consciousness towards servile labor, towards the trades and business generally, and towards the pecuniary reward for work.

If now in conclusion we turn to a brief consideration of the influence of this social philosophy of Carlyle and Ruskin, we shall find reason to believe that it told powerfully upon a wide circle of intellectual and social leaders during the years from 1835 to 1880. This was a period in English life of unrest, criticism, and transition. As Arthur Hugh Clough wrote in 1848, there seemed to be

"Only infinite jumble and mess and dislocation."

To most people, particularly to the working classes, as to Dickens's Stephen Blackpool in *Hard Times* (1854), the industrial world was "a' a muddle." Even at the end of the period, Matthew Arnold, most discerning and dispassionate of observers, declared in his essay *Equality* (1878): "We are trying to live on with a social organization of which the day is over." The government during this time had no far-reaching policy of social reform. Parliament, under the influence of liberal-utilitarian policies, was a good

deal less actively engaged in creating new agencies
of control than in removing old disabilities against
Catholics, Jews, and Dissenters, and old restrictions,
such as the Corn Laws, the Navigation Laws, and
the various import duties that were hampering
freedom of trade.[1] It was the formative period for
organized labor, marked up and down by many acute
industrial disturbances, which served, however, to
warn the public of the growing strength of trade
unionism.[2] Employers, almost to a man, were still
militantly individualistic, declaring that the administration of industry belonged to them and that they
would deal with the workers only as individuals.[3]
Karl Marx was not much felt as a force in the English
world of labor before 1880. The Fabians had not yet
organized, and Henry George's *Progress and Poverty*,
a book of tremendous significance, was not published
until 1879. In the intellectual circles of that time
two groups were conspicuous above all others, the
utilitarians and the men of the Oxford movement.

[1] There was of course always a certain political current in favor of state
interference, stronger towards the end of the period than at the beginning.
Factory Acts were passed from time to time to regulate hours of labor or
conditions; and in 1870 the great Education Act was passed and amended
in 1876, making elementary education compulsory. It is interesting to
find that Carlyle was one of the earliest advocates of state control. At a
time when there was wide-spread opposition to the Poor Law Amendment
Act of 1834, which first established a central control of poor relief, Carlyle
(in *Chartism*) welcomed the law: "supervised by the central government,
in what spirit soever executed, is supervisal from a centre."

[2] In 1868 occurred the first meeting of the Trade-Union Congress. In
1871 the Trade Unions Act recognized the legality of unions; and in 1875
the repeal of the Criminal Law Amendment Act (passed in 1871, virtually
making unionism illegal) fully established collective bargaining as legal.
The Independent Labor Party was not formed until 1892.

[3] *Cf.* Webb, *History of Trade Unionism*, 250.

One, chiefly commercial, held up the glories of English industry and trade, and preached material progress; the other, chiefly clerical, glorified the Church as the savior of society: and neither group voiced the great social stirrings of the people. Even John Stuart Mill, in some respects the most humane and most prophetic intellect of his time, and the high priest of the Liberals, never entirely shook off the effects of his earlier and narrower utilitarianism. "*Laissez-faire*," he said in his *Principles of Political Economy*, "should be the general practice: every departure from it, unless required by some great good, is a certain evil." [1] Economics, in utilitarian circles at least, was not yet socialized, and if social problems were discussed at all the discussion was generally carried on in the high and dry atmosphere of Ricardian principles—rent, value, consumption, production, profits, losses,—an atmosphere far removed from the dust and din of the toiling masses who had come into existence in the wake of the industrial revolution.

Into this atmosphere Carlyle and Ruskin came as with the effect of an electric storm, bringing men once more face to face with the elemental forces of life and arousing within them the hope of a better day. From 1835, for twenty-five years, Carlyle (to consider him first) was the dominant literary personality of England. Coming into his presence, out of the academic or social life of early Victorian times was, as Lady Ashburton remarked, "like returning from some conventional world to the human race." His books, his

[1] *Principles*, 950: Ashley's Edition of 1909.

lectures, his home, were the sources and center of an extraordinary personal force that fell powerfully upon many intellectual and spiritual leaders of that day, old and young, but chiefly young. The voice of Carlyle to the generations of college men in 1840–1850 was no doubt mainly a voice to awaken and thrill, but it carried tidings of the oppressed poor and a very definite report that all was not well in the great outside world of industry. *Sartor Resartus*, the *Essays*, *Past and Present*, were indeed a new charter of freedom to the men of the English and Scottish universities. But they were more; for they proclaimed the spirit of democracy even while they condemned the method of democracy. As Professor MacCunn says: "It would be nearer the truth to affirm that though all the political predictions which Carlyle ever penned were falsified, though he were proved wrong in his forecasts and Mill and Mazzini right, he would still remain one of the great political writers of the century. . . . For the root and the fruit of democracy—what are they but the recognition of the worth, dignity and possibilities of the individual life, however flickering and obscure? Carlyle joins hands with Mill and Mazzini here. He outdoes them. No writer in our literature, it is safe to say, has done more for this, the essence of the democratic spirit, than this sworn foe of political democracy." [1] It is difficult to believe that readers of Car-

---

[1] MacCunn, *Six Radical Thinkers*, 163–4. Mazzini, too, recognized (1843) the democratic spirit of Carlyle: "Amidst the noise of machinery, wheels, and steam-engines, he has been able to distinguish the stifled plaint of the prisoned spirit, the sigh of millions." (*Essays*, 115.)

lyle could have escaped these social implications in his thought. Emerson recognized them fully in his review of *Past and Present* in the *Dial*. "It is a political tract," he said, "and since Burke, since Milton, we have had nothing to compare with it. . . . The book of a powerful and accomplished thinker, who has looked with naked eyes at the dreadful political signs in England for the last few years."[1] Lecky, the historian, who was far from being a Carlylean, considered Carlyle's social influence upon his generation to have been very great, particularly in his resistance to *laissez-faire*, in his support of the cause of increased government regulation, and in his championship of education, emigration, and better relations between masters and men. "It will be found," said Lecky, "that although he may not have been wiser than those who advocated the other side, yet his words contained exactly that kind of truth which was most needed or most generally forgotten, and his reputation will steadily rise."[2] The testimony of Edward Caird, successor to Jowett as Master of Balliol, is to much the same effect. Caird was a student at the University of Glasgow in 1850–1856, and at Oxford in 1860–1863. Carlyle, he says "was the greatest literary influence of my student days. . . And undoubtedly, at that time, Carlyle was the author who exercised the most powerful charm upon young men who were beginning to think. . . . Nor was he merely a student who cast new light on the past; he was inspired with a passion for social reform,

---

[1] Emerson, *Works*, Centenary Edition, XII, 379.
[2] *Carlyle's Message to his Age* (1891), in *Historial Essays*, 106.

which at least in this country,[1] was then felt by few.
He expressed, almost for the first time in English,
that disgust at the mean achievements of what we
call civilization, that generous wrath at the arbitrary
limitation of its advantages, that deep craving for a
better order of social life, which is the source of so
many of the most important social and political
movements of the present day." [2] It is needless to
accumulate testimony where the evidence is so pre-
ponderatingly in the same scale, but one further
statement may perhaps be allowed, since it comes
from a critic who in his thinking was much nearer to
Mill than to Carlyle, and whose opinion therefore has
exceptional weight,—the statement of Leslie Stephen.
In his *English Utilitarians* he says: "It must be
allowed, I think, that such men as Carlyle and
Emerson, for example, vague and even contradictory
as was their teaching, did more to rouse lofty aspiration and to moralize political creeds, though less for
the advancement of sound methods of inquiry, than
the teaching of the Utilitarians." [3]

[1] Caird was addressing the Dialectic Society of the University of Glasgow.
[2] *The Genius of Carlyle*, in *Essays on Literature and Philosophy*, I, 233-4.
The biographer of Caird says that "throughout his career as Master he
delivered impressive lay-sermons on social problems in the College Hall,
and occasionally at Toynbee Hall." (*D. N. B.*) Since he was all his life
an admirer of Carlyle, may we not believe that even as Master the old
influence was at work?
[3] *English Utilitarians*, III, 477. Stephen acknowledged the influence of
Carlyle upon himself. In letters to C. E. Norton he said: "Certainly
there is no one now (1880) who is to the rising generation what Mill and
Carlyle were to us. . . . Nobody, I think, could ever put so much
character in every sentence. . . . It seems to me as if he had fuel enough
to keep a dozen steam-engines going. . . . He fascinates me like nobody
else." (Maitland's *Life and Letters of Leslie Stephen*, 341, 377-8.) Steph-

Who, the reader may ask, were the men touched as Stephen has described in this extraordinary tribute? They were mainly the young intellectuals, as we have seen, beginners in the voyage of life, who, as Froude has told us in his great biography, were drifting without chart or compass and whom Carlyle brought to land. "To the young, the generous, to every one who took life seriously, who wished to make an honorable use of it," says Froude, "his words were like the morning reveille. . . . Amidst the controversies, the arguments, the doubts, the crowding uncertainties of forty years ago, Carlyle's voice was to the young generation of Englishmen like the sound of 'ten thousand trumpets' in their ears." And he adds

en's brother, Sir James Fitzjames Stephen, although a follower of Mill, was strongly drawn to Carlyle. He found the later Mill "sentimental," and he turned sympathetically to Carlyle, whose writings in their "contempt for haphazard, hand-to-mouth modes of legislation, the love of vigorous administration on broad, intelligible principles, entirely expressed his own feeling." (*Life of Sir James Fitzjames Stephen*, by Leslie Stephen, 315.)

Among many other statements as to the social influence of Carlyle, the following may be cited: "It was not his mission to legislate, but to inspire legislators. Every man who since his time has tried to lift politics above party has owed something directly or indirectly to his influence, and the best have owed the most." (Richard Garnett, *Life of Carlyle*, 72.) "One of Mr. Carlyle's chief and just glories is, that for more than forty years he has clearly seen, and kept constantly and conspicuously in his own sight and that of his readers, the profoundly important crisis in the midst of which we are living. The moral and social dissolution in progress about us, and the enormous peril of sailing blindfold and haphazard, without rudder or compass or chart, have always been fully visible to him, and it is no fault of his if they have not become equally plain to his contemporaries." (Morley, *Miscellanies*, 137.) "His great and real work was the attack on Utilitarianism. . . . It is his real glory that he was the first to see clearly and say plainly the great truth of our time; that the wealth of the state is not the prosperity of the people. . . . In this matter he is to be noted in connection with national developments much later; for he thus became the first prophet of the Socialists." (Chesterton, *Victorian Age in Literature*, 55.)

that in the practical objects at which Carlyle was aiming Carlyle was more radical than the radicals! [1] If we inquire who belonged to this company of elect spirits, we can readily recall the names of many, each long since placed in his niche of fame. There was Emerson, who made his pilgrimage to Scotland in 1833 to talk with the solitary thinker whose *Essays* had already helped to quicken his own awakening thought. There was John Stuart Mill, a man utterly different from Carlyle, but a man whose hard-won victory over the cramped utilitarianism in which he had been reared owed encouragement from the mystic radical of Craigenputtock. In his *Autobiography* he generously acknowledged "Carlyle's earlier writings as one of the channels through which I received the influences which enlarged my early narrow creed. . . . The wonderful power with which he put (his truths) forth made a deep impression upon me, and I was during a long period one of his most fervent admirers; but the good his writings did me, was not as a philosophy to instruct, but as poetry to animate." [2] There were Charles Buller and John Sterling, early removed by death from a stage on which they were destined to play brilliant parts; each of whom, along with many others, came under a fascination best expressed by Sterling a few weeks before his end in a letter to Carlyle: "Towards me it is still more true than towards England that no man has been and done like you." [3] There were Maurice and Kingsley

---

[1] *Life of Carlyle*, III, 248–251.

[2] *Autobiography*, 174, 175. *Cf. Letters of Mill*, I, 28.

[3] Carlyle's *Life of Sterling*, 229. Sterling's full-length appreciation of Carlyle was his essay in the *London and Westminster Review* for 1839. In

and Dickens, all of whom at one time or another felt
the energizing power of the Chelsea Prometheus.[1]
And there were Froude and Ruskin, foremost among

his letters to Emerson there are a number of enthusiastic references to
Carlyle: *Correspondence of Emerson and Sterling*, 17, 26, 34, also, E. W.
Emerson's introductory note. Charles Buller (1806–1848) was one of the
most brilliant members of the radical group of his day, including Roe-
buck, Mill, Grote, Molesworth, and Macaulay. Carlyle tutored him in his
youth during months from August, 1822, to the summer of 1824. "When
we hear," says Richard Garnett, "that Charles Buller's principal fault
was then (*i. e.*, in student days) considered to be indolence, and remember
that he lived to frame in conjunction with Edward Gibbon Wakefield the
Durham Report, the charter of Colonial self-government, and died
President of the Poor Law Board, with his foot on the threshold of the
Cabinet, we may conclude that Carlyle's influence was precisely what he
required." (*Life of Carlyle*, 35.) Carlyle's parting memorial to Buller in
the *Examiner* for December, 1848, is full of the love of an older for a
younger friend. "In the coming storms of trouble one radiant element
will be wanting now. . . . He was not the man to grapple, in its dark
and deadly dens, with the Lernæan coil of Social Hydras; perhaps not
under any circumstances: but he did, unassisted, what he could; faithfully himself did something, nay something truly considerable."
[1] The Christian Socialists, Maurice and Kingsley, were as unlike
Carlyle in certain directions as Mill was in others, and yet they too were
strongly influenced. "Maurice says he has been more edified by Carlyle's
Lectures than by anything he has heard for a long while, and that he has
the greatest reverence for Carlyle, but that it is not reciprocal, for he is
sure Carlyle thinks him a 'sham.' " [From a letter of Strachey (1838),
quoted in *Life of Maurice* by his son, I, 250.] In a notable letter (1862)
written to J. M. Ludlow, after Maurice had had a long conversation
(with many differences) with Carlyle, Maurice refers to Carlyle as "a man
who has taught *me* so much." (*Ibid.*, II, 404). Kingsley was far nearer to
Carlyle than was Maurice, both in temper and thought, and owed far
more to Carlyle's stimulating force. He read the *Essays* and the *French
Revolution* while an undergraduate at Cambridge and was "utterly
delighted." His biographers testify to the "remarkable effect" (the
words are Mrs. Kingsley's) on his mind of the writings of Carlyle. *Alton
Locke*, probably Kingsley's most effective work for social reform, was
refused by the first publisher to whom it was offered and it was then
accepted by Chapman through the friendly offices of Carlyle, who was
"right glad myself to hear of a new explosion, a salvo of red-hot shot
against the devil's dung-heap from that particular battery." (*Charles
Kingsley, Letters and Memorials of his Life*, 128.) Readers of *Alton Locke*
do not need to be reminded how much of Carlyle it contains. Dickens

disciples, of whom further account here would be superfluous. The roll could easily be extended, as all students of Carlyle know, but we may well break it off with a brief reference to two other names. One is the name of W. E. Forster, Bradford manufacturer, social reformer, Gladstonian statesman, and author of the Elementary Education Act of 1870 already several times referred to. Forster knew Carlyle intimately and acknowledged his influence freely. "If Carlyle's companionship," he said in 1847, "has had any mental effect upon me, it has been to give me a greater desire and possibly an increased power to discern the real 'meanings of things,' to go straight to the truth wherever its hiding-place, and sometimes his words, not so much by their purport as by their tone and spirit, sounded through me like the blast of a trumpet, stirring all my powers to the battle of life." "Carlyle's writings," says Forster's biographer, "exercised their fascinating influence over his mind, and every day of his life during his first decade at Bradford (*i. e.*, 1842–1852) seemed to be marked by a new stage in the growth of his active interest in the social politics of the time." [1]   The other name,

was a fervent admirer of the Chelsea sage. To him he dedicated *Hard Times* (1854), and owed much to him for the inspiration of one of his best Christmas stories, *The Chimes* (1844). "I would go at all times," said Dickens, "farther to see Carlyle than any man alive." The *French Revolution* he read, as he says in his extravagant way, "for the 500th time," and of course drew from it no little of the inspiration that helped to create *A Tale of Two Cities* (1859).

[1] *Life of Forster*, by T. Wemyss Reid, 119, 81. It was Carlyle's mention of Thomas Cooper, a famous Chartist, that brought Forster into touch with Cooper. Forster was very active in Chartist meetings and disturbances, especially at Bradford, and was deeply and influentially interested all his life in social conditions.

presently to be mentioned more prominently in connection with Ruskin, is that of William Morris, who
as a young man heard and believed the gospel of work
as preached in the early writings of Carlyle. Morris
read Carlyle at Oxford, and according to his biographer, Mackail, Carlyle shared with Ruskin the
strongest influence that Morris received from prose
authors, an influence that held him to the end.[1] In
the *Oxford and Cambridge Magazine*, published in
1856 by undergraduates mainly under the leadership
of Morris, there were five articles of review and
praise of Carlyle,[2] to whom (the writer says) "we
owe that growing seriousness of tone, which has now
won a place even in novels, and from kindred minds
(for example Kingsley's) receives an expression only
less ardent than his own. . . . To me they (*i. e.*,
Carlyle's thoughts and counsels) appear practical in
the highest sense; planted in the very loftiest conception of human duty and destiny, and in a clear discernment of the divine Laws written in the main
facts of every Social matter that he examines. . . .
So practical are they, that I often wish that Carlyle
had not been one of England's Writers, but one of
England's Governors!"[3] Youthful enthusiasm could
scarcely go further. It was well, no doubt, that the
enthusiasm *was* youthful and would sober down with

[1] *Life of Morris*, I, 219; *cf.* also, II, 28, 76. In 1885 when Morris sent
his list of the "Best Hundred Books" to the *Pall Mall Gazette* (the list
contained but fifty-four titles), he included "Carlyle's Works" in a place
with Sir Thomas More and Ruskin. (*Collected Works of Morris*, XXII,
intro. XVI.)

[2] Although probably not written by Morris they could hardly have
appeared without his approval.

[3] *Oxford and Cambridge Magazine* (bound volume), 669, 770.

age. But where shall we look for better evidence of the fire that Carlyle kindled in the hearts of young England from 1835 to 1860?

It was from 1860 onward that Ruskin's influence began to count most for social and economic reform. By this time the voice of Carlyle had become, as Arnold declared, "sorely strained, over-used, and misused," and his direct effect as a personal force had begun to wane. Ruskin's personality, although distinguished in an eminent degree, never captured his contemporaries as did the personality of Carlyle. But his thought, apart from its stimulating moral quality, has been more fruitful than Carlyle's, because it has carried with it a richer and more definite social program, a program already fulfilled in various ways. His writings, particularly *Unto This Last* and *Time and Tide* came upon many minds like a new gospel and awakened within them lasting impulses for direct social action. Illustrations of this effect have already been offered in previous chapters, including reference to such workers as Frederic Harrison, F. J. Furnivall, Arnold Toynbee, and Miss Octavia Hill.[1]

---

[1] Harrison, Ruskin's biographer in the *English Men of Letters* series, has recorded numerous testimonies of his debt to Ruskin: *e. g.*, "Ruskin's essays *Unto This Last* which I read as they appeared in numbers in the *Cornhill Magazine* in 1860, filled me as with a sense of a new gospel on this earth, and with a keen desire to be in personal touch with the daring spirit who had defied the Rabbis of the current economics." (*Autobiographical Memoirs*, I, 230.) Furnivall, when a young man, met Ruskin (in 1849). "Thus began," he says, "a friendship which was for many years the chief joy of my life." (*D. N. B.*) It was Furnivall who brought Ruskin into touch with Maurice, and thus into active relations with the Working Men's College. Arnold Toynbee, whose connection with the Hinksey Diggers has already been described, lectured to popular audiences on economic questions (the lectures are now gathered into the notable volume, *Industrial Revolution*), and lived for a time in quarters in Lon-

"Probably none of his experiments," says Ruskin's principal biographer and editor, Sir E. T. Cook, "will have had so permanent and so fruitful an influence towards the solution of modern problems as the demonstration which he enabled Miss Octavia Hill to give in model landlordism. Ruskin was fond of preaching what has been called the 'slum crusade' in his lectures at Oxford, and the movement for University and College 'Settlements' owes not a little to his exhortations." Cook's evidence of the power of *Unto This Last* is no less pertinent. Although this book sold slowly at first (the edition of 1862 was not exhausted in ten years), its circulation greatly increased when the publication of it was transferred in 1873 to Mr. George Allen. "A few years later," says Cook, "Ruskin re-issued the book on his own account, and the rate of sale during the following thirty years was 2000 per annum. Ruskin was told of a working man who, being too poor to buy the book, had copied it out word for word. Subsequently a selection of extracts, sold at a penny, was circulated widely among the working classes, and the book has been translated into French, German, and Italian. . . . When the Parliament of 1906 was elected, there was a great hubbub about the large contingent of Labor Members, and an ingenious journalist sent circulars to them asking them to state, What were the Books that had Influenced them? Some said one, and some another; but the book which appeared in the greatest

don East End, working for the poor and seeking to understand their life. Toynbee Hall, in East London, the pioneer institution in Settlement work, was named after him, as a tribute to his educational and social work among the poor.

number of lists was Ruskin's *Unto This Last*."[1]
Additional proof of Ruskin's effect upon the working
class is furnished by William Morris in his lecture on
Art and Socialism (1884): "Apart from any trivial
words of my own, I have been surprised to find such a
hearty feeling toward John Ruskin among working-
class audiences: they can see the prophet in him
rather than the fantastic rhetorician, as more super-
fine audiences do. That is a good omen, I think, for
the education of times to come." It was a good omen
indeed, and the ferment has been working since then,
through various Ruskin Societies (organized "to
encourage and promote the study and circulation of
Mr. Ruskin's writings"), and through the Ruskin
College, at Oxford, a notable institution for teaching
working men, and established as a direct result of
Ruskin's influence.[2]

Ruskin's teaching has told no less steadily and
effectively upon economic doctrine, according to the
reports of accredited English witnesses. Mr. J. A.

---

[1] *Works*, XVII, *intro.*, CXI; Cook, *Life of Ruskin*, II, 13–14.

[2] See Hobson's appendix on Ruskin Societies and the Work, in *John Ruskin, Social Reformer*, 326–328; also an article in the *Fortnightly Review* (1900, v. 67, p. 325) on *The Ruskin Hall Movement*. In the *Survey* for August 30, 1919, is the report of a speech in New York, by Miss Margaret Bondfield, "official representative of the British Trade Union Congress," on how British labor began to educate itself. Among other things she says: "Ruskin College in Oxford, though it is pretty stodgy, and though the students there, while they are *in* Oxford, are not *of* Oxford, has played its part in labor education. Trade unions send up students who are expected to come back and give the union the advantage of their knowledge. Frank Hodges made a brilliant success there, and then went back to digging coal. Young as he was, he soon was put in as general secretary of the great Miners' Federation, and his brilliance, together with the power of Robert Smillie, the president, have lately enabled the federation to make history."

Hobson, perhaps the foremost of these and himself a Ruskinian in many ways, counts as the most distinguished services of Ruskin his insistence upon a standard of human well-being as a substitute for the monetary standard of wealth. "This assertion of vital value as the standard and criterion," says Mr. Hobson, "is, of course, no novelty. It has underlain all the more comprehensive criticisms of orthodox political economy by moralists and social reformers. By far the most brilliant and effective of these criticisms, that of John Ruskin, was expressly formulated in terms of vital value. . . . This vital criterion he brought to bear with great skill, alike upon the processes of production and consumption, disclosing the immense discrepancies between monetary costs and human costs, monetary wealth and vital wealth. No one ever had a more vivid and comprehensive view of the essentially organic nature of the harmony of various productive activities needed for a wholesome life, and of the related harmony of uses and satisfactions on the consumptive side. His mind seized with incomparable force of vision the cardinal truth of human economics, viz., that every piece of concrete wealth must be valued in terms of the vital costs of its production and the vital uses of its consumption, and his most effective assault upon current economic theory was based upon its complete inadequacy to afford such information." [1] Mr. Ernest Barker, still more recently (1915), has recorded his opinion to much the same effect. Ruskin's teaching,

[1] *Work and Wealth* (1914), 9. *Cf. John Ruskin, Social Reformer,* 89, 309, and preface.

he says, "has influenced the doctrine of pure economics. It has helped to turn economists since the days
of Jevons from the theory of production to the theory
of consumption; it has helped to correct the old
emphasis laid on saving, and to give more weight to
spending; it has helped vitally to modify the old
conception of value as mainly determined by cost of
production, and to give more scope to the influence of
utility in the creation of value. Nor has Ruskin's
teaching only influenced economic science; it has also
affected the theory and the practice of politics. . . .
And the vogue of his writings enabled him, perhaps
more than any other writer, to help men to shed the
old distrust of the State, and to welcome, as men
since 1870 have more and more welcomed, the activity of society on behalf of its members. If Ruskin
was not the begetter of English Socialism, he was a
foster-father to many English Socialists." [1]

First among these was William Morris, master of
modern craftsmen. "The whole of the Socialism with

[1] *Political Thought from Spencer to To-Day*, 195–6. *Cf.* Chesterton:
"He was not so great a man as Carlyle, but he was a much more clear-
headed man. . . . On this side of his soul (*i. e.*, social side) Ruskin
became the second founder of Socialism." [*Victorian Literature*, 67–8.
Cf. also opinion of Geddes (in *John Ruskin, Economist*, 42); Ingram (in
History of Political Economy, 1915 ed.); and Stimson (in *Quarterly
Journal of Economics*, II, 445.] According to Mr. Bernard Shaw, Ruskin
did not influence the Fabians: "It is a curious fact that of the three great
propagandist amateurs of political economy, Henry George, Marx, and
Ruskin, Ruskin alone seems to have had no effect on the Fabians. Here
and there in the Socialist movement workmen turned up who had read
Fors Clavigera or *Unto This Last;* and some of the more well-to-do no
doubt have read the first chapter of *Munera Pulveris*. But Ruskin's name
was hardly mentioned in the Fabian Society. My explanation is that,
barring Olivier, the Fabians were inveterate Philistines." (*History of the
Fabian Society*, by Pease, 263.)

which Morris identified himself so prominently in the eighties," says Mackail, "had been implicitly contained and the greater part of it explicitly stated, in the pages of *Unto This Last* in 1862, when Morris had just begun the work of his life as a manufacturer. . . All his serious references to Ruskin showed that he retained towards him the attitude of a scholar to a great teacher and master, not only in matters of art, but throughout the whole sphere of human life."[1] Reference has already been made, in a previous chapter, to the powerful effect which *The Nature of Gothic* had upon Morris, in the Oxford days. In his introduction to the Kelmscott Edition (1892) of this famous manifesto—"one of the very few inevitable utterances of the century," he called it—he recorded his opinion that the social teaching of Ruskin was more significant than his entire criticism of art itself. "Some readers will perhaps wonder," he wrote, "that in this important chapter of Ruskin I have found it necessary to consider ethical and political, rather than what would ordinarily be thought the artistic side of it. I must answer that, delightful as is that portion of Ruskin's work which describes, analyzes, and criticises art, old and new, yet this is not after all the most characteristic side of his writings. Indeed, from the time at which he wrote this chapter here reprinted, those ethical and political considerations have never been absent from his criticism of art; and, in my opinion, it is just this part of his work, fairly begun in *The Nature of Gothic*, and brought to its culmination in that great book *Unto This Last*, which has had the

[1] *Life of Morris*, II, 201, I, 220.

most enduring and beneficent effect on his contemporaries, and will have through them on succeeding generations."[1]   Readers of Morris who are also readers of Ruskin will hear reverberations of the master's thought in almost every lecture and essay that Morris produced on the subject of art or socialism, often accompanied with generous acknowledgments; for Morris took no pains to conceal a main source of his inspiration. His whole attack upon modern life corresponds exactly with Ruskin's. He assailed the ugliness of it, the loss of instinct for beauty among people to-day, the "bestial" economics, the degradation of the worker by machine labor; and he followed up his attack with a stern prophecy that a day of change must come when mankind would become an association of workers, each realizing the freedom of his soul in joyful labor; and with an equally stern demand for a return to simplicity in life as a preparation for the new order. Like Ruskin, too, Morris discovered in medievalism, in the old guilds and in Gothic architecture, a clue to the way out of the labyrinth in which contemporary society had become lost. Extending the notion of art as Ruskin had extended it, he valiantly preached the gospel of the democracy of art, upon a threefold text, namely, that work must be worth doing, that it should be of itself pleasant to do, and that it should be done under such conditions as would make it neither over-wearisome nor over-anxious.

This message, either as Morris delivered and practiced it or as it came directly from Ruskin, has made

[1] *Works*, X, 461-2.

notable impressions in two quarters, neither of which can be quite passed by in a general summary such as the present one,—the Arts and Crafts Movement and present day Guild Socialism. The Arts and Crafts Movement, as it came to be named by Mr. Cobden-Sanderson, grew out of the work of the Arts and Crafts Exhibition Society, which held its first exhibition of decorative art in London in 1888. The Society was created by a group of young artists drawn together under the inspiration of Morris for the purpose of bringing about (to quote Mackail) "a Renaissance of the decorative arts which should act at once through and towards more humanized conditions of life both for the workman and for those for whom he worked. . . . The way here, as in so many other instances, had been pointed out by the far-ranging genius of Ruskin long before any steps were, or could be, taken towards its realization." [1] Thus if Morris and his followers begot the movement, it was Ruskin, as Mr. Cobden-Sanderson has aptly said, who "begot the begetters." [2] The movement, however, was not only for the purpose of renewing interest in the decorative arts; it was also an endeavor to see what could be done towards the reconstruction of industry by the creation of small associated workshops, wherein designer and artificer should be one person and not two (or more), and wherein common traditions of craft might be established and machines rather than men should be made the slaves. The most conspic-

---

[1] *Life of Morris*, II, 196, 201.

[2] *Arts and Crafts Movement* (1905), 12. The statement of the purposes of the movement by Mr. Walter Crane, in his introduction to *Arts and Crafts Essays* (1893), is shot through with Ruskinism.

uous expression of this aim has probably been the Guild of Handicraft, established in East London in 1888, by Mr. C. R. Ashbee, an enthusiastic disciple of Ruskin and Morris.[1] "The Guild had its beginnings," says Mr. Ashbee, "in the years 1886–7 in a small Ruskin class, conducted at Toynbee Hall."[2] Its aims and its achievements alike, according to its founder, have all along been due to the inspiration of Ruskin and Morris. And it has constituted a most challenging experiment, for it has sought to realize in small shops under co-operative control all the virtues of the medieval guild system, including quality-production before quantity-production, fellowship and happiness in work, permanence of status, concentration of force without the deadening subdivision of labor, and the education of the consumer.

These purposes (or most of them),[3] united with a demand for the overthrow of capitalism and the wage-system, find a more significant expression to-day in the program of a remarkable movement in England known as Guild Socialism. Originating in 1906 with the publication of an article in the *Contemporary Review* by Mr. A. R. Orage and a book on the *Restoration of the Gild System* by Mr. A. J. Penty, the movement has drawn to itself a number of

[1] In 1902 the Guild was moved to the country, at Campton, Gloucestershire. In 1907, after practically twenty years of substantial life, it was in financial straits. I regret to say that I have been unable to follow its history since the time of Mr. Ashbee's record in *Craftsmanship in Industry*, 1908.

[2] *An Endeavor Towards the Teaching of John Ruskin and William Morris*, (1901), 1.

[3] Guild Socialism does not advocate as a national policy small-scale production in local workshops.

brilliant thinkers and writers, who are not only
waging war upon competitive industry, but who are
also fighting a battle for ideals of labor which go back
to Morris, and from him to Ruskin.[1] Mr. Penty, who
has been called "the prophet of the Guild idea," [2] and
whose approach to labor problems appears to be
decidedly in the spirit of art and medieval craftsmanship, is an avowed follower of Ruskin and Morris.
Our only hope, he says, in solving the social questions
of to-day "lies in some such direction as that foreshadowed by Ruskin"; whose guild idea he therefore
takes up, reduces to practical outlines, and makes a
basis for a re-creation of the present industrial order.[3]
Cole and Hobson are following a different path, but
their eyes are set upon the same goal,[4] for their ideal-

[1] For a full account of the movement the reader is referred to the books
on Guild Socialism, the most notable of which thus far published are:
National Guilds (1914), by S. G. Hobson; *Old Worlds for New* (1917), by
Penty; *Self-Government in Industry* (1918), by Cole; *Guild Principles in
War and Peace* (1918), by S. G. Hobson; *The Meaning of National Guilds*
(1919), by Reckitt and Bechhofer. In a word the school stands for the
ownership of industry by the state, but for its management by the workers, who are to be organized locally, sectionally, and nationally, according to industries (organization by craft will cross-section organization by
industry), into democratic units known as guilds. "The title of *Guild* has
implicit in it several unique industrial attributes: it means that public
recognition is accorded to the body, that the monopoly of its particular
trade is vested in it, that all its members have an equal and free status as
associates in it; also, that the Guild spirit in work is revived." (Reckitt
and Bechhofer, 304.)

[2] *Ibid.*, 396.

[3] See his preface to *Restoration of the Gild System*. Penty also fully
recognizes the pioneer work of Morris and the men of the Arts and
Crafts Movement. *Cf. Old Worlds for New*, Ch. XII; also Reckitt and
Bechhofer: among the influences upon Guild Socialism "we should find
the craftsman's challenge and the blazing democracy of William Morris."
(*Intro.*, XIII.)

[4] Penty has now joined them in favoring *national* guilds as a step
towards *local* guilds. (Reckitt and Bechhofer, 397.)

ism again is the unassailable idealism of Ruskin and
Morris. "I share to the full," says Cole, "William
Morris's happy conviction that joy in life, and art as
the expression of that joy, are fundamental, and, if
you will, natural, to free men and women. I believe
that, if men and women were set free, as they might
be, from economic necessity, they would set with new
manhood about the creation of the good life." [1] Thus
the fire that Ruskin lighted in his *Nature of Gothic*,
the fire that inflamed the heart of Morris, burns still,
and will burn, until the evils of our industrial civilization are utterly and everlastingly consumed.

It is a good many years now since Carlyle and Ruskin first went forth to combat these evils. As we look
out upon the world to-day, a world still bent under
the wounds and burdens of a frightful war, can we say
with any truth that the standard under which they
fought has gone forward? If industry was large in
their time, it has expanded to dimensions almost
beyond computation now. Material progress has
advanced with ever accelerating speed, until whole
continents seem to be like nothing so much as vast

---

[1] *Labor in the Commonwealth*, 220; *cf.* also on the work of Morris, *Self-
Government in Industry*, 119–121, 280, 302. As to the idealism of the
Guild Socialists note the following two or three statements out of scores:
"The case for Guild Socialism is based upon an unchanging faith that
man's motives and hopes, freed from the contamination of poverty, will
replenish the world with unsuspected richness and variety of wealth and
life" (*National Guilds*, 211); "Let us look at industry, not as a science
apart, but as a vital function of communal life" (*Labor in the Commonwealth*, 33); "Not art for the rich or the poor, not art for art's sake; but
the spirit of the true and the beautiful entering into our industrial life;
production no longer a grinding burden but a pleasure, limited only by
Nature and our necessities." (*Guild Principles*, 170.)

networks of manufacturing systems, woven together to minister to the newly-created necessities or luxuries of congested populations. The genius and energy of man, supported by the factory system and by machine labor, those giant offspring of the industrial revolution, are rapidly mastering the resources of the earth. The smoke and din of the world's workshops are omnipresent, and the morning or evening march of its toilers is heard in every ear.

Out of the darkness and confusion of these times in which we are living, are there no lights to point the way, no voices lifted for social justice and human fellowship? There are, many of them, as wise observers know. On every hand, from the council rooms of capital, from the debating halls of labor, from the press, from the pulpit, from club, and school, and home, everywhere, even from the assemblies of statesmen met to restore the nations to peace, there comes the word that the present order must give way to a better one. And although different leaders or groups place the emphasis differently, the full meaning of this message is fourfold:—the conservation, at all costs, of the human factor in industry; increased collective control, or ownership, in the interest of a vast body of dependent consumers; increased partnership of labor with capital, in management and profits of industry, tending always towards fuller democratic control by labor, as labor proves its capacity; and, finally (last to come but of most value when it arrives), the opportunity for expression in work of the creative impulse, a consummation which will set the worker free and will realize for him the highest gifts of life,—joy and fellowship in daily toil,—and will realize for society a genuine revival of art. The number of those who are now thinking of this program and striving for the fulfilment of it is legion. Fifty and more years ago the number was few, and they were prophets. None among that small company spoke out more powerfully or wisely than Carlyle and Ruskin. For with all their shortness of vision in some directions, they saw far more clearly than the majority of their contemporaries, and they set forth in language of incomparable power, what was coming and what must come. They were, in truth, heralds of the better order.

APPENDIX

SINCE the foregoing chapters were written and sent to press there have come into the writer's hands three small commemorative volumes of addresses, letters, and studies in connection with the centenary of Ruskin's birth; observed by a public meeting February 8, 1919, at the Royal Society of Arts, London, and by an exhibition of his drawings at the Royal Academy in the autumn of the same year. The volumes are: *Ruskin Centenary Addresses*, edited by J. H. Whitehouse, Oxford University Press, 1919; *Ruskin Centenary Letters*, edited by J. H. Whitehouse, Oxford University Press, 1919; *Ruskin The Prophet and Other Centenary Studies*, edited by J. H. Whitehouse, E. P. Dutton and Co., 1920. Among many striking tributes in these volumes to Ruskin as a social force, the following may be quoted as perhaps the most notable:

(1) "A great deal of his inspiration came from Carlyle, but it was changed in the process, passing through a mind so different as Ruskin's was, and it made a more direct, sympathetic, and emotional appeal to many people than the same fundamental principles had made when they were stated with the fiercely vigorous abruptness of Carlyle himself. Perhaps it is in that direction that he has most told upon what I may call the younger half of the generation to which he belonged. The older half of the generation to which most of us here belong was impressed chiefly by his writings upon Art and upon Nature, but those who are still below sixty years of age have probably

been more affected by his ethical teachings. In this respect he did make a great difference to his time, and has been the parent of many movements, many new currents of opinion, which have been playing backwards and forwards over the face of the country during the last twenty-five or thirty years." (Lord Bryce, *Addresses*, p. 5.)

(2) "It is as an interpreter, not of art but of life, that he now stands. Here his influence has been, and continues to be, immense. It is perhaps greater, so far at least as England is concerned, than that of any other single thinker or teacher. His social doctrine was germinal: it colors the whole movement of modern thought, and shapes the whole fabric of modern practice. . . . Our whole social legislation, and the whole attitude of mind of which legislation is the result, have since followed, haltingly and fragmentarily, the principles then asserted for the first time. Nor have sixty years lessened their vital and germinal force. Much of what was then taken for monstrous paradox has become accepted truth, the mere commonplace of social organization. Much more still awaits fulfilment, and remains to us what it was for him, an obscure and terrible inspiration, a sound of trumpets in the night. . . . He is the prophet of the Socialist movement; he taught its leaders and inspired their followers. But the doctrines of Socialism, whether in its bureaucratic or its anarchic form, were to him false and even deadly." (J. W. Mackail, *Addresses*, pp. 11, 14, 21.)

(3) "Ruskin's life plan includes all that is vital, all that is real, in work and life to-day. His influence has permeated the whole world of artistic creativeness. But what was perhaps more significant still to me was the discovery that Ruskin perceived in the industrial world of his day the premonitory tremors of the vast upheaval which now threatens the whole world, the whole of civilization, the whole of our life, our ideals, our religion, and everything else. The organization in the midst of which we have been living, to which we have got accustomed, is being shaken to its very foundations, and who

knows that it may not fall in ruins about us. Yet one cannot feel, or think, or believe that it is going to fall in ruins, because after all, although Ruskin foresaw and foreshadowed and wrote clearly about the very thing that has fallen upon us, he did at the same time indicate the cure for the industrial evil. And that remedy which is in our own hands is, briefly, to return again to a creative life, to individual, collective, and co-operative productivity. We must, as Carlyle says, 'produce, produce, be it but the infinitesimalist product'—we must produce. Ruskin never wearied of reminding us that there is no way of learning all and quickly about anything but by the labor of our hands. Years before Stanley Hall, his pupils, and other American writers taught that muscular activity influences mental growth, Ruskin was teaching the same thing more beautifully, and therefore perhaps more truly. Ruskin shows that the man who builds his own house, tills his own ground, makes his own furniture, has more wealth and more essential culture than he who only makes fortunes by the labors of others. Workers have learnt by Ruskin's precept and their own practice that the basis of craftsmanship is vital morality, vital religion. Creative work is philosophy in being. That is why the great teachers of the world have all been craftsmen. . . .

"It has occurred to me to suggest that of all the schemes of reconstruction which are before the world to-day, and before ourselves in particular, the most promising are those schemes which, consciously or unconsciously, are giving effect to Ruskin's ideal as outlined in the constitution of St. George's Guild, and seek to plant both able and disabled soldiers on the land and to give them opportunities of craft activity, to help them to make a happy, productive, and real life for themselves, and in so doing to give to England again some degree of that beauty of creative activity which she possessed in the earlier periods of her history. The scheme of the St. George's Guild might well now be carried into effect, with the aid and help of all artists and craftsmen of to-day, the help of the Art Workers' Guild, the Arts and Crafts Society and other handicraft societies, and the Royal Academy. If all artists would combine to urge upon all the authorities the necessity of establishing at least a few real, recon-structed, reconstituted villages, towns, districts, whatever limitation you may prefer, if they would urge the recon-struction of some few centres, however small at first matters not, in which the soldiers who are returning from the front, wounded and sound, could settle and live a rational, Ruskinian, and therefore natural life, then real effect might be given to Ruskin's ideal of a new order of production, and his three graces, his three beauties of life, his three cardinal virtues, admiration, hope, and love, might again flower among the ruins of the world and something would have been done to heal the wounds which war has made." (Henry Wilson, President of the Arts and Crafts Exhibition Society, *Addresses*, 28–29; 32–33.)

(4) "To-day official recognition is given to the princi-ples Ruskin expounded. Codes have been widened, and although much progress has yet to be made in con-nexion with our whole system of national education, that which has taken place is precisely on the lines which Rus-kin laid down. He urged, for instance, so far back as 1857 that drawing should be taught as an integral branch of education. He pleaded for the inclusion of music and noble literature as essential things in education. He de-sired that all schools in themselves should be beautiful. He desired to form standards of taste and judgment by surrounding children with beautiful things. He fought against the idea that education was something to be con-fined to class-rooms or in buildings, and he made a noble plea for the value of the outdoor life and scenes of natural beauty in all schemes of education. All these expressions of educational principles have been in part at least realized. The bare and ugly school-rooms of the past are replaced by buildings furnished in many cases on the lines indicated

by Ruskin. Pictures, sculpture, color, architecture, are realized to be great instruments of education. Drawing was made a compulsory subject in elementary schools in 1890. Even the introductions issued by the Board of Education to the various editions of their code now give expression for the guidance of school managers to the Ruskinian views we have set forth. . . . Ruskin's teaching in this connexion (i. e., handicrafts) has made steady headway in our educational life. Most of the developments on the lines of his teaching, so far as younger children are concerned, have taken place in the secondary schools of England and Scotland. . . . No teacher before Ruskin had been so successful in the ultimate appeal which he made to unlettered people. Some educational thinkers had taught some of the things Ruskin taught and before he wrote. But they made no popular appeal. Ruskin's strength, after all, came from the fact that he appealed to the conscience of the entire nation. The widest response to his appeal came from the working classes. They have always been the greatest readers of his books. His language made to them something of the same popular appeal as did the prose of the Bible to an earlier age." (John Howard Whitehouse, *Addresses*, 50–51, 55, 64.)

(5) "The close connection of the decay of art with faulty social arrangements was his great discovery. Ugliness in the works of man is a symptom of disease in the State. This was Ruskin's conviction, and we may call it his discovery. . . . As an art-critic he had taught that beauty is fundamentally a matter of right values, and that all ugliness has its root in a false or mean or vulgar standard of values. But conduct also is determined by our standard of values, which alone gives life its meaning. If our values are perverted, our social order, in which our notions of good and evil express themselves, will be perverse and bad, and there will be no beauty in what we do or in what we make." (Dean Inge, *Studies*, 25, 26.)

(6) "If to-day Labor leaders and social reformers in general are quite as keenly set upon reducing the hours

of labor and otherwise diminishing the pressure of the machine upon the man who tends it, we have to thank men like Ruskin and Morris for much of this revolt. Not even yet have psychologists succeeded in making us recognize the amount of vital damage done by setting men and women to spend most of their time and energy in some single narrow routine—not merely the painful fatigue and conscious or unconscious atrophy of other productive capacities, but the narrowing of the capacity for enjoyment which comes from this over-specialization. Not more productivity, but more liberty from industry, should be the chief demand of humanist reformers to-day, and they should boldly announce the gospel of Ruskin as theirs. . . . *Time and Tide* and *Fors* are full of suggestions keenly prophetic of the new social-economic order which is even now pressing through the broken shell of the nineteenth-century individualism. Skilled manual labor, with the apparent exception of agriculture, he relegates to a guild system not very different from the Guild Socialism which to-day appears in many quarters to be displacing both the traditional Trade Unionism and the State Socialism of last century. . . . In economic, as in educational reform, he was no barren prophet of denunciation, but a true leader towards a land of promise. Long before scientific pedagogy had worked out the psychology of the relations between brain and hand work, Ruskin had recognized their fundamental importance and had demanded the union of the workshop and the schoolroom. When nature and art, in any real sense, were taboo in our schools, he exposed their vital value, not merely or mainly as subjects in a curriculum, but as pervasive and suggestive influences in the atmosphere of education. A minimum wage based upon the wholesome maintenance of the worker and his family, a shorter working day, the housing problem, the revival of rural life, and such specific reforms as smoke abatement and the prevention of river pollution, owe an immense and often unrecognized debt to Ruskin's early advocacy." (J. A. Hobson, *Studies*, 92, 94, 96.)

INDEX

WITHDRAWN

JUN 2 7 2024

DAVID O. McKAY LIBRARY
BYU-IDAHO